AF324670

Race and Identity in Hispanic America

Race and Identity in Hispanic America

The White, the Black, and the Brown

Patricia Reid-Merritt and Michael S. Rodriguez

An Imprint of ABC-CLIO, LLC
Santa Barbara, California • Denver, Colorado

Library of Congress Cataloging-in-Publication Data

Names: Reid-Merritt, Patricia, author. | Rodriguez, Michael S., author.
Title: Race and identity in Hispanic America : the white, the black, and the brown / Patricia Reid-Merritt and Michael S. Rodriguez.
Description: First edition. | Santa Barbara : Praeger, an imprint of ABC-CLIO, LLC, [2020] | Includes bibliographical references and index. |
Identifiers: LCCN 2019051204 (print) | LCCN 2019051205 (ebook) | ISBN 9781440867842 (hardcover) | ISBN 9781440867859 (ebook)
Subjects: LCSH: Hispanic Americans—Ethnic identity. | Hispanic Americans—Race identity. | Latin Americans—Ethnic identity. | Latin Americans—Race identity.
Classification: LCC E184.S75 R45 2020 (print) | LCC E184.S75 (ebook) | DDC 305.868/073—dc23
LC record available at https://lccn.loc.gov/2019051204
LC ebook record available at https://lccn.loc.gov/2019051205

ISBN: 978-1-4408-6784-2 (print)
       978-1-4408-6785-9 (ebook)

24 23 22 21 20   1 2 3 4 5

This book is also available as an eBook.

Praeger
An Imprint of ABC-CLIO, LLC

ABC-CLIO, LLC
147 Castilian Drive
Santa Barbara, California 93117
www.abc-clio.com

This book is printed on acid-free paper ∞

Manufactured in the United States of America

To my father—Memory begins in the mind,
but lives in the heart.

And to my mother—who always wanted the very best for me
and my eight siblings, whom she cherished the most in life.

Contents

Preface

There are two contributing writers to this manuscript. We share many similarities, but our journeys to this point have been different.

I am an African American female born during the baby-boom generation. I came of age during the civil rights and black power movements, when a certain level of racial consciousness was required for the rite of passage into young adulthood. Throughout my life, I was always aware of race and color issues that plagued America in general and the black community in particular. In my four-decade tenure as a college professor, I have presented hundreds of lectures and dozens of papers and have written several books focusing on the issue of race. For me, race is a defining factor in American life—predetermined at birth and remaining a powerful influence until death.

I was raised in Philadelphia, Pennsylvania, where neighborhoods, for the most part, were racially and ethnically segregated. There were heavy concentrations of black, white, Italian, Jewish, and Hispanic residents throughout the city. When I traveled outside of my own West Philadelphia community and into the then primarily Puerto Rican neighborhoods, people spoke to me in Spanish. I thought this was unusual, but when I observed the people in Philadelphia and the nearby Camden, New Jersey, areas, it made a lot of sense. We were, after all, multicolored communities that looked very much alike. I may have been mistaken for being a member of the Hispanic community, but there was never any doubt that my identity was solidified as black and female. Barring medical intervention, I will remain black and female until the day I die.

I first began to seriously ponder the question of race and identity in the Hispanic community during a multicultural program at Stockton University. A colleague, Dr. Pedro Santana, stood up and introduced himself as an individual who embraced three bloodlines. "I am Latino! My heritage is African, Indian, and European." While I understood this to be true, I was also aware of the emerging discussions in the Latino community about racial and ethnic identity.

In the summer of 2014, the Caribbean Cultural Center African Diaspora Institute, in conjunction with the Inter American University of Puerto Rico, launched the Community Arts University without Walls project. Dr. Marta Moreno Vega created the credit-earning certificate program. The program was designed for those interested in the impact and role of cultural arts in engaging issues of social justice within diverse communities. More specifically, the course of study would focus on the legacy of the civil rights movement, addressing issues of cultural equity and social and economic justice in Puerto Rico. I wear multiple hats and assume many different social roles. And as a social worker, performing artist, black cultural nationalist, and African-centered scholar, I knew this was the perfect opportunity for me to visit Puerto Rico to examine the impact of race and racism on the Puerto Rican community. It was during the very first session that the instructor explained (in Spanish), "The latest census data indicates that eighty percent of the people in Puerto Rico racially identify themselves as being white. Helping them to understand aspects of our African heritage is part of the challenge." I felt confused. I remained in Puerto Rico for two weeks. I saw lots of diversity but very little evidence that the population of the island was overwhelmingly white. Examining the race question for the Hispanic community was a project that I would consider some time in the near future.

The publication of *Race in America: How a Pseudoscientific Concept Shaped Human Interaction* (2017) and *A State-by-State History of Race and Racism in the United States* (2018) laid the foundation for this work. As an African American female, I have been impacted by a multitude of issues surrounding race and racism. I was enthusiastic about undertaking this project, but I would not do so without collaborating with a scholar from the Hispanic community. I turned to my Stockton University colleague, Dr. Michael Rodriguez.

*   *   *

"So, where are you from?"
My response: "Texas."
"No, where are you really from?"
My response: "Um . . . San Antonio?"

"So, what part of India are you from?"
My totally baffled response: "I'm actually from Texas, I'm Mexican American."

"So, what aspect of Chicano politics are you doing your thesis on?"
My perplexed response: "Uh . . . It's actually on John Rawls's *A Theory of Justice.*"

I often reflect on these three seemingly unrelated moments in my life. The first exchange has occurred many times throughout my life, the second a few, and the third once. What ties them together is my utter surprise that how I define who I am (i.e., my identity) is not completely in my own hands. I, we, are also other-defined, not just self-defined. As a student of politics and the intersections of race and politics, I have had a keen intellectual understanding for decades that our identities, in part, are also defined by others—how they see us, how they define us, and ultimately how they interact with us. But to accept that reality at a deep, ontological level is an entirely different matter because it means others have a claim on how my identity is defined; our relationship shapes (defines) my identity, just as it does theirs. It is both frightening and thrilling to accept that who I am—who you are—is not entirely up to me or you. Identity formation is, oddly enough, a truly democratic process; we all participate in defining ourselves, as well as each other.

I am a fourth- or fifth-generation American of Mexican descent. I am an English-dominant, bilingual Tejano, Chicano, Latino, Mexican American whose childhood memories of watching *The Brady Brunch* are as seared into my being as watching (Mario Moreno) Cantinflas movies at the drive-in with my family. I also listened to the country music of Roy Clark, Dolly Parton, and Porter Wagoner (yes, I confess to watching *Hee-Haw* as a kid!), and the Southern rock music of Lynyrd Skynyrd and ZZ Top. I grew up knowing that we can be this and that and that, not just this or that. Living multiple, overlapping, and interlacing identities can be discombobulating, but it is also deliciously liberating. I agree fully with the Ghanaian-English philosopher Kwame Anthony Appiah that we create, recreate, and invent ourselves; that is our freedom, power, and autonomy. However, we confront the other-definition of ourselves that others gently or even violently hoist upon us—most often without our consent or even awareness. Identity formation is also thrilling because we issue a daily, standing invitation for others to participate in the wonder of defining who we are.

One of the benefits of having lived for several decades is the wonderful discovery that the process of defining my ethno-racial identity is never quite over—until, of course, it's over (if you know what I mean). But, it's also an open-ended invitation to others to be a part of that process. I grew up in a Mexican American family beyond the city limits of San Antonio, Texas. The community (Losoya) was predominantly Mexican American, as was my school district. I started working in the fields at an early age and excelled in school, graduating first in my class in both junior high and high school. I earned graduate degrees in political science, worked as a dean, and have now had the profound honor of being a professor for over a dozen years. I live in an interracial home with a spouse who is African American and three Afro-Latino children (and three insouciant cats). My home, my culture/s, and my country are all still working out what it means to be who we are. This volume is our humble effort to advance a more nuanced understanding of how race and identity shape and reshape Hispanic America. That effort necessarily involves understanding the ethno-racial dynamics in the countries from whence we come. It also involves exploring how this country, this hegemon of the Western Hemisphere, impacts identity formation for Hispanic Americans through its geographic, historical, and metaphorical proximity to Latin America (Mexico, Central and South America, and the Caribbean).

We want to thank all of those who supported us in this effort. A special thanks and appreciation to senior editor Kim Kennedy White. Kim guided us through the process and remained patient as we stumbled through a number of delays as we edged toward completion of this work. Our special thanks to Jaishree Thiyagarajan who skillfully saw this project to completion. We also wish to thank all the support staff at Praeger; from cover design to final edits, they helped to make the product look good.

Several of our Stockton University colleagues read parts of the manuscript and provided us with valuable feedback. Our heartfelt thanks and appreciation go out to Dr. Meryawilda Colon, Dr. Arnaldo Cordero-Roman, Dr. Arleen Gonzalez, and Dr. Pedro Santana. As our colleagues often reminded us, "We're in this thing together."

We were also fortunate to have the help and support of graduate assistant Stephanie Smith, MSW. We are grateful for the time and energy she spent on researching issues surrounding race in Hispanic America. Stephanie's skillful ability to search the internet and locate contemporary issues of concern was superb.

Finally, to our family members: We thank you for your support and apologize for taking so much time away from family responsibilities as we worked diligently to complete this project. Your continued love and support are priceless.

Patricia Reid-Merritt, DSW
Michael S. Rodriguez, PhD
April 2020

Introduction

> Please allow me to introduce myself. My name is Juan and I am a white Puerto Rican!
>
> —Juan, age 26

The need and/or desire to proclaim himself a "white" Puerto Rican was not the introduction I'd expected from this twenty-six-year-old male student on the very first day of class. The course—Race, Ethnicity, and Diversity—is a required one for social work majors but is popular among other students seeking to explore the many questions and issues surrounding race. Having taught this course on the university level for the past four decades, I was more than familiar with students' struggles and anxieties around racial identity. The black, white, Asian, and Indian students possessed some general sense of clarity or understanding about their membership in a particular racial group. However, the same could not be said for many of the Latin, Spanish-speaking, or mixed-race students who expressed genuine confusion about locating themselves in one of America's rigid racial categories. "My race is Latino," a light-brown-skinned student offered during the first day of discussion. "I am Latina, but I am black," responded a female student of a much darker hue. "Why do people question me and look at me in a strange manner when I tell them that I am Hispanic?" The discussion grew more challenging as students shared their understanding of racial classifications: What does it mean to be white, black, or brown in America? Are Asians and Indians the same? What is the difference between an ethnic group and a racial group? And what about the Hispanics? How do Hispanic Americans respond to the racial question?

This introductory chapter examines issues surrounding race and identity in Hispanic America. It offers a broad overview of America's Hispanic population, highlighting the importance of ethnic identification in the Spanish-speaking community, as well as the geographic locations and homogeneity of their respective communities. In addition, this chapter examines the socially constructed concept of race within the global and national context and the social and political implications of racial classifications, and it offers a framework for understanding racial and ethnic identity in Hispanic America.

Who Are the Hispanic Americans?

While the concept of race forms the basis of identity for most Americans, understanding race and identity in the United States of America is far more complicated for Hispanics than for members of other racial groups. For one, the terminology used to describe this population is controversial, misleading, imprecise, and ever-changing. It is further convoluted by the nation's extensive history of racial intermingling and the continuous flow of immigrant groups from countries whose definitions of race, ethnicity, and culture remain fluid.[1] It was during the early 1970s when the U.S. government first used the term *Hispanic* to describe a person's region of origin. Hispanics were individuals coming from Mexico and South or Central America. Mexicans were, by far, the largest of America's Spanish-speaking immigrant population. However, Hispanics also included newcomers from Cuba, Costa Rica, the Dominican Republic, Guatemala, Honduras, Nicaragua, Panama, and El Salvador. Hispanics also arrived from areas further south, including Bolivia, Chile, Colombia, Ecuador, Paraguay, Peru, and Venezuela. The term *Hispanic* refers to an ethnic designation, not a racial one. The common denominator for these groups was the language (Spanish) of the country of origin. And while Puerto Ricans were also included as Hispanics, they were not immigrants, but rather American citizens migrating off the island to the mainland.[2]

Disagreement over the use of the term was swift and immediate. Many chose not to embrace the nomenclature, preferring to identify themselves based on the country of origin. Mexican Americans were particularly vocal, declaring themselves *Chicanos*—Mexico descendants born in the United States of America—a term that existed prior to the 1970s but was popularized during the civil rights movement.[3] As the number of immigrants from further south of the border increased, many expressed dissatisfaction with the use of the term *Hispanic* and preferred *Latino* instead, as many of the new arrivals were from Latin American countries. However, Latino is not synonymous with Hispanic or Spanish-speaking America. Brazilian Americans, for example, are part of the Latino community. Portuguese, not Spanish, is the official language of the Brazilian people and the language most widely spoken in South America.[4] Belize, a Central American country bordered by Guatemala and Mexico, offers another example. The former British colony's official language is English. For the purpose of examining the experiences of the Spanish-speaking population in the United States of America, we have chosen to use the word *Hispanic* to focus the discourse on their unique historical and contemporary social journeys. However, we are fully cognizant of the way in which Hispanic and Latino (and now Latinx) are often used interchangeably in the American lexicon.

The varied histories of the Spanish-speaking countries not only reveal great similarities but also great differences. For example, the use of the Spanish language in the New World speaks to a period of conquest and domination by European invaders that began to unfold at the very end of the fifteenth century. In very much the same way that the British eventually dominated the North American continent (making English the unofficial language of the United States of America), it was the political might of Spain that resulted in its domination of Central and South America.[5] Indigenous populations, including the Aztec, Maya, Mixtec, Otomi, and Taino Indians, were the original inhabitants of the area.[6] The introduction of the international slave trade throughout the region and the intermingling of Europeans, Indians, and Africans in the repopulation of the area produced descendants of a darker hue, thus resulting in the often-used term *people of color.* In countries like Mexico, El Salvador, Colombia, Honduras, Peru, and Paraguay, these mixed-race populations are identified as Mestizo. Their common plight was that they were viewed and treated as less desirable by the dominant, socially powerful, "lighter" members of the population. While the social, political, and economic development in each country has varied (which we will discuss in detail in subsequent chapters), a common denominator was the conquest and eventual domination by Europeans from Spain. The politically powerful created and implemented a new world order—one in which Europeans and their descendants nurtured the concept of race, racial differences, and the superiority of whites over all people of color, including the indigenous, African, and mixed-race populations.

Race in the Global Context

One could easily argue that the concept of race emerged in the global context. Before the global launch of European explorations that began in earnest in the sixteenth century and continued for more than three hundred years, questions about race were irrelevant. Human societies were homogeneous in nature. As Patricia Reid-Merritt indicates in *Race in America*:

> Prior to the 16th century, contact between continentally unique populations was limited: Indigenous peoples populated the Americas; Asians the Orient; Africans the African continent; and, Caucasians, Europe. However, with the rapid expansion of European exploration into the New World, human beings, or more accurately the Europeans, would begin to view the others as different, and ways in which we could explain these differences began to coalesce around the concept of race.[7]

Human beings are naturally curious about "others," and curiosity about variations among human groupings has followed different investigatory paths. Over the next two centuries, race developed into a pseudoscientific concept utilized, primarily, to justify the dehumanization of various globally unique categories of the human population. Many would look to science to offer an explanation as to why one human population appeared to perform in more "socially superior" ways than the others.

The work of Swedish-born zoologist and physician Carolus Linnaeus marks the beginning of scientific efforts to understand and classify the natural world. His 1758 publication of *Systema Naturae* (tenth edition) was viewed as a groundbreaking intellectual achievement.[8] The focus of Linnaeus's work was on understanding differences in the animal, plant, and mineral kingdoms. His conclusion: there was a hierarchy of development in the natural world. The animal kingdom emerged at the top, with human beings at the very forefront of the evolutionary ladder. Other scientists attempted to build on his work in their efforts to explain human differences.

Obvious variations in skin color, facial features, skull size, body types, and other observable characteristics led some to conclude, rather falsely, that there were, in fact, separate and distinct groups of human beings. Polygenetic theories would argue that the differences in physical appearances were due to the separate origins of the human species.[9] It was the German scientist Johann Friedrich Blumenbach who, in the late eighteenth century, provided the first racial classification system.[10] Blumenbach postulated that the human race was divided into five distinct groups: Caucasians, Mongolians, Malayans, Ethiopians, and Americans.

> Thus, the skin hues of white, yellow, brown, black, and red were associated with the different races, and Blumenbach, a member of the Caucasian group, concluded that whites were the most highly developed and the

original descendants of mankind. The other groups, viewed as savage, backward, underdeveloped, with lower levels of intelligence and social functioning, had suffered from the degenerative effects of poor diets and living in harsh physical environments.[11]

Given the global expansion of the exploitation and trafficking of humans and the need to justify unimaginable human indifference to suffering, the politically powerful attempted to marry the idea of race to a biological and human hierarchy. If a hierarchal existence was present in the natural world, did one also exist among humans? Did not "nature" provide evidence explaining the perceived superiority of one group over the others? Without any scientific proof or evidence, from its earliest inception, America constructed a society in which whites were viewed as the superior group; they were granted a privileged social status. In contrast, people of color were viewed as inferior. They were forced to accept a socially subordinate status, which limited their opportunities for social advancement.

While some looked to science, others looked to biblical explanations for differences, and similarities, among the human species. This was a popular approach among Christians, and America was emerging as an overwhelmingly Christian nation. For the monogenetic creationists, all life began with Adam and Eve.[12] In Genesis 2:3, Adam was the first man that God created, "in the image" of God Himself. Recognizing Adam's loneliness, God created Eve from one of Adam's ribs. Adam and Eve, the progenitors of human life, were represented as the Europeans, who dominated in the Western world. Others, with different colors and physical features, could also be explained by utilizing biblical text.[13]

The Curse of Ham or the Curse of Canaan is discussed in Genesis 9, where the word *slave* is introduced. Genesis 9:25–27 states: "And Noah said 'Cursed be Canaan! A slave of slaves, a slave to his brothers! Blessed be God, the God of Shem, but Canaan shall be his slave. God prosper Japheth . . . But Canaan shall be his slave.'"[14] Was this not a reference to the newly enslaved population in the Americas? The curse carried the mark of blackness, a biblical reference frequently cited by the slave-holding Christians in America to justify the perpetual enslavement and dehumanization of African people and their descendants.

The story of the Tower of Babel in Genesis 11:1–9 offered another explanation as to why human beings are different.[15] The people of Shinar joined together to build their own stairway to Heaven. Fearing his diminishing power as the almighty, God punished the people by giving each a different tongue, thus inhibiting their ability to communicate. Each group was forced onto new lands, occupying different regions of the Earth. "Divine intervention" resulted in the scattering of human beings throughout the world. God was, ultimately, responsible for producing human populations in different colors and speaking in different tongues.

Still, others sought different theoretical and pseudoscientific explanations for the obvious differences in the racial groups. For the phrenologists, different sizes of the human skull offered proof of distinct racial groups. Larger skulls presented a greater capacity for higher learning and intellectual achievement. Again, Europeans would emerge at the top of the evolutionary ladder. Moreover, "There were false notions of pure races, and subsequent arguments about mongrel races, often described as lower, savage breeds that needed to be conquered and tamed by the dominant race. But there appeared to be little doubt that differences among the races were significant, and that the power and dominance of the Caucasians were, indeed, a part of the natural world order."[16]

Exploring New Worlds

From the sixteenth through the nineteenth centuries, Europeans were global explorers. They traveled to all the world's continents, their presence proving particularly devastating to those in Africa and the Americas. The Caucasians seized the land and controlled the social resources, thus emerging as the dominating political force in the New World. In a little more than 150 years after Christopher Columbus's contact in the region, the native populations in North America, Central America, and throughout the Caribbean were systematically diminished, stripped of their land and social resources. They endured forced labor while being denied basic human rights. In addition, hundreds of thousands of Africans were forcibly transported from the west coast of Africa to the Americas as part of the international slave trade, resulting in the depopulation and underdevelopment of the African continent.[17]

The Europeans sought social, moral, and legal justification for the ongoing assault and exploitation of Africa and the Americas. This social and economic exploitation resulted in the enslavement of hundreds of thousands of Africans and Native Americans and their descendants. In fact, the enslaved African descendant population had become the mainstay labor of the developing colonies and formed the basis of wealth for the aristocratic agricultural societies of both the North and the South. The false notion that Africans and the indigenous Native American populations were a subcategory of human beings, or separate and distinct races, was conveniently embraced. It was used as the rationale for cultural domination and all resulting forms of social oppression and human humiliation that followed. Thus, race and racial discrimination were among the basic founding principles of American society.

Over time, the concept of race was socially constructed to reflect the existence of geographic or global human populations with distinguishable physical characteristics. These characteristics are innate or "genetically transmitted," resulting in consistent patterns of skin color, hair and body type, and other forms of observable characteristics throughout the population. With the naked eye, one could see great similarities in the skin color, shape of the eyes, and hair and body types of diverse human populations. Europeans were fair-skinned with straw-like hair. Those living in Asia had bright skin tones with unique, slanted eye shapes; the Africans were dark-hued with broad facial features and tightly curled hair; and the Native Americans possessed reddish skin tones, chiseled facial features, and long, rich black hair. There is no doubt that from a purely scientific point of view, there is just one race, the human race; however, human beings are not monolithic. As the Europeans emerged as leaders in the global order, this politically powerful and dominant racial group arbitrarily assigned a negative social value to those whose physical appearance differed from their own.

Race in America and the Emergence of White Supremacy

In the United States of America, concepts related to race and racial superiority are deeply interwoven into the American social fabric and are based on the notion of white supremacy.[18] White supremacy is the belief that white people are superior to all other people of color; their domination in the social, economic, and political realms offers "proof" of their superiority. However, not all of America's white citizens were among the emerging middle and upper classes. There were poor white Americans. Yet the existence of enormous populations of poor whites did little to deter their beliefs in the superiority of whites; given the opportunity, they, too, would eventually rise to the top. Furthermore, lower-class whites may have been economically impoverished and lacked political power, but they could take comfort in knowing that they were still white Americans! As noted by numerous historians, Europeans boarded the ships as British, French, Spaniards, Portuguese, Irish, and Italians, but once in America, it was important to embrace a "white" identity.[19]

These racist ideals and the belief in the desirability of whiteness resulted in the implementation of racist social practices that produced deleterious effects on people of color. A pattern of social separation emerged from the very beginning. New generations of Americans were socialized to believe that the separation of the races in living arrangements, employment, politics, power, and all forms of social interaction was the new social norm. Over time, these patterns of social living were embedded in the American psyche.

Historically, racial classifications have been used to elevate one group over another, distribute social resources, concentrate power and wealth in the hands of a few, create divisions among the people, segregate populations, and limit opportunities for the development of human potential. Race serves as a major social indicator, helping to assess the social status and physical conditions of members of the society. Most importantly, race provides a sense of social identity to many American citizens by falsely promoting the view that membership in one group is superior to all others. From the very beginning, the United States of America legislated racial classifications, making clear legal distinctions between the human rights of three main groups: the African, the European, and the Native American. These ubiquitous de jure and de facto rules and social customs were clear to most. However, among the Spanish-speaking groups, the Mexicans would be the first to discover that attempting to comply with the nation's racial categorization system would prove most challenging.

Mexican Americans: The "Other" Whites

The descendants of Mexico have had a particularly unique racial experience in the United States of America. Mexican Americans are the largest Spanish-speaking population in America, comprising nearly two-thirds of the Hispanic community.[20] As fully explained in chapter 3, determining the racial classification for the Mexican American was fraught with ambiguity from the very beginning, highlighting one of the difficulties in proclaiming a national or ethnic group as a race.

The first group of Mexican Americans were indigenous to the area. The Spaniards began their invasions into Mexico during the sixteenth century. For nearly two hundred years, the Mexicans were victims of repeated waves of European and U.S. aggression, resulting first in the European domination of Mexico and then in the loss of Mexican territory to the ever-expanding United States of America. Originally, the area that we now call Texas was part of Mexico, and it was occupied by indigenous Indian populations. After a series of takeover events, many Mexicans, who never traveled beyond the confines of their homesteads, awakened to the reality of their new status as citizens of the United States of America. In 1836, the Republic of Texas, controlled by a white majority, declared its independence from the Republic of Mexico. The 1845 Texas annexation incorporated the Republic of Texas into the United States of America, with Texas later admitted to the Union as the twenty-eighth state. In 1848, the Treaty of Guadalupe Hidalgo ended the Mexican-American War. Large sections of Mexico were now part of the United States of America, including California, New Mexico, Arizona, Nevada, Wyoming, and Colorado. Once citizens of Mexico, those who decided to stay were now citizens of the United States of America, with the guarantee that they would be granted the rights and privileges of U.S. (white) citizenship. Unfortunately, American racism produced a different result.[21]

Mexican Americans were legally classified as white by state and federal courts. But as noted by Cybelle Fox and Thomas Guglielmo, "it was clearly a subordinate form of whiteness."[22] As further highlighted in chapter 3, Mexican Americans, marked by both the Spanish language and their darker hue, were placed in the category of "other" and faced discrimination on an ongoing basis. The first Mexican Americans were neither migrants nor immigrants. However, once joined by new waves of immigrants from Mexico, the Mexican Americans (those born in America) also faced segregation—created by de facto rules and customs rather than codified in law—in education, employment, housing (barrios), and public facilities. Many of the Southwestern states, including California, Arizona, and Texas, once home to the Mexicans, now created separate schools for Mexican and Mexican American children. Their experiences would mirror that of the African Americans. Over time, Mexican Americans were denied full access to public facilities, including restaurants, movie theaters, swimming pools, and recreational areas. Their questionable status and privilege as white Americans would continue to be an issue of concern throughout the remainder of the twentieth century.

Since its founding, the United States of America has experienced four major immigration waves. The British, Germans, and Scotch-Irish dominated the first wave in the colonial era. The second wave, during the post–American Revolutionary and pre–Civil War era, sent millions of Germans, Irish, and Scandinavians to our shores. At the turn of the twentieth century, the third wave resulted in ten million new immigrants, dominated by those coming from Italy, Poland, and Greece. However, it is the fourth, contemporary wave of immigration, the largest in our nation's history, which has resulted in millions of future U.S. citizens coming not from Europe, like the first three waves, but from the Caribbean and Central and South America.[23] These predominantly Spanish-speaking populations from south of our border are often described as "people of color," but, depending on the place of origin, may also be classified as white, Afro-Mexican, Afro-Latinos, or black Hispanics.

The notion of Hispanics as a single racial group is a misnomer. The large percentage of "brown" people coming from south of the boarder is reflective of the long, extensive history of racial mixing, or miscegenation, that has occurred over time. As Justin Garcia notes:

> The vast physical diversity found among Latinos derives from the colonial history of Latin America, in which male European conquistadors engaged in sexual and marital unions with indigenous and African females on a scale that far exceeded that which occurred in British colonial North America. Over the centuries, this amalgamation produced physically blended and phenotypic diverse populations throughout the Spanish-speaking empire . . . Mexicans, Puerto Ricans, and other Latinos whose ancestry consists of significant admixture between Europeans, Amerindians, and Africans—to varying degrees, depending on which nation or region of Latin America one's heritage derives from—pose a major conceptual challenge to an American society that thinks of race in terms of concrete, clearly discernible categories.[24]

It is this amalgam of European, Amerindian, and African ancestry that we now identify as *miscegan*—the multiracial, blended, brown people of the world.[25] As indicated above, this population has emerged after generations of racial intermingling. It is difficult or near impossible to declare oneself as Caucasian, Indian, or African. It is this "brown" population that when asked to racially identify themselves on census forms are far more likely to select the category of "other," given their discomfort in proclaiming their racial group to be white, black, or native.[26]

Hispanic America

As indicated previously, there is tremendous ethnic diversity in the Hispanic community. During the fourth wave of immigration, millions of Hispanics arrived from Mexico, joined by those from Cuba and a migrating population from Puerto Rico. While the Mexican American, Cuban American, and Puerto Rican populations continue to represent the largest Spanish-speaking groups in the United States of America, increasing numbers of immigrants from El Salvador, Guatemala, Costa Rica, Colombia, the Dominican Republic, and other Spanish-speaking nations have joined them. Their journeys toward full American citizenship are quite dissimilar. For example, Mexicans have played an integral part in the history and development of the United States of America; the expansion of the Cuban American population is linked directly to the Cuban revolution and the disastrous consequences of the Bay of Pigs; and Puerto Ricans have been declared citizens since 1917, when the United States of America acquired the island and granted it commonwealth status. Those from El Salvador, Guatemala, Costa Rica, Colombia, the Dominican Republic, Honduras, Ecuador, Peru, Nicaragua, Venezuela, and Argentina are more recent arrivals to the United States of America. Today, there are an estimated fifty-seven million Americans who indicate they are of Hispanic or Latino origin.[27] When asked to self-identify their racial group, most prefer to indicate an ethnic identity. Given their preference to cling to an ethnic heritage (I am Puerto Rican, Chicano, Cuban), discussions about the emergence of a "transnational Latino identity" may be premature. As with the Mexican American experience, it is the language, as well as the immigrant status, that has become racialized. The repeated experiences of the Spanish-speaking population with segregation and discrimination, coupled with a disproportionately higher poverty rate and marginalization in low-skill, low-status occupations, have resulted in many concluding that they, too, are victims of American racism.

While there is a Hispanic presence in most states, the Hispanic ethnic populations are largely concentrated in ten states: Arizona, California, Colorado, Florida, Illinois, New Jersey, New Mexico, New York, Pennsylvania, and Texas. "Eighty-six percent of Mexican Americans make their homes in five Southwestern states: Texas, California, New Mexico, Arizona, and Colorado. Texas and California account for more than 50 percent of the total Hispanic population in the United States of America. About two-thirds of Puerto Ricans residing in the United States of America are in the New York City area, including nearby New Jersey. About 60 percent of Cuban Hispanics reside in Florida, with the heaviest concentration in Dade County (Miami). Another 20 percent are in the New York–New Jersey area, particularly in Union City, New Jersey. Illinois also has large numbers of Mexicans, Puerto Ricans, and Cuban Hispanics—mostly in Chicago."[28] These heavy areas of concentration can best be described as ethnic enclaves, where one's racial and ethnic identities are reinforced by the homogeneous nature of the residential communities.

In examining questions surrounding race and identity in Hispanic America, we will focus on seven groups: Puerto Rican, Mexican, Cuban, Dominican, Costa Rican, Guatemalan, and Colombian Americans. Their sizable numbers, in addition to their geographic locations, will allow us to investigate their collective journeys toward immersion and assimilation into American culture and/or their unique approaches to embracing and reinforcing their ethnic and cultural heritage.

Notes

1. Roth, 2012.
2. Gonzalez, 2011.
3. Rosales and Rosales, 1997.
4. Arreola, 2004.
5. Kamen, 2004.
6. Cline, 2000; Jones, 2000.
7. Reid-Merritt, 2017, p. 4.
8. Linnaeus, 1758.
9. Stocking, 1968.
10. Bhopal, 2007.
11. Reid-Merritt, 2017.
12. Trasancos, 2016.
13. Genesis 2:3.
14. Genesis 9:25–27.
15. Genesis 11:1–9.
16. Reid-Merritt, 2017, p. 6.
17. Rodney, 2011.
18. Kendi, 2016; Bonilla-Silva, 2001; Dobratz and Shanks-Meile, 2000.
19. Grant, 1970; Daniels, 2011; Ignatiev, 2008.
20. Ennis, Ríos-Vargas, and Albert, 2011.
21. Reid-Merritt, 2017.
22. Fox and Guglielmo, 2012, p. 328.
23. Schaefer, 2018.
24. Garcia, 2017, p. 160.
25. Reid-Merritt, 2017.
26. CTL News, 2014.
27. U.S. Census Bureau, 2017.
28. Lamar University, 2015, p. 1.

References

Arreola, Daniel (2004). *Hispanic Spaces, Latino Places: Community and Cultural Diversity in Contemporary America*, Houston: University of Texas Press.

Bhopal, Raj (2007). "The Beautiful Skull and Blumenbach's Errors: The Birth of the Scientific Concept of Race," *BMJ* 335: 1308.

Bonilla-Silva, Eduardo (2001). *White Supremacy and Racism in the Post-Civil Rights Era*, Boulder: Lynne Rienner Publishers.

Cline, Sarah (2000). "Native Peoples of Colonial Central Mexico," in *The Cambridge History of the Native Peoples of the Americas*, Bruce G. Trigger and Wilcomb E. Washburn, eds., Cambridge: Cambridge University Press, 2: 187–222.

CTL News (2014). "Hispanics More Likely to Choose 'Other Race' in U.S. Census—Prefer to Be Identified by Country of Origin," https://ctlatinonews

.com/hispanics-more-likely-to-choose-other-race-in-u-s-census-prefer-to-be-identified-by-country-of-origin/.

Daniels, Roger (2011). *Coming to America: A History of Immigration and Ethnicity in American Life*, 2nd ed., New York: Harper Perennial.

Dobratz, Betty A., and Stephanie Shanks-Meile (2000). *White Power, White Pride!: The White Separatist Movement in the United States*, Baltimore: Johns Hopkins University Press.

Ennis, Sharon R., Merarys Ríos-Vargas, and Nora G. Albert (2011). "The Hispanic Population: 2010," U.S. Census Bureau, https://www.census.gov/prod/cen2010/briefs/c2010br-04.pdf.

Fox, Cybelle, and Thomas Guglielmo (2012). "Defining America's Racial Boundaries: Blacks, Mexicans, and European Immigrants, 1890–1945," *American Journal of Sociology* 118: 327–379.

Garcia, Justin D. (2017). "Hispanic/Latino Identity as Racial Misnomer," in *Race in America: How a Pseudoscientific Concept Shaped Human Interaction*, Patricia Reid-Merritt, ed., Santa Barbara: Praeger, 155–180.

Gonzalez, Juan (2011). *Harvest of Empire: A History of Latinos in America*, New York: Penguin Books.

Grant, Madison (1970). *Passing of the Great Race, Or, the Racial Basis of European History* (American Immigration Collection, Series 2), Buffalo: Ayer Co Publishers.

Ignatiev, Noel (2008). *How the Irish Became White* (Routledge Classics, vol. 137), 1st ed., Oxford: Routledge.

Jones, Grant D. (2000). "The Lowland Maya from the Conquest to the Present," in *The Cambridge History of the Native Peoples of the Americas*, Bruce G. Trigger and Wilcomb E. Washburn, eds., Cambridge: Cambridge University Press, 2: 346–391.

Kamen, Henry (2004). *Empire: How Spain Became a World Power, 1492–1763*, New York: HarperCollins.

Kendi, Ibram X. (2016). *Stamped from the Beginning: The Definitive History of Racist Ideas in America*, New York: Nations Books.

Lamar University (2015). "Hispanic Heritage Month," https://www.lamar.edu/diversity-inclusion/hispanic-heritage/2015.html.

Linnaeus, Carolus (1758). *Systema naturae per regna tria naturae: secundum classes, ordines, genera, species, cum characteribus, differentiis, synonymis, locis* (in Latin), 10th ed., Stockholm: Laurentius Salvius.

Reid-Merritt, Patricia, ed. (2017). *Race in America: How a Pseudoscientific Concept Shaped Human Interaction*, Santa Barbara: Praeger.

Rodney, Walter (2011). *How Europe Underdeveloped Africa*, Baltimore: Black Classic Press.

Rosales, F. Arturo, and Francisco A. Rosales (1997). *Chicano! The History of the Mexican American Civil Rights Movement* (Hispanic Civil Rights), 2nd rev. ed., Houston: Arte Publico Press.

Roth, Wendy (2012). *Race Migrations: Latinos and the Cultural Transformation of Race*, Stanford: Stanford University Press.

Schaefer, Richard T. (2018). *Racial and Ethnic Groups*, 15th ed., Boston: Pearson-Prentice Hall.

Stocking, George W. (1968). *Race, Culture and Evolution: Essays in the History of Anthropology*, New York: Free Press, 38–40.

Trasancos, Stacy A. (2016). *Particles of Faith: A Catholic Guide to Navigating Science*, Notre Dame: Ave Maria Press.

U.S. Census Bureau (2017). "Facts for Features: Hispanic Heritage Month 2017," https://www.census.gov/newsroom/facts-for-features/2017/hispanic-heritage.html.

CHAPTER TWO

From Whence We Come?

Introduction

Who are all of these people, where did they come from, and how did they get here? Since the passage of the 1965 Immigration and Nationality Act, the United States of America has experienced a surge in immigration. During this most recent (fourth) historical wave of immigration, an unprecedented number of these newcomers hail from south of the U.S. border. This chapter examines trends in immigration from Spanish-speaking countries of the Western Hemisphere.

Becoming Hispanic

A common experience of Hispanic Americans, regardless of citizenship status, is the disquieting inevitability of encountering the presumption by others that Hispanics are from somewhere else (i.e., of being *in* but not *of* this country). The poignant irony of such moments is that individuals who are, in fact, descendants of immigrants often hold this presumption, particularly Euro-descendant Americans. A secondary and quite commonplace presumption is that Hispanics are an immigrant population, though only slightly more than one-third of Hispanics in the United States are foreign-born, and Puerto Ricans—the second largest Hispanic group—are not by definition immigrants. A vast majority of Hispanics (approximately three-fourths) are also U.S. citizens by virtue of being born in the country (birthright citizenship or through naturalization). Once immigrants are naturalized, they cease being immigrants and are then full U.S. citizens. They may claim an immigrant identity in terms of

lineage or prior citizenship in another country, but they are nonetheless still identified as immigrants by the ethno-racial majority. The characterization of Hispanics as an immigrant population is factually inaccurate and underscores the reality that identity is formed not just by self-definition but also other-definition. A feature of the former is that Hispanic (or Latino/Latinx) is not the primary descriptor of identity for most

Hispanics; instead, it is their sense of affinity with a specific nationality. Ethnic identity remains strong, even for many Hispanics born and raised in the United States. Moreover, successive generations of Hispanics increasingly identify themselves as American, and for those who designate themselves as "white" in the census questionnaire, the association is not merely to a specific phenotypical profile, but with Americanization more generally (i.e., identifying as someone who is both *in* and *of* this country).

Both aspects of identity formation further compound, and certainly complicate, what it means to be Hispanic in the United States. Does the term *Hispanic* connote a clearly discernible demographic group? What anchors Hispanic identity? Is it a pan-ethnic culture and identity, or are Hispanics an amalgam of various ethnic groups whose primary sense of identity is nationality (i.e., being Mexican, Cuban, Costa Rican, Dominican, Puerto Rican, etc.)? Perhaps the term is more appropriately a transnational term that is, to be geographically specific, also (Western) hemispheric. Like all other inhabitants of the hemisphere, Hispanics are quite literally of the Americas and Americans (or Americanos) in the broadest sense of the term. The unfortunate appropriation of the term *American* by the United States certainly muddles the possibility of a more transnational, hemispheric sense of identity for Latin Americans. In a sense, one response to the question *From whence we come?* is that Hispanics are from here—the Americas.

This initial response to the framing question points to a central paradox between how Hispanics are defined by non-Hispanics (other-definition) and their own self-definition. On the one hand, Hispanics are generally—and erroneously—other-defined in rather homogenous terms as having: (1) a common primary language (Spanish); (2) a collective, transnational identity (Hispanic); (3) a similar immigrant experience (foreign-born or first-generation); and (4) a primary affinity for the left side of their dual identity (be that Mexican American, Cuban American, Colombian American, etc.). The error in this other-definition is twofold. The first problem is the mistaken assumption that the homogeneity ascribed to Hispanics as a group is more essential to their self-definition than the specific nationalities to which they have a particular affinity. The additional problem is that this homogeneity is counterposed against the purported homogeneity of Americanism (i.e., to be American means embracing mono-lingualism, mono-culturalism, and mono-nationalism). The false dichotomy between being Hispanic and being American fuels the other-definition of Hispanics as being anathema to Americanism, at least from the standpoint of many in the ethno-racial majority.

The other side of the paradox, the lived experience—and hence, the self-definition—of Hispanics in the United States, diverges quite dramatically from their other-definition by non-Hispanics. Survey research by the Pew Research Center indicates that the perception that Hispanics share a primary common language is incorrect. Approximately 36 percent of Hispanics describe themselves as bilingual, 25 percent mainly use English, 38 percent mainly use Spanish, and among English-speaking Hispanics, overall 59 percent are bilingual.[1] Despite the increase in English-language proficiency (due largely to younger Hispanics) and the fact that subsequent generations of Hispanic parents are speaking less Spanish with their children, Hispanics are not moving toward the monolingualism that the traditional model of assimilation expects. Moreover, an overwhelming sense (95 percent in 2016)[2] among Hispanics is that speaking Spanish is important for future generations; interestingly, nonetheless, a clear majority of Hispanics (71 percent)[3] also believe that speaking Spanish is not necessary to be considered Latino. What underlies these seemingly inchoate set of trends is a clearly discernible fact about Hispanic identity in the United States, namely that bilingualism will remain an important, though not *the* defining, feature of what it means to be Hispanic in the United States. The idea that full acculturation into the American mainstream requires mono-lingualism, mono-culturalism, and an exclusive (i.e., U.S.-centric) sense of national identity will be increasingly difficult to sustain.

Hispanic American

Bilingual and bicultural Hispanics—particularly those born and raised in the United States—are often mildly amused by the surprised reactions of non-Hispanics upon learning that their Hispanic acquaintances are no less Americanized than themselves. The film *Selena* captures the irony of such moments. After releasing an English-language single, Selena enjoyed a hearty laugh with her siblings over comments by members of the music industry that expressed astonishment at how quickly she had learned English. Though she sang in Spanish for most of her short career as the Queen of Tejano music, Selena was a predominantly English-speaking native of South Texas who was fully acculturated into American popular culture.

The cognitive dissonance that underlies such reactions emerges from three failures of recognition. The first is the failure to recognize that being both American and Hispanic is not a binary, zero-sum proposition (i.e., the more one is of something, the less he or she is of something else).

Indeed, Selena embodies the proposition that enacting both identities generates more, not less, cultural capital. Her musical career became the pathway for her to become fully proficient in Spanish while simultaneously embodying a bicultural sense of being American that millions of fans could emulate. The second is a failure to recognize that cultural identity formation—for individuals and groups—does not unfold within isolated compartments, or silos, but at the intersections of cross-cultural engagement among the various Hispanic groups and more generally between Hispanics and the broader American culture. On one level, the cultural intermixing (*mezcla*) among various Hispanic ethnicities is producing an emerging (pan-ethnic) Hispanic identity that is quite specific to the United States, though the primary referent for Hispanic identity in the United States remains the nationality of particular Hispanic groups (be they Mexican, Cuban, Costa Rican, and the like). At another level, the *mezcla* of U.S. Hispanic cultures with American popular culture is also engendering a nascent Hispanicization of the latter. These multiple, cross-cutting, and transcultural hybridities among Hispanics, and between Hispanics and American culture, capture Octavio Paz's poignant characterization of the United States as the Republic of the Future.[4]

The self-definition Hispanics construct for themselves is therefore more nuanced and multilayered than the monolithic other-definition that serves as the prism through which Hispanics are often perceived. Hispanic self-definition is based on a triad of affinities—to specific national-origin groups, to an embrace of Americanization, and to a generalized (pan-ethnic) sense of being Hispanic. The interplay of these affinities informs how Hispanics construct their self-definition. Moreover, the prospect of ameliorating the paradox between that self-definition and how Hispanics are other-defined depends on the capacity, indeed the willingness, of non-Hispanics to recognize how Hispanics define themselves from their own standpoint.

An ongoing debate among students of immigration is whether Hispanic immigrants will emulate Euro-descendants in assimilating into American culture by relegating their ethnicity to the private sphere of family, community, and co-ethnics. The traditional assimilationist model empowers immigrants to maintain a semblance of symbolic ethnicity in the form of dual identities (Polish Americans, Italian Americans, Irish Americans, and the like), as long as their identity is anchored to the right of the hyphen. A corollary of the assimilationist model is that the process of absorbing an ethno-racial minority or immigrant group into mainstream American culture is unidirectional; the former is absorbed into the latter.

The presence of Hispanic Americans challenges this traditional understanding of becoming American. Two-thirds of Hispanics are U.S.-born and are immediately acculturated into American culture, but they are also Hispanicizing elements of popular culture in the United States. The nationalization of Latino music, cuisine, and celebrations such as Cinco de Mayo and Día de los Muertos, as well as the prevalence of (Hispanic and non-Hispanic) Spanish-speaking Americans, suggest the United States is experiencing a level of reciprocal acculturation that is unlike the assimilation of Euro-descendant immigrants. Regional variations of Hispanicization, such as the emergence of the bicultural genre of Tejano Rock in Texas, are bicultural and bilingual in production and popular appeal (e.g., Los Lonely Boys). Another response to the question *From whence we come?* is that Hispanics come from the sociocultural phenomenon of Hispanicization that is influencing the national identity of the United States, a process of cultural intermixing (*mezcla*) among various Hispanic nationalities and more broadly between Hispanics and the popular culture of the United States.

Place and Region

This response to the framing question of this chapter points to the centrality of place in Hispanic identity. At a macro level, the United States represents a multicultural venue with broad latitude for various Hispanic and non-Hispanic groups to enact transcultural identities and politico-cultural coalitions. The affective dimension of certain religious, cultural, or political movements has a centripetal effect of coalescing Hispanics across their various nationalities (for example, Hispanic Heritage Month, the Americanization (and commercialization) of Cinco de Mayo, the approximately fifty National Puerto Rican Day parades throughout the country, the transcultural celebrations of Día de Los Muertos, Día de la Virgen de Guadalupe, and Fiesta de los Reyes Magos, as well as Hispanic coalitions that engage in immigrant rights advocacy). At the micro level, the centrality of place is also expressed by ascribing a particular Hispanic identity to specific locales—for example, Tejanos (Texas), Californios (California), Nuyoricans (New York), Spanish (New Mexico), Boriqua (Puerto Rico), Dominicans (New York), Cubanos (Florida and New Jersey), Chicanos (Southwest U.S.), Colombians (New Jersey and New York), etc. The centrality of place for Hispanic identity means that affinities for local culture have a deeper resonance in terms of ethno-racial identity than the pan-ethnic category *Hispanic*.

However, even regional enclaves of Hispanics reflect the broad geographical dispersal and intermixing among Hispanic groups. The

Hispanic presence in San Antonio, Texas—the seventh largest city in the United States—is perceived almost exclusively as Mexican American. The city was part of Mexico before Texas became an independent republic and later annexed as the twenty-eighth state in 1845. However, almost one in ten of San Antonio's Hispanic population of over one million is not of Mexican descent; they are Puerto Rican, Cuban, Colombian, or another South American nationality.[5] Data compiled by Pew Research Center indicate that cities with long-standing associations with particular Hispanic groups are becoming increasingly diverse in their Hispanic populations. The proportion of Cuban Americans in the Miami metropolitan region has decreased to a slight majority (54 percent); and, while Puerto Ricans are still the largest Hispanic group in the New York City metropolitan area, they comprise only 28 percent of the area's Hispanic population; slightly more than one in five are Dominican American.[6]

The increasing diversification of Hispanic enclaves and the broader Hispanicization of the United States do not mean the country is the place where Jose Vasconcelos's racial fantasy of *raza cosmica* (the universal race) will be realized. Instead, the United States is uniquely situated as *the* place in the Western Hemisphere where Hispanic ethnicities are reinvigorated through interethnic engagement with each other and the broader popular culture, as well as through ongoing infusions of immigrant co-ethnics. In a more metaphorical sense, the United States is also *the* place where the (pan-ethnic) Hispanicization of both Latin American nationalities in the United States and the broader American popular culture will continue to mediate how the triad of affinities unfolds, i.e., the affinities to specific national-origin groups, to an embrace of Americanization, and to a generalized (pan-ethnic) sense of being Hispanic. The manner of this unfolding within the United States will also determine whether the paradox between self- and other-definitions of Hispanic identity will be ameliorated or exacerbated.

Geopolitical Locations

The question *From whence we come?* also implicates the proximity of Latin American nationalities to the historical project of forging national identity in the United States. National identities take shape through the specific trajectories of historical experience and formative myths that form the narrative frameworks for ascribing meaning to those experiences; both are integral dimensions of the nation-building project. A formative myth of the United States is that we are a nation of immigrants. Indeed, the United States is a truly global nation through the extraordinary ethno-racial, linguistic, and cultural diversity that immigration has engendered. Immigration to the United States has spurred unprecedented economic growth, the revitalization of urban communities, and positive population growth. Birthright citizenship for the children of immigrants and the comparative ease of naturalization (albeit with inexplicably lengthy wait periods and exorbitant costs) enable immigrant families to enjoy the blessings of citizenship within a generation of their arrival. The narrative arc of formative myths in popular culture invariably points in an upward and positive direction. However, the "nation of immigrants" narrative also has the countervailing historical reality of the forced migration of enslaved Africans and the violent and systematic displacement of indigenous populations. It also includes the incorporation of nonwhites through military conquest, mass deportations of undocumented immigrants in the 1930s, 1950s, and the early decades of the twenty-first century, as well as the explicit manipulation of immigration policy to exclude or limit non-European people (the Naturalization Act of 1790 excluding aliens who were not free white persons). The Chinese Exclusion Act of 1882 and racially restrictive measures in immigration legislation enacted in 1917 and 1924 are also profound distortions of America's stated commitment to an open and egalitarian constitutional democracy.

From a contemporary point of view, the paroxysms of anti-immigrant and nativist furor that fueled political polarization during the Obama and Trump presidencies may appear to be unique historical moments, but they are quite consistent with recurrent episodes of targeting or racializing immigrants as existential threats to the American way of life. Immigrants are often racialized as the threatening *Racial Other*. Authorized and unauthorized Hispanic immigrants as well as naturalized and U.S.-born Hispanics bear witness to a vitriolic political discourse in the United States that denigrates them as the *Foreign Other*. Thus, another response to the question *From whence we come?* is that Hispanics also come from the (Janus-faced) paradoxical historical experience of immigration in the United States.

Immigration from Latin America to the United States is transnational migration, just like European immigration to the United States. However, while the latter is also transoceanic and declined dramatically after the 1920s, the former is intra-hemispheric and contemporaneous and disproportionately frames immigration politics and discourse in the United States. For instance, Mexicans and Central Americans are almost exclusively associated with "illegal" immigration in terms of unauthorized border crossing. However, virtually half of undocumented immigrants in the

United States entered the country legally (i.e., immigrants who gained legal entry through points of entry like airports) and overstayed their visas. The hemispheric context of Hispanic immigration to the United States also means that the geographic proximity of Latin American countries to the United States makes the presence of Hispanics in the United States inextricably linked to the hegemonic machinations of the United States throughout Latin America. This includes the legacies of the Monroe Doctrine, Manifest Destiny, the U.S.-Mexican War, the Spanish-American War, military interventions and regime change in the Caribbean, from Mexico to Chile, as well as the treatment of immigrants as mere units of production through the Bracero Program. Thus, another response to the question *From whence we come?* is that Hispanics are inextricably linked to the nation-building project that made the United States a global power, through the geographical and geopolitical proximity of specific Latin American nationalities to this country.

Historical Antecedents

Hispanic immigrants arrive in the United States with far more (metaphoric) proximity to the United States than is generally recognized, in terms of the historical presence and impact of American power in the Western Hemisphere and Caribbean. The Mexican dictator Porfirio Diaz is known to have quipped, "Poor Mexico, so far from God, so close to the United States."[7] The mere presence of Mexican Americans and Puerto Ricans in the United States, unlike other Hispanic groups, is rooted in the imposition of territorial jurisdiction through military conquest; the border quite literally crossed them. For Mexican immigrants entering the United States legally or illegally, many points of destination were historically part of Mexico, and millions of present-day Mexican Americans descend from Mexicans who lived in the Southwest before it was incorporated into the United States. Other Hispanic groups, like Costa Ricans, Cubans, Dominicans, Guatemalans, or Colombians, arrive in, and integrate themselves into, the United States with a different sense of proximity. Like Mexico and Puerto Rico, Cuba and the Dominican Republic share a certain geographic proximity to the United States. The former is only ninety miles from the nearest U.S. coastline, and the latter is only 237 miles (air travel distance)[8] from U.S. territorial jurisdiction (Puerto Rico). However, both countries are closely intertwined with the historical trajectory of the United States as a global power. The explosion that sank the battleship USS *Maine* in the harbor of Havana, Cuba, triggered the three-month Spanish-American War, which resulted, with the signing of the Treaty of Paris, in the United States acquiring the Spanish colonial possessions of Puerto Rico, Guam, and the Philippines.[9] This critical, historical juncture enabled the United States to project its military and diplomatic power well beyond the Western Hemisphere. Puerto Rico was initially incorporated into the United States as an unorganized territory. Puerto Ricans became U.S. citizens in 1917 through the Jones Act (just in time to serve in World War I), and the island nation became a commonwealth of the United States through its 1948 constitution.[10] Guam remains an unincorporated territory of the United States, with ongoing efforts to acquire commonwealth status, like Puerto Rico. Since 1950, native Guamanians (or Chamorros) have been U.S. citizens. Like Puerto Rico, Guam has limited political enfranchisement and representation in Congress.[11] The United States initially intended to maintain the Philippines as a colonial possession, but a bloody, three-year conflict erupted between 16,000 Filipino fighters and 120,000 U.S. soldiers, with more U.S. soldiers killed (4,200) than in the Spanish-American War.[12] After World War II, the Philippines secured independence from the United States on July 4, 1946.

Cuba has also had close (even dangerous) political proximity to the United States. Throughout the Cold War, there was palpable conflict between the United States and the Soviet Union, including the humiliating failure of the CIA-sponsored Bay of Pigs invasion and the (near-apocalyptic) standoff over the placement of Russian nuclear missiles sites on Cuban soil. The adversarial posture between the two superpowers also shaped immigration policy toward Cuba, including the preferential treatment of Cuban refugees (mass emigration in the immediate aftermath of the Cuban Revolution, expedited green cards through the 1966 Cuban Adjustment Act, the Mariel boatlift of the 1980s, and the 1995 wet-foot, dry-foot policy).[13]

As noted, the Dominican Republic also has a certain geographic proximity to the United States and, like Cuba, a long-standing and complicated proximity to American hegemony in the Western Hemisphere. The United States imposed direct administrative control over customs revenues and repeatedly intervened militarily, from 1912 to 1965, for economic (protection of investments and debt repayment) and geopolitical (stemming German influence in the Caribbean during World War I and preventing a domino-theory effect of the Cuban Revolution during the mid-1960s) motivations.[14] Guatemala, Costa Rica, and Colombia do not have the same geographical proximity to the United States as Mexico, Puerto Rico, Cuba, and the Dominican Republic, but as subsequent chapters outline, they are all (geopolitically) proximate to the project of American nation building in the Western Hemisphere. This includes U.S.

involvement in the civil conflict that severed what is now Panama from Colombia (1903–1904), the direct and indirect support of the armed revolt against the Teodoro Picardo government in Costa Rica (1948), and the CIA-orchestrated overthrow of the democratically elected government of Jacobo Arbenz in Guatemala (1954).

The historical precursor to the modern geopolitical interlacing of Latin America with U.S. hegemony was the triad of civilizational clashes between European colonial powers (Spanish and Portuguese) on the one hand, and Mesoamerican, Andean, and African civilizations on the other. A cruel irony of applying the misnomer of the New World to the Western Hemisphere is that Mesoamerican and Andean civilizational development predates the establishment of viable European societies. By the mid-sixteenth century, Spain's *conquista* of Mesoamerican and Andean civilizations was firmly established from Mexico to South America; within another hundred years, the indigenous populations of the region had declined between 80 and 90 percent, which precipitated the forced importation of African slaves as early as the sixteenth and seventeenth centuries. Benign phrases like "Discovery of the New World," "New World Encounters," or "the Columbian Exchange" elide the enormity of the human catastrophe that engulfed present-day Latin America. What is euphemistically referred to as "Columbian Exchange" certainly created an unprecedented triad of transatlantic commercial trade between the Americas, Europe, and Africa. However, the cornerstone of this epochal period of economic development was an equally epochal triad of human calamity. The contributing factors included the African slave trade, which brought more than ten million enslaved Africans to Latin America and the Caribbean, the enslavement of indigenous people in the Americas, and the large-scale decimation of Indians by European diseases to which they had little to no immunity.

Hispanic Ancestry: Indigenous Americans and Enslaved Africans

The forced importation of millions of enslaved Africans into present-day Latin America, the superimposition of colonial rule and a racial *casta* system on indigenous societies through military conquest, and the enslavement and decimation of indigenous populations by pandemic diseases brought to the Americas by Europeans produced a human disaster that is nonpareil. The historical crosscurrents of economic development and human devastation had an even deeper and broader impact on Latin America (Mexico, the Caribbean, and Central and South America) than the British colonies had along the Eastern seaboard of North America.

The devastation of indigenous civilizations in the Americas that pre-cipitated the forced migration of enslaved Africans throughout Latin America created a discernible African diaspora throughout present-day Latin America. Despite historical efforts to deny, diminish, and even denigrate the Afro-descendant population in various Latin American countries, Africans in the Americas became part of the transracial *mestizaje* (miscegenation) and sociocultural intermixing (*mezcla*), along with Spaniards/Portuguese (and other Europeans) and indigenous populations. The result was a mixed-race population of color. The historical tendency of several Latin American countries to describe their nation's population as white and *mestizo* (i.e., European and Indian) is belied by the discernible African presence in the Americas. The phenotypical features of Afro-descendants throughout Latin America; the linguistic and cultural hybridity integrated into Spanish dialects, cuisine, music, and dance; and the syncretism of Yoruba-based religions in Latin America (Santeria and Candomblé) are undeniable though still not fully recognized.

Present-day Latin America is also a product of the ongoing legacy of pre-Columbian indigenous populations. That influence is not limited to historical artifacts and archaeological sites but is an integral part of the multiracial, multilingual, and multicultural profile of Latin America. Although Spanish and Portuguese are the most common languages of Latin America, hundreds of indigenous languages are currently spoken in Latin America, some by only a few thousand persons (Popoluca) and others by millions (Quechua and various Mayan languages). The linguistic and cultural hybridity and religious syncretism of indigenous (pre-Columbian) communities, coupled with the parallel impact of the African diaspora on present-day Latin America, mean that the question of *From whence we come?* necessarily implicates the crosscurrents of civilizational clashes and sociocultural intermixing that formed modern-day Latin America. A proper understanding of the historical lineage of Hispanic Americans cannot therefore privilege Europeans and mestizos while excluding or diminishing the Africans and indigenous peoples from the projects of nation making and national identity formation.

Twenty-First Century Hispanic American

A final rejoinder to the question of *From whence we come?* is to explore where Hispanic Americans are presently. That response, however, is not without challenges. Unfortunately, the U.S.-centric approach to education creates a certain intellectual myopia among students that is compounded by sensationalized and partisan news coverage for the general public.

Current controversies and crises like immigration, race relations, and demographic change in the United States are decoupled from historical, regional, and global developments. Consequently, the saliency and urgency that attach to polarizing issues are perceived as being without precedent. For instance, despite hyperbolic political rhetoric that the country is being overrun by "illegal" immigration, the immigrant share of the U.S. population in 2010 (13 percent) was consistent with historical standards and even notably below the peak of 15 percent in 1890. Much of the twentieth century witnessed a steady decline in the overall percentage of foreign-born Americans to as low as 5 percent in 1970.[15] However, in large part due to changes in immigration policy after enactment of the landmark Immigration and Nationality Act of 1965, the flow of immigrants to the United States, especially from Latin America and Asia, increased significantly starting in the 1970s. Indeed, immigration from Latin America and South and East Asia has completely overwhelmed immigration from Europe and Canada. The Pew Research Center notes that prior to the 1970s, immigration to the United States was predominantly from Europe and Canada; in 1960, 84 percent of the US foreign-born population was from Europe and Canada and only 14 percent was from Latin America (including Mexico) and South and East Asia. By 2016, the relative proportions among these nationalities had virtually flipped: 13 percent came from Europe and Canada, while 78 percent came from Latin America and South and East Asia.[16] The share of the foreign-born population from Latin America has steadily increased from 1960 (4 percent) to a high of 25 percent in 2016, whereas the share of Mexicans in the foreign-born population peaked at 29 percent in 2010–2011 and decreased to 26 percent in 2016.

The Migration Policy Institute estimated that in 2010, the top five states with the largest overall immigrant population in 2010 were (in order of descending rank) California, New York, Texas, Florida, and New Jersey. The top two states are also California (27 percent) and New York (22 percent), in terms of the proportion of a state's population that is immigrant; New Jersey (21 percent) is ranked third, while Florida and Nevada were fourth and fifth (both at 19 percent.[17] The most populous states in the United States continue to receive the largest number of immigrants; however, the geographic distribution of immigrants arriving in the country is changing the demographic profile of less populous states, particularly in the South. Between 2000 and 2010, none of the top five states with the largest percent increases in immigrants were among the top ten most populous states, but they were all either in the Deep or Upper South (Alabama, South Carolina, Tennessee, Arkansas, and Kentucky).[18] The geographic distribution of immigrants is a function of the points of entry for immigrants but is also due to domestic migration after their arrival in the United States. The U.S.- and foreign-born Hispanic population in the United States follows a similar trajectory of geographic concentration and dispersal. Hispanics are heavily concentrated in the most populous states in the country. Approximately thirty-seven of the fifty-eight million Hispanic Americans live in California, Texas, Florida, New York, and Illinois. However, between 2000 and 2015, some of the fastest rates of growth in a state's Hispanic population occurred in other states—Arizona, New Jersey, Colorado, and Georgia. The highest rate of growth for any state in the country was Georgia (11.8 percent).[19]

The following chapters offer nationality-specific case studies of the historical, sociocultural, and ethno-racial dynamics that frame the current presence of Hispanics in the United States, in terms of how ethno-racial identity is formed. The chapters focus specifically on Mexican Americans, Puerto Rican Americans, Cuban Americans, Guatemalan Americans, Costa Rican Americans, Dominican Americans, and Colombian Americans. While these seven focus groups are among the largest of the Spanish-speaking communities, the diversity of ethnic nationalities that is part of Hispanic American extends well beyond them. However, a focus on these seven groups provides a compelling rationale for linking the discourse on race and identity for Hispanic Americans to the processes of national identity formation in the nations from whence Hispanics have come to the United States. The specific scope of the book does not permit a comprehensive or encyclopedic analysis of how immigration from all (Spanish-speaking) Latin American countries shapes the ethno-racial identity of Hispanics in the United States. The criteria for selecting some, but not all, Hispanic groups in the United States were: (1) to ensure national-origin diversity from throughout Latin America—North America (Mexico), Central America (Guatemala and Costa Rica), South America (Colombia), and the Caribbean (Puerto Rico, Cuba, and the Dominican Republic); (2) to provide a range of demographic profiles in terms of population, socioeconomic status, and race; and (3) to include Hispanic groups that highlight different themes in the discourse on race and identity in Hispanic America.

Americans and the Americas

An additional methodological note concerns the national-origin groups that comprise Hispanic America, in terms of nomenclature, and which Latin American nationalities are part of Hispanic America. The book refers to specific national-origin groups in the United States as hyphenated

Americans—regardless of citizenship status or levels of assimilation or acculturation—for example, Colombian Americans or Dominican Americans. To be a Hispanic American, within the analytic frame of this book, is quite simply to be a resident of the United States who self-defines as belonging to one of the nineteen Spanish-speaking nationalities of Latin America listed below. The (nationality-specific) Hispanic groups encompass both U.S.-born and foreign-born residents of the United States. Additionally, the remaining discussion in this chapter contains references to immigrants from specific Hispanic nationalities; those references are specifically to foreign-born U.S. residents of a Hispanic nationality, not the entire group that includes U.S.-born individuals.

Latin America is understood conventionally as encompassing Mexico and countries (or dependencies) of Central and South America and the Caribbean that speak a Romance language.[20] That general definition includes Brazil (Portuguese) and French Guiana (French). Central and South America also include countries where non–Romance languages are the primary or official language—Suriname (Dutch), Belize (English), and Guyana (English). In the Caribbean, Spanish is the primary or official language in Puerto Rico, Cuba, and the Dominican Republic.

Brazil is the largest country of South America in terms of land area and population. The country also has the largest population of Afro-descendants in South America and comprises the fourth largest population of South American immigrants in the United States—451,000 in 2017.[21] However, the book's definition of Hispanic America is limited to national-origin groups in the United States with historical, linguistic, and cultural roots in Spanish-speaking countries (i.e., nation-states or nations) of Latin America (i.e., North America, Central America, South America, and the Caribbean). Additionally, the book assigns the term *Spanish-speaking* to countries where Spanish is the primary or official language. Belize, for example, is not included as a Spanish-speaking country because its official language is English; however, Spanish is widely used in the country and taught in public schools. A final methodological note concerns Puerto Rico. As an island nation, Puerto Rico is a distinct geographical entity with its own cultural and historical uniqueness and quite a strong sense of nationhood. However, as a commonwealth of the United States, it does not have the legal status of an independent nation-state. The book refers to Puerto Rico as a Spanish-speaking (Caribbean) nation of Latin America.

The previous methodological caveats mean that in the book, the term *Hispanic America* refers to national-origin groups in the United States with cultural, linguistic, and historical ties to the following nineteen

Spanish-speaking countries of Latin America (North America, Central America, and the Caribbean: (1) Mexico; (2) Puerto Rico; (3) Cuba; (4) Dominican Republic; (5) Guatemala; (6) Costa Rica; (7) Colombia; (8) El Salvador; (9) Honduras; (10) Nicaragua; (11) Panama; (12) Argentina; (13) Bolivia; (14) Chile; (15) Ecuador; (16) Paraguay; (17) Peru; (18) Uruguay; and (19) Venezuela. Countries one through seven, which include all three Spanish-speaking countries of the Caribbean (Puerto Rico, Cuba, and the Dominican Republic), are analyzed in the main chapters of the book.

The Spanish-speaking countries of South America far exceed their counterparts in Central America in terms of land area and population. However, the latter contribute to a much higher number of immigrants in the United States than the former. In 2017, there were approximately 2.5 million immigrants in the United States from Spanish-speaking countries of South America; in contrast, there were approximately 3.3 million immigrants alone from Central America in 2015.[22] A majority of virtually all Hispanic American groups, except Panamanian Americans, that claim a Central or South American nationality are immigrants (or foreign-born). The difference between the two regions is quite small—59 percent of Spanish-speaking Central Americans in the United States are foreign-born, whereas, the same is true for 61 percent of Hispanic Americans who claim a South American nationality.[23] As noted, Panamanian Americans are the exception—only 40.8 percent are immigrants. Among Hispanic Americans who identify with Central or South American nationalities, Venezuelans have the highest percentage of foreign-born (70.6 percent). Hispanic Americans who identify with the Spanish-speaking Caribbean countries of Cuba and the Dominican Republic have a slightly lower proportion (55.2 percent) of foreign-born than Central and South Americans. The commonwealth status of Puerto Rico means that virtually all Puerto Ricans are U.S.-born, though 1.8 percent are indeed foreign-born.[24] Additionally, and despite stereotypes to the contrary, approximately two-thirds of Mexican Americans are U.S.-born.

As noted, there are more immigrants from Central America in the United States than from South American. The same pattern holds more generally for Hispanic groups who identity with Spanish-speaking nationalities from Central and South America, including immigrants and U.S.-born Hispanics. The overwhelming majority (85 percent) of Hispanic Americans (U.S.- and foreign-born) who identify as Central American claim one of the three countries that make up the Northern Triangle of Central America (El Salvador, Guatemala, and Honduras). These Hispanic Americans far outnumber the total number of U.S. residents who self-identify with all nine Spanish-speaking countries of Latin America—4.4 million and

3.4 million, respectively.[25] Similarly, three South American nationalities also account for the vast majority of Hispanic Americans who claim a Spanish-speaking nationality from that region. Colombians, Ecuadorians, and Peruvians comprise 75 percent of all Hispanic Americans who identify as South American.

This book devotes an entire chapter to Guatemalans, one of the top three Central American groups. The other two Central American national-origin groups in the United States, El Salvador and Honduras, together represent 58 percent of Central Americans in the United States. In comparative terms, the three million Salvadorans and Hondurans in the United States is approximately equal to 90 percent of all (Spanish-speaking) South Americans in the United States. Salvadorans are the single largest Hispanic group in the United States from either Central or South America. The only other comparable group is Cuban Americans. In 2015, there were 2.2 million Salvadoran Americans and 2.1 million Cuban Americans.[26] This book also devotes an entire chapter to Colombian Americans, one of the top three (Spanish-speaking) South American groups in the United States. The other two South American groups, Ecuadoran Americans and Peruvian Americans, together account for 40 percent of all South Americans in the United States.

As noted, the top three Central American groups (Guatemalan Americans, Salvadoran Americans, and Honduran Americans) in the United States vastly outnumber the top three South American groups (Colombian Americans, Ecuadoran Americans, and Peruvian Americans)—4.4 million and 4.2 million, respectively. Their demographic profiles also differ quite markedly in some important respects. The top three Central American groups are generally younger than their South American counterparts; the median age for the former is 28.6 years and 34 years for the latter. This group of Central Americans is also far less likely to have a college education than South Americans; only 8.6 percent of the former have attended college, while 28.6 percent of South Americans have done so. The top three groups of Central Americans in the United States are also less likely to be English-proficient than their South American counterparts—47.6 percent and 60 percent, respectively.

A higher proportion of Colombian Americans, Ecuadoran Americans, and Peruvian Americans have attained U.S. citizenship than Guatemalan Americans, Salvadoran-Americans, and Honduran-Americans have; 68.7 percent of the former are U.S. citizens, while 54 percent of the latter are. The top three South American groups in the United States have higher average incomes ($50,633) than their Central American counterparts ($39,447); consequently, they also have markedly lower levels of poverty—16 percent for South Americans and 25.3 percent for Central Americans. Income and poverty are generally correlated with homeownership. That pattern holds true for these groups of Central and South Americans in the United States. The latter have a homeownership rate of 44 percent, whereas only about one-third of Central Americans (32 percent) own homes.

The consistent pattern in divergent socioeconomic circumstances between these two groups of Central and South Americans poses serious challenges for policy makers, advocacy groups, and community-based organizations. The top three Central American groups in the United States are much larger in population and notably younger than the top three groups of South Americans. Unless this gap in the relative levels of integration into the American mainstream is ameliorated, the socioeconomic conditions of Central Americans, particularly immigrants and their families, will be made increasingly precarious by the highly polarized and often vitriolic discourse surrounding immigration politics in the United States. Central American immigrants, particularly from the Northern Triangle countries of El Salvador, Guatemala, and Honduras, are especially vulnerable because they represent a highly disproportionate number of immigrants seeking entry and asylum into the United States as they flee persecution, political and gang violence, and economic displacement. Central American immigrants have become grist for the political mill of seemingly irreconcilable debates about twenty-first century American immigration policy. The focus of the debates shifts from funding a border wall, the trauma of family separations at the border, and the virtual imprisonment in administrative detention centers under conditions that are prima facie violations of human rights and international law. Moreover, there are legal questions that focus on the summary refusal to process asylum petitions and the precariousness of life and liberty that Immigration and Customs Enforcement (ICE) raids impose on immigrant families (many of whom are U.S. citizens).

The question *From whence we come?* contains a poignant saliency not just for Central Americans in the United States, but also for Americans more generally. The push-pull factors that bring thousands of Central Americans to the U.S. border with Mexico are not reducible to the political vicissitudes of one U.S. presidential administration or another. These factors are more intricately woven into the historical proximity that Central American countries, particularly countries of the Northern Triangle, share with the United States. All three countries of the Northern Triangle were profoundly affected by the geopolitical proxy wars between the United States and the Soviet Union—a legacy that remains largely unknown in the public imagination of the United States but that is indelibly imprinted in the political memory of these Central American countries. The United States orchestrated the overthrow of the democratically elected government of Jacobo Arbenz in Guatemala in 1954 because of suspected sympathies with Communism. The coup leader (Colonel Carlos Castillo Armas) was installed as president with direct support from the Eisenhower administration. His regime rescinded many of the progressive land and social reforms initiated by the deposed Arbenz government. Castillo's assassination in 1958 and the subsequent autocratic rule of General Miguel Ydigoras Fuentes precipitated a devastating, thirty-six-year civil war that claimed over two hundred thousand lives; the vast majority of the causalities were indigenous Mayans. The Guatemalan government prosecuted a violent war against its own citizenry, with direct logistical, financial, and intelligence support from the United States. A similar Cold War proxy civil war erupted in El Salvador during the 1980s and resulted in over seventy-five thousand deaths and social and political instability that lingers into the twenty-first century. As it was in Guatemala, the United States was intimately involved in supporting and training government forces that prosecuted "a bloody, brutal, and dirty war."[27] El Salvador is still grappling with the national trauma of the El Mozote massacre, in which over twelve hundred men, women, and children were killed in a government operation that was unwritten by direct U.S. funding and counterinsurgency training. The war forced thousands of Salvadorans to seek asylum in the United States under the Temporary Protected Status (TPS) program. When that program was suspended during the Clinton administration, hundreds of Salvadorans were deported from the United States—an action that precipitated much of the gang violence that is commonly associated with Central American immigrants.[28] Honduras also became a flashpoint in the Cold War geopolitics when the United States used bases in that country to prosecute a covert war by the Contras against the Sandinista regime in Nicaragua. The covert operations resulted in over thirty thousand deaths,[29] created regional instability and displacement, spurned international condemnation and protests against U.S. intervention in Central America, and threatened the Reagan presidency when the Iran-Contra hearings disclosed unconstitutional and illegal actions by senior U.S. government officials. Apart from the political Cold War machinations that enveloped Honduras during the 1980s, the country has also suffered from climate-related disasters. It sits in the middle of what is referred to as the Central American hurricane belt. Extreme weather events like Hurricane Mitch (1998) have a devasting impact on countries like Honduras and exacerbate conditions that lead to immigration to the United States by reversing decades of economic development.

The Temporary Protected Status program has been a vital lifeline for over two hundred thousand Central American (climate) refugees from Honduras and El Salvador. Central American immigrants who have resided in the United States for decades under TPS protection, however, are in a precarious and vulnerable position, as concerted efforts have been undertaken to end the TPS program.

Conclusion

The pitched saliency of immigration politics in the United States are a cautionary tale for Americans of all political persuasions. The imperative to study and analyze why immigration—particularly immigration from the southern half of the Western Hemisphere—is such a divisive issue in the American body politic challenges us to broaden the question *From whence we come?* as Hispanic Americans to include a more somber, self-reflective question for all Americans: *What have we wrought?*

Notes

1. Krogstad and Gonzalez-Barrera, 2015.
2. Krogstad, 2016.
3. Lopez, 2016.
4. Gardels, 2017.
5. "Hispanics in San Antonio."
6. Brown and Lopez, 2013.
7. Carroll, 2017.
8. DistanceFromTo.
9. History.com, 2019.
10. Weber, 2017.
11. *Encyclopaedia Britannica*, "Guam."
12. United States History, "Insurrection in the Philippines."
13. Batalova and Wong, 2017.
14. U.S. Department of State Archive, "Dominican Republic, 1916–1924."
15. Batalova and Lee, 2012a.
16. Radford and Noe-Bustamente, 2019.
17. Batalova and Lee, 2012b.
18. Ibid.
19. Flores, 2017.
20. *Encyclopaedia Britannica*, "List of Countries in Latin America."
21. Zong and Batalova, 2018.
22. Estimates based on author's calculations of data compiled by the Migration Policy Institute, see Zong and Batalova (2018) and Lesser and Batalova, 2019.
23. Ibid.

24. Ibid.

25. Estimates based on author's calculation of data compiled by Pew Research Center; see Flores, López, and Radford (2017).

26. Ibid.

27. Bonner, 2018.

28. Ibid.

29. Sánchez, 2007.

References

Batalova, Jeanne, and Alicia Lee (2012a). "Frequently Requested Statistics on Immigrants and Immigration in the United States," Migration Policy Institute, https://www.migrationpolicy.org/article/frequently-requested-statistics -immigrants-and-immigration-united-states-2#1b.

Batalova, Jeanne, and Alicia Lee (2012b). "Frequently Requested Statistics on Immigrants and Immigration in the United States," Migration Policy Institute, https://www.migrationpolicy.org/article/frequently-requested-statistics -immigrants-and-immigration-united-states-2#6.[0]

Batalova, Jeanne, and Zie Wong (2017). "Cuban Immigrants in the United States," Migration Policy Institute, https://www.migrationpolicy.org/article/cuban -immigrants-united-states.

Bonner, Raymond (2018). "America's Role in El Salvador's Deterioration," *The Atlantic*, https://www.theatlantic.com/international/archive/2018/01/trump-and -el-salvador/550955/.

Brown, Anna, and Mark Hugo Lopez (2013). "Mapping the Latino Population, By State, County, and City," Pew Research Center, https://www .pewhispanic.org/2013/08/29/iv-ranking-latino-populations-in-the -nations-metropolitan-areas/.

Carroll, Rory (2017). "So Far from God, So Close to the U.S.: Mexico's Troubled Past with Its Neighbour," https://www.theguardian.com/us-news/2017 /feb/01/donald-trump-us-mexico-relations-history.

DistanceFromTo. https://www.distancefromto.net/distance-from-dominican-repub lic-to-puerto-rico.

Encyclopaedia Britannica. "Guam," https://www.britannica.com/place/Guam.

Encyclopaedia Britannica. "List of Countries in Latin America," https://www .britannica.com/topic/list-of-countries-in-Latin-America-2061416.

Flores, Antonio (2017). "How the U.S. Hispanic Population Is Changing," Pew Research Center, https://www.pewresearch.org/fact-tank/2017/09/18/how -the-u-s-hispanic-population-is-changing/.

Flores, Antonio, Gustavo López, and Jynnah Radford (2017). "2015[0][0], Hispanic Population in the United States Statistical Portrait: Statistical Portrait of Hispanics in the United States," Pew Research Center, https:// www.pewresearch.org/hispanic/2017/09/18/2015-statistical-information -on-hispanics-in-united-states-current-data/.

Gardels, Nathan (2017). "White Supremacy Is a Lost Cause," *The Washington Post*, August 24, https://www.washingtonpost.com/news/global-opinions/wp/2017/08/24/white-supremacy-is-a-lost-cause/?utm_term=.819b182a7ef3.

"Hispanics in San Antonio," accessed July 12, 2019, https://www.mysanantonio.com/sacultura/conexion/article/Hispanics-in-San-Antonio-2192950.php.

History.com (2019). "The USS Maine Explodes in Cuba's Havana Harbor," accessed July 13, 2019, https://www.history.com/this-day-in-history/the-maine-explodes.

Krogstad, Jens Manuel (2016). "Rise in English Proficiency among U.S. Hispanics Is Driven by the Young," Pew Research Center, https://www.pewresearch.org/fact-tank/2016/04/20/rise-in-english-proficiency-among-u-s-hispanics-is-driven-by-the-young/.

Krogstad, Jens Manuel, and Ana Gonzalez-Barrera (2015). "A Majority of English-Speaking Hispanics in the U.S. Are Bilingual," Pew Research Center, accessed July 9, 2019, https://www.pewresearch.org/fact-tank/2015/03/24/a-majority-of-english-speaking-hispanics-in-the-u-s-are-bilingual/.

Lesser, Gabriel, and Jeanne Batalova (2019). "Central American Immigrants in the United States," Migration Policy Institute, https://www.migrationpolicy.org/article/central-american-immigrants-united-states/.

Lopez, Mark Hugo (2016). "Is Speaking Spanish Necessary to Be Hispanic? Most Hispanics Say No," Pew Research Center, https://www.pewresearch.org/fact-tank/2016/02/19/is-speaking-spanish-necessary-to-be-hispanic-most-hispanics-say-no/.

Radford, Jynnah, and Luis Noe-Bustamente (2019). "Facts[0][0] on U.S. Immigrants, 2017: Statistical Portrait of the Foreign-Born Population in the United States," Pew Research Center, https://www.pewresearch.org/hispanic/2019/06/03/facts-on-u-s-immigrants/.

Sánchez, Alex [0][0](2007). "Honduras Becomes U.S. Military Foothold for Central America," North American Congress on Latin America (NACLA), https://nacla.org/news/honduras-becomes-us-military-foothold-central-america.

United States History. "Insurrection in the Philippines: Independence from America as well as Spain," https://www.u-s-history.com/pages/h830.html.

U.S. Department of State Archive. "Dominican Republic, 1916–1924," https://2001-2009.state.gov/r/pa/ho/time/wwi/108649.htm.

Weber, Tim (2017). "What Does Being a U.S. Territory Mean for Puerto Rico?" National Public Radio (NPR), https://www.npr.org/2017/10/13/557500279/what-does-being-a-u-s-territory-mean-for-puerto-rico.

Zong, Jie, and Jeanne Batalova (2018). "South American Immigrants in the United States," Migration Policy Institute, https://www.migrationpolicy.org/article/south-american-immigrants-united-states.

CHAPTER THREE

Mexican Americans and Ethno-Racial Identity

My Mexican American family has lived in Texas for more than six generations. We were Mexicans before we were Americans. I was given an American name, not a Mexican one. My family felt that is was important to adopt white American customs. I was the darkest of all the siblings and was often reminded that skin color was meaningful.

—Charles, age 45

Introduction

Students of American history, culture, and race relations are generally quite familiar with the brilliant prescience of W. E. B. Du Bois in asserting that the problem of the twentieth century is the problem of the color line. Du Bois also posed the chilling question about an ontological aspect of African American identity (i.e., double consciousness): "How does it feel to be a problem?" A twenty-first century iteration of this question for Mexican Americans, and Hispanics more generally, is how does it feel to be *in* but not *of* this country? The question contains a deep historical irony because Mexican Americans were incorporated into the United States as citizens after the annexation of Texas and acquisition of ceded territories following the U.S.-Mexican War; hence the often sardonic quip that Mexican Americans did not cross the border—the border crossed them.

This chapter proceeds through several stages of analyzing Mexican American identity. The first outlines the demographical (descriptive), nomenclatural (naming), and ontological (sense of being) dimensions of Mexican American identity in the United States. The nomenclatural and ontological dimensions rely on an important conceptual distinction between the self-defined and other-defined elements of individual and group (ethno-racial) identity. The second stage addresses Mexican American identity from an historical standpoint. The objective of this section is to establish that the incorporation of Mexicans into the United States as citizens is central to understanding the racialization of Mexican Americans on the basis of national origin. Racialization on the basis of national origin is not unique to the Mexican American experiences. A comparative review of three Supreme Court cases involving Asian Americans (*Ozawa v. United States* [1922]; *United States v. Bhagat Singh Thind* [1923]; and *Gong Lum v. Rice* [1927]) is included to illustrate how the constitutional norms of equal protection have at times failed to extend the blessings of constitutional democracy by validating the racialization of other ethno-racial minorities. Conversely, the last section of the chapter highlights four cases in which constitutional norms have indeed overridden the racialization of Mexican Americans (*In Re Rodriguez*, 1897; The Lemon Grove Incident, 1931; *Westminster v. Mendez*, 1947; and *Hernandez v. Texas*, 1954).

Racialization

Mexican Americans have been rendered strangers in a familiar land through a process of racialization. The assertion is not predicated on presuming that Mexican Americans are a race, though the 1930 census included "Mexican" as a racial category. Racialization is a sociopolitical phenomenon that perceives and treats a class of persons according to readily identifiable markers of identity such as phenotype, culture, or national origin. Thus, a group can be racialized, though it may not constitute a "race" in the traditional understanding of the term. The idea that race has a biologistic basis has been largely discredited, but it continues to function as an organizing principle for social and political organization as well as identity formation.[1]

When ideas of race, culture, or national origin are deployed with the sanction of government authority (i.e., state action) to exclude or disadvantage members of racial, ethnic, or national-origin groups, these groups are being subjected to another feature of racialization. The overarching objective of racialization is to construct an ethno-racial minority as the foreign or despised *other*. That objective is realized through: (1) systematic exclusion of an ethno-racial minority on an identifiable marker of identity like national origin, as in the case of Mexican Americans; (2) ethno-majoritarian social norms that contain "generalized assertions" about the essential character of an ethno-racial minority; and (3) alignment between those social norms and state action. Asymmetries in power between an ethno-racial minority, like Mexican Americans, and an ethno-racial majority, like whites, means that processes of racialization illuminate not just intergroup dynamics but the essential character of constitutional democracy in the United States.

What Identity Is: Demographical, Nomenclatural, and Ontological

Ethno-racial identity is demographical, nomenclatural, and ontological. The first consists of a descriptive profile of a group's demographic characteristics; the second represents how individuals and groups name themselves and are named by the broader society; and the third signifies an individual's or group's sense of being (i.e., their sense of being or essential character). Demographical identity is relatively straightforward as an empirical matter; census and survey data reveal a fairly accurate picture of a group's presence in a society, in terms of their proportion of the population and socioeconomic characteristics. *Latinos*, the more popularized term now being used to replace the word *Hispanic*, are the largest ethno-racial minority group in the country. The Pew Research Center notes that in 2016, Latinos accounted for 18 percent of the national population, or 58 million out of 323 million U.S. residents.[2] Mexican Americans are by far the largest Latino group in the United States; in 2015, there were 36 million persons of Mexican heritage in the country, which accounts for slightly less than 63.3 percent of all U.S. Latinos in 2015, when there were 56.5 million Hispanics.[3] While immigration discourse is fixated on unauthorized border crossings at the U.S.-Mexico border, only about one-third (32 percent in 2015) of Mexicans in the United States are foreign-born, just two percentage points below the proportion of all foreign-born Latinos (34.4 percent in 2017).[4] The number of naturalized but foreign-born Mexicans means that 77 percent of all Mexican-heritage individuals are U.S. citizens.

The Pew Research Center ranks the fourteen largest Hispanic groups in the United States according to various socioeconomic factors.[5] Mexican Americans rank first in population but fourteenth in median age, twelfth in terms of being foreign-born, fourth in terms of high school completion, twelfth among Hispanic groups holding a bachelor's degree, fourth in terms of English proficiency, fourth in terms of citizenship (birthright or naturalization), tenth for median household income, fifth in terms of poverty, fifth for lacking health insurance, and fourth in terms of homeownership.[6]

The sheer size of the Mexican American population, in relation to other Hispanic groups, suggests that the generalized perception by non-Hispanics of what Latino identity means in the United States will be largely shaped by the demographic and socioeconomic characteristics of Mexican Americans. The overall proportion of Latinos who are of Mexican heritage will continue to increase for years, as will the proportion of all Americans who are Mexican American (presently approximately 12 percent of the U.S. population). Though they are overwhelmingly U.S. citizens and largely English-proficient, Mexican Americans are younger (median age), significantly less educated (high school graduation rates and postsecondary education), and markedly poorer (poverty rate, median household income, health insurance coverage, and homeownership) than Americans more generally. Though Mexican Americans increasingly see themselves as being American, their demographical profile will continue to provide fodder for elements of the ethno-racial majority that frame their presence in the United States as being *in* but not *of* the country.

The nomenclatural (naming) and ontological (sense of being) dimensions of identity-formation are both endogenous (self-defined) and exogenous (other-defined).

The self-defined aspect of ethno-racial identity is measured by the decennial census in a two-step process. First, the 2010 Census asked all Americans to sort themselves ethnically as either Hispanic/Latino or non-Hispanic/Latino. Second, the census questionnaire prompted Americans to self-identify according to fifteen categories of race and to indicate whether they are of one race, two or more races, or some other race.[7] Virtually all (94 percent) Hispanic respondents self-defined their racial identity as consisting of one race. More than half (53 percent) of those reporting one race indicated they were white; among the 14.5 million Hispanics who identified themselves as "some other race, 44.3 percent defined that category as Mexican (which includes Mexican American and the national-origin term *Mexico*). The next highest category (Hispanic) accounted for only 22.7 percent of respondents indicating some other race.[8] The Pew Research Center uses a different methodology than the U.S. Census Bureau to estimate the multiracial population in the United States; the former estimates the population to be 6.9 percent,[9] whereas the latter puts the proportion of multiracial Americans at 2.7 percent of the U.S. population.[10] The inclination among many Hispanics, and many multiracial Americans more generally, to identify as "some other race" makes it the third largest race category in the United States, according to Pew's methodology, and slightly above the fourth largest racial group (Asian Americans, at 5.9 percent).[11] This demographic feature of race identity in the United States is predicated on the census's designation of Hispanics as constituting an ethnic category, not a race.

The idea that race is anchored in a singular racial category has deep resonance among Hispanics, whether that category is white, some other race, Hispanic, or a specific nationality. Another common feature among Hispanics, and Mexican Americans more specifically, is the tendency to see ethnicity and race as intersecting, if not interchangeable, categories of identity. Despite efforts by the federal government to draw a clear line of demarcation between ethnicity (two categories: either Hispanic/Latino or non-Hispanic/Latino) and race (fifteen categories in the 2010 Census), many Hispanics conceptualize race and ethnicity as overlapping, if not synonymous, categories of identity. The racialization of an ethnic minority group by nonmembers is also predicated on a similar conceptual blurring of race and ethnicity, hence the term *ethno-racial*.

Another dimension of how Hispanics, in general, and Mexican Americans in particular, conceptualize ethno-racial identity is that for many Hispanics, being white is associated more with being acculturated as an American than with the phenotypical features of Anglo Americans.[12] Survey data on Mexican American views about identity illustrate the point. Successive generations of Mexican Americans increasingly self-define themselves as American, not because of trans-generational changes in phenotypical markers but due to a broadening and deepening sense of acculturation—as distinguished from assimilation. While only 3 percent of Mexican immigrants describe themselves as American, (two-thirds say they are Mexican and 29 percent use the term Hispanic/Latino), in contrast, 45 percent of third-generation Mexicans see themselves as American.

A follow-up question by the Pew Latino survey suggests that ethno-racial identity for Mexican Americans is conceptualized in terms of acculturation, not phenotype. The survey asked Mexican American respondents whether they considered themselves "a typical American or very different from a typical American."[13] While 29 percent of Mexican immigrants considered themselves typical Americans, 60 percent of second-generation Mexicans did so, and 71 percent of third-generation Mexicans characterized themselves as typical Americans. Such divergent trend lines reflect changes in how Mexican Americans self-define themselves from one generation to the next. Mexicans in the United States decreasingly describe themselves as Mexican or Hispanic/Latino while increasingly considering themselves as American more generally and as "typical" Americans more specifically. That slightly more than half of Mexican Americans indicate they are white in the census race question suggests their response reflects the lived experience of becoming acculturated Americans, though vestiges of seeing Anglo Americans as quintessentially "American" still persist.

If identity for Hispanics is more accurately characterized as ethno-racial identity, the conceptual link between race and ethnicity is national origin.[14] Only a quarter of Hispanics, in general, refer to themselves as either Hispanic or Latino, but slightly more than half (51 percent) use their family's country of origin, and about one-fifth simply refer to themselves as American (another national-origin term). Framing Hispanic identity in terms of national origin is actually consistent with the government's own construction of what it means to be Hispanic. When the federal government first mandated the categorization and collection of data on Hispanics in 1976 (Public Law No. 94-113), it defined being Hispanic by national origin (e.g., being "Mexican, Cuban, Puerto Rican, Central American, South American, and other Spanish-speaking country origins").[15] That framing informs the ethnicity question on the U.S. Census. When Americans are asked to identify themselves ethnically as either Hispanic or non-Hispanic, the former are further prompted to link their Hispanicity with national-origin categories. In one fell swoop, the government defined *Hispanic* as an ethnic term, structured the census survey question on ethnicity in a pan-ethnic manner, yet attributed a transnational meaning to the term *Hispanic* by absorbing various nationalities into that "ethnic" category. In 1997, an Office of Budget and Management (OMB) directive compounded the lack of conceptual clarity by adopting the term *Latino* for purposes of data collection, thereby making it, at least officially, interchangeable with *Hispanic*. The government's construction of the terms *Hispanic/Latino* is not entirely incongruent with how Hispanics view either term. More than two-thirds of Latinos see *Hispanic* as a pan-ethnic category, while less than one-third see being Latino as a common culture. Slightly more than half of Hispanics have no preference for either term, thereby reinforcing their interchangeability, and among those who state a preference, Hispanics are almost twice as likely to prefer that term to *Latino* (33 percent and 14 percent, respectively).[16]

The third dimension of identity, ontological identity (sense of being), can be framed in multiple ways. An individual's or group's (self-defined) sense of being can be expressed as: (1) a singular identity (e.g., "Yo soy

Chicano/I am Chicano"); (2) sequentially linked identities (e.g., "I am first an American, then Mexican, then . . . "), polycentric identities (e.g., "Being American, Mexican, and Catholic are equally central to my identity"), or concentric identities (e.g., "Being myself, Catholic, Mexican, American, a global citizen are layered in expanding circles of identity and affinity"). The idea that ontological identity should be entirely self-defined has an obvious appeal. It seems self-evident that an individual knows their essential character better than anyone else or at least that the final arbiter should be the self. The philosopher Kwame Anthony Appiah argues that ontological identity is not static; individuals freely choose, create, invent, and reinvent themselves. Identity formation in this context does not unfold in a scattershot manner, nor do individuals concoct their sense of being out of whole cloth. Instead, the network of embedded relationships that anchor our lived experience shapes how our identity is formed. Appiah refers to this process of identity formation, particularly as it pertains to immigrants, as "rooted cosmopolitanism."[17] He believes migrants are not compelled to abandon their roots (i.e., assimilate); they take their roots with them as the freely create, choose, invent, and reinvent their sense of being as they engage new forms of human experience in their newly adopted homes (i.e., they acculturate).[18] Indeed, he personally exemplifies this cosmopolitan ethic of acculturation as both Ghanaian and—not *or*—English. The cosmopolitan ethos Appiah describes is reflected in the intra- and intercultural dimensions of the terms *Hispanic/Latino/Latinx*. These terms are not defined by any one Hispanic ethnicity; instead, the hybridity and sociocultural intermixing between the various ethnicities that comprise Hispanic America underscores the intra-cultural dimension of being Hispanic/Latino/Latinx. Moreover, the Hispanicization of U.S. popular culture suggests that the terms are also intercultural—i.e., between Hispanics generally and the mainstream popular culture of the United States. The intra- and intercultural dimensions of being Hispanic/Latino/Latinx, as well as the racialization of Hispanics as an ethno-racial group, explain why Hispanics are increasingly referring to themselves with the multiracial term *people of color.*

The other-defined aspect of ontological (essential character) identity is more explicitly political than Appiah's (self-defined) rooted cosmopolitanism, particularly when the balance of power between ethno-racial minorities, like Mexican Americans, and the ethno-racial majority is so profoundly asymmetrical. This enables the latter to superimpose onto the former its own construction of what Mexican American identity means, in terms of defining the essential character of Mexican Americans. This process of other-defined identity formation has two important components: (1) the historical relationship between Mexican Americans and the broader American polity; and (2) majoritarian social norms that are reinforced by government action in the form of legislative, bureaucratic, and judicial determinations. These components operate in tandem to produce social norms that effectively racialize Mexican American identity as the *foreign other*. A prevalent nomenclatural norm is to reserve for Mexican undocumented immigrants the highly pejorative term *illegals*, a moniker not applied to almost half of the undocumented population in the United States (i.e., individuals who reside in the country with expired visas). A prevalent ontological norm is the widespread presumption that Mexican Americans are either recent immigrants or first-generation citizens, hence the familiar probing question about one's heritage upon making an acquaintance: "Yes, but where are you really from?" Another ontological norm is the generalized assertion that Hispanics, and Mexican Americans more specifically, either reject or are incapable of assimilating fully into the culture of the ethno-racial majority. Another generalized assertion is the (other-defined) norm that national origin is the essential character of Mexican Americans, not a pan-ethnic identity (Hispanic/Latino), citizenship status, or level of acculturation into American culture. The perniciousness of this norm is manifest in the historical treatment of Mexican Americans by the ethno-racial majority (repression, de facto discrimination, deportation, repatriation, and segregation) without regard to citizenship status or acculturation.

Being Mexican American: Historical Identity

Being Mexican American does not refer merely to national origin (Mexico) or phenotype (i.e., being brown). As the largest Hispanic group in the United States, Mexican Americans are playing a highly visible role in the Hispanicization of American popular culture. Mexican Americans are an interesting case study of that process because their presence in the United States has defied clear-cut categorization. Mexican Americans have been designated as white, other white, and as a distinct racial group. Mexican Americans are predominantly *mestizos*, the progeny of indigenous and Spanish intermarriage and miscegenation. However, the biracial connotation of the term fails to recognize the significant Afro-descendant lineage in Mexican history and culture. As one of the major ports of entry for the Atlantic slave trade (particularly through Veracruz), New Spain was supplied with Africans by slave traders to supplant the decimated indigenous populations. The Afro-Mexican presence is primarily concentrated in rural areas of the Mexican states Veracruz, Guerrero, and

Oaxaca. Mexico's census bureau estimates that 1.2 percent (or 1.4 million Mexicans) of the population self-identifies as Afro-Mexican, though many Afro-descendants were absorbed into the general population through intermarriage.[19] Afro-Mexicans are increasingly asserting their own ethno-racial identity in the United States, even coining the term *Blaxican* to reflect their multi-raciality.[20]

In addition to challenging the view that race is unilinear, the Mexican American presence in the United States is also complicating traditional notions of the nation-making project in the United States. Mexicans fought alongside Anglos for Texas's independence, but they were enemy combatants (U.S.-Mexican War), potential adversaries (during the Mexican Revolution), and targets of systematic dispossession of landed wealth and political disenfranchisement in the Southwest while being legally defined as white.

For Mexican Americans, the arc of history does not quite bend along a singular trajectory. On the one hand, as the Chicano historian Rudy Acuna notes, Mexicans in the United States have been treated "as a class apart from the dominant race" since the U.S.-Mexican War.[21] On the other, Mexican Americans were officially designated as *white* or *other white* after their incorporation into the United States following the annexation of Texas and the Treaty of Guadalupe Hidalgo. The only explicit exception to this de jure classification was the brief historical moment when Mexicans were categorized as a distinct race in the 1930 Census.[22] Notwithstanding this official classification, Mexican Americans were subjected to a "Juan Crow" version of Jim Crowism, a system of (ethno-racial majority) social norms that rendered Mexican Americans as second-class members of society—even those who were citizens by virtue of incorporation, birthright citizenship, or naturalization.[23] While these norms were reinforced by state action (i.e., government authority), countervailing norms—particularly in the federal judiciary—contributed to the dismantling of Juan Crow practices and broadened (Fourteenth Amendment) protections for ethno-racial minorities, like Mexican Americans, through a series of important, if relatively unknown, cases in the federal judiciary. Another countervailing norm is the implicit jus soli (right of soil) principle in American jurisprudence (judicial opinions, federal law, treaty law, and constitutional guarantee) that Mexicans in the United States are collectively entitled to citizenship, naturalization, and immigration.

The conventional understanding of the jus soli principle, in the American context, is that it was codified as a constitutional guarantee of birthright citizenship when the Fourteenth Amendment was ratified in 1868. The relevant passage of the amendment provides that "all persons born or naturalized in the United States and subject to the jurisdiction thereof, are citizens of the United States and of the State wherein they reside."[24] The importance of the amendment is multilayered. First, it nationalized the power of defining citizenship and naturalization in the hands of the federal government. Second, it subordinated citizenship in the various states to (the paramount) citizenship in the United States. Third, it framed citizenship in the various states as a derivative guarantee of citizenship in the United States. If an individual was a citizen of the United States, by birth or naturalization, they were also automatically a citizen of the state in which they resided. Fourth, the Fourteenth Amendment effectively eviscerated the (pre–Civil War) power states wielded to deny citizenship and political rights to free and enslaved African Americans, thereby also invalidating the *Dred Scott* decision. In this extraordinarily racialized decision, Chief Justice Roger B. Taney articulated the notion that free and enslaved blacks could not, by nature, be citizens of the United States and that states had authority to decide the status of citizenship within their jurisdictions.[25]

Contemporary debates on birthright citizenship and naturalization for DACA (Deferred Action for Childhood Arrivals) recipients have drawn appropriate attention to the Citizenship Clause of the Fourteenth Amendment. What has also been overshadowed is the historical fact that even before the Citizenship Clause and the Naturalization Act of 1870 became the law of the land, Congress had already conferred a collective grant of naturalization and birthright citizenship on Mexicans residing in newly annexed or incorporated territories of the Southwest. Even prior to the annexation of Texas, Mexicans (i.e., Tejanos) living in the newly formed Republic of Texas were granted citizenship but with the caveat of pledging loyalty to Texas.[26] Congress's annexation of Texas in 1845 extended U.S. citizenship to all Texans, including Texans of Mexican descent. Another collective grant of citizenship was conferred on Mexicans in ceded territories, under Articles VIII and IX of the Treaty of Guadalupe Hidalgo. Mexicans in the ceded territories were required within a year of ratification to decide whether to return to Mexico or remain in the United States with protection of property and political rights. Mexicans who did not explicitly declare their intention but remained in the United States would be automatically granted U.S. citizenship. The grant of citizenship was not limited temporally only to those Mexicans living in the United States at the time of annexation and incorporation, but to their progeny as well, thereby conferring birthright citizenship on Mexican Americans. The wholesale naturalization of Mexicans living in the United States and conferral of birthright citizenship to future generations of Mexican

Americans were thereby established well before the Citizenship Clause of the Fourteenth Amendment was ratified in 1868. The limiting principle for (national-origin) incorporation into the United States was residency in newly acquired territories or an annexed state. However, not all residents were incorporated as citizens of the United States; free and enslaved African Americans and Indians were excluded from citizenship.

The incorporation of Mexicans into the United States highlights the racialized dimensions of citizenship based on the jus soli claim of being both *in* and *of* this country. Since the Naturalization Act of 1790, only free white persons who immigrated to the United States were eligible for naturalization because they were presumptively *of* this country. Naturalization would make them both *in* and *of* the United States. Free and enslaved Africans and Indians, though certainly *in* the United States, were presumptively not *of* the country and therefore categorically excluded from citizenship on the basis of race. Why were incorporated Mexicans not excluded from citizenship like African Americans and Indians? Mexico would certainly not have acceded to the Treaty of Guadalupe Hidalgo if Mexicans in the ceded territories had been rendered not only stateless but possibly enslaved like African Americans. Denying incorporated Mexicans citizenship on the basis of race would have been absolutely anathema to abolitionist forces in the United States already staunchly opposed to expanding slavery geographically.

The politically expedient policy of extending citizenship to incorporated Mexicans on the nonracial basis of (Mexican) national origin was paradoxical on many levels. First, the immense expansion of the United States could not have been secured without citizenship for incorporated Mexicans; but the expansion ultimately precipitated the dissolution of the Union through civil war. Second, race was no longer the exclusive criterion for citizenship in the United States because national origin became a pathway to citizenship for incorporated Mexicans. However, national origin immediately became the basis for methodically eviscerating the property and political rights of incorporated Mexicans through dispossession of land, social segregation, political disenfranchisement, and state-sponsored racial violence (e.g., Texas Rangers). Third, the "legal" equality between whites and incorporated Mexicans that shared U.S. citizenship implied was immediately undercut by the wholesale racialization of Mexican Americans as the *foreign other*. Their essential character (i.e., identity) was defined by the ethno-racial majority as being *of* another country— and of a country that had just been at war with the United States. The long-standing (racialized) presumption that (Mexican) national origin is more essential than U.S. citizenship in Mexican American identity illuminates another persistent and racialized assertion: Mexican Americans are either reluctant or incapable of fully assimilating into American mainstream culture. The historical paradox of Mexican American identity is that despite being U.S. citizens since incorporation, the racialized norms of the ethno-racial majority have defined their presence in the United States as the *foreign other.*

The racialized norms of the ethno-racial majority are often reinforced by government action and imposed on ethno-racial minorities. Two Supreme Court cases illustrate the point: *Ozawa v. United States* (1922) and *United States v. Bhagat Singh Thind* (1923). The central issue in both cases was whether the self-defined identity of two individuals (from Japan and India, respectively) as white sufficed to make them eligible for naturalization. In both instances, the Supreme Court privileged the definition of *white persons* held by the ethno-racial majority. Since the Naturalization Act of 1870, only whites and persons of African nativity and descent were eligible for naturalization. The binary racial framework that limited eligibility for naturalization to whites and persons of African descent was reinforced by these two cases and the subsequent 1924 Immigration Act but failed to clarify the status of persons who were deemed neither white nor of African descent. The significance of *Ozawa* and *Thind* is that the Supreme Court determined that the arbiter of what it means to be white would, in the first instance, be the common or popular understanding of the ethno-racial majority and the federal judiciary in the second instance for difficult cases that fell within a zone of uncertainty. The self-definition of individuals in question would hold no determinative value. The Supreme Court conceded that while Takao Ozawa was qualified for citizenship by character and education (i.e., assimilation), he was nonetheless racially ineligible. The court reasoned that the "popular understanding" of being white was whether an individual belonged to the Caucasian race. The racial metric was not an individual's capacity to assimilate into white culture but whether that individual bore the phenotypical markers of whiteness.[27] However, the court conceded a certain malleability to the term *white* by imagining a zone of indeterminate outline that included persons who were not clearly eligible or ineligible for naturalization on the basis of racial phenotype. The decision about which individuals would fall in or out of this zone would not be determined by an individual's self-defined sense of being (their ontological identity) but by the "gradual process of judicial inclusion and exclusion."[28] Indeed, the court rejected Ozawa's contention that he was assimilable.

A year later, the Supreme Court issued a similar ruling in *United States v. Bhagat Singh Thind,* in which, despite Thind's own assertion of being white for purposes of naturalization, the court employed the same "common understanding" test to find Thind ineligible for naturalization on the basis of phenotype. The Supreme Court reasoned that the "physical group characteristics of the Hindus render them readily distinguishable from the various groups of persons in this country commonly recognized as white."[29] The court concluded that naturalization statutes would be interpreted in accordance with the understanding of the common man, i.e., members of the ethno-racial majority, in terms of phenotype and which groups were unassimilable. Four years later, the Supreme Court reiterated its constitutional preference for privileging the racialized norms of the ethno-racial majority in *Gong Lum v. Rice*, 275 U.S. 78 (1927).

The case involved Chinese American children in the Mississippi Delta who were barred on the first day of school from the Rosedale Consolidated High School because the school board adopted a policy of segregating all nonwhite students into separate (colored) schools. The Lum family was initially successful at the trial court, where a writ of mandamus ordered the school to readmit the Lum children. The decision was appealed to the Supreme Court of Mississippi, which rejected the Lum family's argument that Chinese Americans were close to whites on the racial continuum by virtue of assimilation. The state's Supreme Court reasoned that Mississippi's constitution was cognizant of only two races (white and colored) for purposes of segregated public education. The court also embraced the school district's argument that as representatives of the (ethno-racial) majority, the state's governing institutions, not members of nonwhite racial groups, should get to decide racial classification. The other-defined identity superseded the self-identity of Chinese Americans. Moreover, the school district argued that the state's dual education system was intended to protect the racial purity of the Caucasian race, a racial privilege the state did not intend to extend to nonwhite races. The U.S. Supreme Court affirmed Mississippi's codification of a binary classification between a pure Caucasian race, on the one hand, and a "colored" category comprised of the amalgamation of nonwhite races, on the other.[30] The court deferred to Mississippi's binary school system—one for whites and another for colored races—by affirming that the state's constitutional scheme of segregated schools was clearly designed to establish separate schools for *only* two races—one white, the other colored. Chief Justice William Howard Taft observed in *Gong Lum* that most of the segregation cases cited in its opinion involved separation of whites and blacks, and he therefore anticipated no reason not to treat Chinese Americans the same as African Americans for purposes of deciding the constitutionality of racial segregation.[31]

The underlying commonality of the *Ozawa*, *Thind*, and *Gong Lum* cases is that the social norms (i.e., common understanding) of the ethno-racial majority superseded the self-defined (nomenclatural and ontological) identity of members of ethno-racial minorities seeking either naturalization or equal access to education. These cases underscore two elements of racialization. The first is systematic exclusion on the basis of some marker of identity; in these three cases, it was racial phenotype. A second element is the generalized assertion by the ethno-racial minority that minority groups are either uninterested or incapable of assimilation into the American culture. The actual assimilation of Ozawa, Thind, and Lum did not overcome the presumption of whites that Japanese, Indians, and Chinese were not fully assimilable. Unless these groups were understood as sharing the same phenotypical markers of being Caucasian, they were perceived as being incapable of fully assimilating into American (i.e., Anglo) culture. They would be *in* but not *of* the country. The link between phenotype and assimilability is also a factor in the racialization of Mexican Americans, but the link is complicated by the historical fact that national origin was the basis upon which they were incorporated into the United States as citizens.

The historical objectives of racializing ethno-racial minority groups have been:

1. To prevent immigration and naturalization (Chinese Exclusion Act, racial quotas for immigration);
2. To protect the racial purity of whites through social separation (segregation in public education, anti-miscegenation laws);
3. To maintain systems of enslavement, peonage, and removal (African Americans, Mexican Americans, and Native Americans); and
4. To render collective grants of citizenship meaningless (Mexican Americans after incorporation and African Americans after the Fourteenth Amendment).

The political dimension of racialization is the alignment between social norms that define the identity of an ethno-racial minority as the foreign or despised *other* and government action to enforce those norms through majoritarian politics. However, the genius of a constitutional democracy is the counter-majoritarian norm that basic rights and guarantees cannot be overridden by hostile majorities. The *Ozawa*, *Thind*, and *Gong Lum* cases are clear examples of how the Supreme Court failed our democracy by deferring to the racialized norms of the ethno-racial majority. Notwithstanding such failures, the larger constitutional trajectory in the

United States has been a gradual dismantling of racialized norms. The civil rights movement of the second half of the twentieth century reinforced the notion that subjecting the rights of minorities to the racial norms of the majority is anathema to a mature political democracy.

Being Mexican American: Who's White and Who's Not?

Four successful constitutional challenges to racialized norms in the United States involved Mexican Americans: *In Re Rodriguez*, the Lemon Grove Incident, *Mendez v. Westminster*, and *Hernandez v. Texas*. These four cases illustrate how nonwhites are conceptualized as the racialized other. The first, *In Re Rodriguez* (1897),[32] occurred decades after the annexation of Texas and the acquisition of ceded territories that incorporated Mexicans into the United States as citizens on the basis of national origin, not race. Only "free white persons" were eligible for naturalization, and thus citizenship, at the time of incorporation, a limitation subsequently expanded in 1870 to include persons of African nativity and descent. The experience of incorporated Mexican Americans established a precedent for granting citizenship on a nonracial basis (i.e., national origin). The exception begged the question of whether a collective claim to citizenship implied a derivative (individual) claim to naturalization. *In Re Rodriguez* federal district judge Thomas Maxey answered in the affirmative. Ricardo Rodriguez was one of many Mexican nationals who immigrated to the United States after the annexation of Texas and the Treaty of Guadalupe Hidalgo. After residing in Texas for a decade, he applied for naturalization. Local politicians opposed his application by claiming Rodriguez was neither white nor African and hence ineligible for naturalization. Judge Maxey conceded that if the case turned simply on racial phenotype, Rodriguez would not be classified as white.[33] However, he asserted that Mexicans had a tacit (individual) right to apply for naturalization as an extension of various discrete, collective grants of citizenship made to Mexicans in the Constitution of the Republic of Texas, the annexation of Texas, congressional resolutions in 1845, and the Treaty of Guadalupe Hidalgo.[34] The body of law, Judge Maxey cited, did not limit citizenship only to those Mexicans who were living in the United States at the time Texas was annexed or the ceded territories were incorporated. His reasoning had two important implications. First, it avoided the logical absurdity of granting citizenship to an ethno-racial minority on the basis of national origin while subsequently denying eligibility for naturalization to the same group on the basis of race. Second, birthright citizenship was conferred to the children of incorporated Mexican Americans, a guarantee of U.S. birthright citizenship to nonwhites well before it was fully constitutionalized through ratification of the Fourteenth Amendment in 1868.

In Re Rodriguez established the nascent constitutional norm that invidious discrimination against ethno-racial minorities on the basis of national origin would elicit heightened judicial scrutiny. That norm was reinforced by another important, though relatively unknown, case involving national-origin discrimination against Mexican Americans. The case, commonly referred to as the Lemon Grove Incident by scholars, occurred as rampant anti-immigrant resentment at the height of the Great Depression triggered repatriation programs and mass deportations of Mexican immigrants and American citizens of Mexican descent. The wholesale segregation of Mexican Americans in public life became the ascendant social norm throughout the Southwest. Mexican American children were separated from predominantly white schools, including schools they had previously attended. The segregation was plenary, regardless of citizenship status and academic proficiency; moreover, the vast majority of Mexican students were native-born citizens.[35] California state officials reinforced the social norm of discriminating against all persons of Mexican descent regardless of citizenship status. Roberto Alvarez notes that the governor of California commissioned a 1930 report (*Mexicans in California*) that reinforced the social norm (i.e., generalized assertion) of perceiving persons of Mexican descent through the prism of nationality, not citizenship. The report also reiterated another prevalent general assertion by whites that Mexicans were either unwilling or incapable of fully assimilating into American culture.[36]

Acting at the behest of the district school board, the principal of the Lemon Grove Grammar School barred the entry of Mexican American school children (a foreshadowing of a similar incident decades later, when segregationist Alabama Governor George Wallace infamously stood at another schoolhouse door to physically bar the enrollment of African American students at the University of Alabama). The Mexican American children at the Lemon Grove school were directed to attend a vastly inferior two-room school building constructed precisely for the purpose of separating the Mexican American school children from their white peers. The Mexican consulate helped secure legal counsel, and the policy was challenged in state court. A committee of parents successfully filed a petition for a writ of mandate to immediately reinstate the children on a non-segregated basis. The Superior Court of California ruled in favor of the Mexican community by ruling that California law did not authorize the segregation of school children on the basis of Mexican nationality or descent. The case was not appealed to the federal judiciary, nor did its finding apply beyond the Lemon Grove School District. However, the case is a compelling illustration of how the constitutional norm of equal protection and nondiscrimination on the basis of nationality overturned a prevalent social norm that racialized Mexican American identity as incompatible with the essential character of American identity.

Sixteen years after the Lemon Grove case, Mexican Americans again successfully challenged public school segregation on the basis of national origin in *Westminster School District of Orange County v. Mendez*, 161 F.2d 774 (9th Cir. 1947). The Westminster School District, along with several other segregated schools named in the lawsuit, used national origin as a proxy for segregating Mexican American children in public schools though they were legally categorized as white under California law. The school district invoked the same rationale as the district had in the Lemon Grove Incident, that the separation was justified by differential levels of academic and language proficiency between white and Mexican American children. The district identified English-speaking ability as the basis for the segregation, but the court averred it was in fact Mexican ancestry. In the lower court decision, *Mendez v. Westminster School District*, 64 F. Supp. 544 (S.D. Cal. 1946), the court had previously ruled that the assignment of Mexican children to the segregated school was categorical; school assignment was not determined by individual results on language proficiency tests but on the basis of ancestry, of which a key marker was a Spanish surname.[37] Since California law did not expressly provide for segregation based on national origin, both federal courts ruled in favor of the Mendez family.

The *Mendez* case is also noteworthy because a year after the decision, California enacted legislation that desegregated the state's entire system of public education. Governor Earl Warren, who five years hence authored the unanimous *Brown v. Board of Education* decision, signed the law. Westminster School District's policy of segregating Mexican American children proceeded from the generalized assumption of the ethno-racial majority that nationality was more central to the identity of Mexican American children than their U.S. citizenship. The Ninth Circuit Court of Appeals ruled in effect that assigning school children on the basis of this social norm violated the more fundamental, constitutional norm that classification without a proper legislative mandate violated due process and equal protection. Because Mexican Americans were legally classified as white under California law, a distinction based on nationality constituted an improper separation "within one of the great races."[38]

The significance of the fourth case, *Hernandez v. Texas*, 347 U.S. 475 (1954), is obscured in part by historical timing; two weeks after

Hernandez, the Supreme Court announced its landmark ruling in *Brown v. Board of Education*.[39] *Hernandez* encapsulates the central elements of the racialization of Mexican Americans. Public officials in Jackson County, Texas, systematically excluded all Mexican Americans from jury duty according to a racialized marker of identity—national origin. Virtually all Mexican American residents of the county were U.S. citizens, but none had been called in the previous twenty-five years for jury service. State law did not classify Mexican Americans as a distinct racial group, so state officials advanced the equivalent of a *reductio ad absurdum* argument that had been previously sanctioned by Texas courts, namely that the wholesale exclusion of Mexican Americans from all-white juries could not constitute racial discrimination since they shared the same race as whites.[40] Accordingly, it would be implausible to argue that Caucasians discriminated against themselves by excluding members of their own race from jury selection. That logical absurdity was compounded by the additional argument by state officials that the only form of discrimination the Fourteenth Amendment addressed was racial discrimination by whites against African Americans. The opinion by Chief Justice Warren categorically rejected Texas's effort to limit the scope of the Fourteenth Amendment's Equal Protection Clause. The court cited an 1880 case for the proposition that arbitrary discrimination against a class of persons on a nonracial basis is also an unconstitutional violation of equal protection.[41] The court's categorical rejection of the "two-class theory" (the Fourteenth Amendment is cognizant only of whites and African Americans) of constitutional interpretation reinforced the proposition that a central element of racialization (i.e., systematic exclusion) can occur on a nonracial basis, like national origin, ancestry, or descent.[42]

The *Hernandez* case, like *In Re Rodriguez*, the Lemon Grove Incident, and *Westminster v. Mendez*, encapsulates all three elements of racialization. Mexican Americans were systematically excluded from an aspect of civic life (jury duty) on the basis of an (other-defined) marker of identity, i.e., national origin. The second element of racialization also found expression in *Hernandez*; Mexican Americans in Jackson County, Texas, were subjected to the (majoritarian) social norm of perceiving all members of an ethno-racial minority through the prism of a generalized assertion: they were presumed to lack the requisite level of civic competence for jury duty. The third element of racialization, i.e., alignment between majoritarian social norms and government action, is also present in *Hernandez*. The local government's systematic exclusion of Mexican Americans from jury duty aligned with the majoritarian norm of constructing Mexican Americans as the despised *other*. The Supreme Court concluded that Mexican Americans were pervasively treated as a separate class by the government and the ethno-racial majority of Jackson County. The local government used national origin (descent) as the method of exclusion for jury duty and segregation in public education. Mexican Americans were barred from certain business establishments and were restricted to segregated restrooms designated for "Colored Men" and "Hombres Aqui" ("Men Here").[43]

Hernandez is also similar to *In Re Rodriguez*, the Lemon Grove Incident, and *Westminster v. Mendez* because the counter-majoritarian, constitutional norm of protecting ethno-racial minorities from racialization by the ethno-racial majority prevailed in all four cases. The Supreme Court did not rule that the Constitution required proportional representation for purposes of jury selection, nor that Hernandez was entitled to have Mexican Americans on his jury because he too was Mexican American. Instead, the court ruled that he was at least entitled to not having members of his own class (i.e., ethno-racial minority) systematically excluded from jury selection. The court recognized that the social phenomenon of classes is not static, nor is it reducible to racial groups. The significance of *Hernandez* is that the Supreme Court concluded that the elements of racialization can be applied to groups on bases other than race in order to deprive them of equality before the law. In those instances, the court asserted it would apply a heightened level of judicial scrutiny, as it did in cases of explicit racial discrimination.

Conclusion

Understanding how Mexican American identity in the United States has been racialized is not simply a matter of historical or academic interest. Current debates about immigration, diversity, crime, drug policy, race relations, and even the maintenance of American prominence on the global stage all implicate the emerging presence of Mexican Americans in the United States. Despite their high levels of acculturation, patriotism, and contributions to American culture and economy, many in the ethno-racial majority harbor resentment and suspicion toward Mexican Americans, and Hispanics more generally. From the ethno-racial majority's viewpoint, "they" (i.e., Hispanics) are not "white," and their mere presence in the United States is constructed as incompatible with whiteness (i.e., being American). The fact that public policy still aligns with the social norms of the ethno-racial majority means that Mexican Americans and Hispanics must remain keenly vigilant in exposing public discourse that racializes ethno-racial minorities.

Public discourse is shaped not just by partisan news outlets, political parties, or think tanks, but also by independent scholars and public intellectuals. Moreover, academia not only informs public discourse but also prepares the next generation of engaged citizens and policy makers. Some current scholars also propagate ideas that resonate deeply with the historical racialization of Mexican Americans and Hispanics in the United States. The nationalist paranoia of the late political scientist Samuel Huntington illustrates this point.[44] He trafficked in the generalized assertion that Hispanics and Mexican Americans (undocumented immigrants, legal immigrants, and citizens alike) reject the Anglo-Protestant values at the heart of the American Dream. He suspected that Mexican Americans, in particular, harbor a collective, ontological identity that aims to remake the country, particularly the Southwest and Hispanic-dominated areas like Miami, into bilingual, bicultural, and binational enclaves more akin to (Catholic) Quebec. Notwithstanding the fact that Mexican Americans are overwhelmingly U.S.-born, he perceived them as an immigrant people whose identity is anchored in Mexico. He defined Mexican American identity not by citizenship or acculturation but by an anti-American disposition that rejects the American Creed, i.e., Anglo-Protestant culture and values. He embraced the version of American exceptionalism in which the United States represents a providentially inspired vision of Heaven on Earth—the "city on a hill" mythology. What enabled this vision to be the essential character of the country is that immigrants sublimated their traditional ethnicity to the American Creed. Huntington feared this vision of American Exceptionalism had been under assault for decades as a (perhaps unintended) consequence of the civil rights movement, the Immigration and Nationality Act of 1965 (which greatly increased immigration from non-Western countries), identity politics, and especially recent immigration trends from Mexico. Huntington argued that several factors contribute to the categorical distinctiveness of Mexican immigration to the United States, in contradistinction to virtually all other immigrant groups. These are the contiguity of the "First World" United States with "Third World" Mexico, the unprecedented scale of Mexican immigration, the "illegality" of Mexican immigration, the regional concentration of Hispanics, the persistence of Mexican immigration, and the historical presence of Mexicans in the United States due to military defeat, occupation, and dispossession at the hands of Anglo-Americans. Huntington feared that Mexican immigration and the reluctance of Mexican Americans to fully assimilate (even third- and fourth-generation Americans) culturally and linguistically suggest that Mexican Americans are enacting a collective historical claim on the Southwest by remaking it in their own image.

Much of what Huntington purported is belied empirically by the (self-defined) demographical, nomenclatural, and ontological identities of Mexican Americans as outlined herein. Huntington is among the most prominent political scientists of the twentieth century and is someone who still commands respect and attention by opinion and policy makers. Immigration restrictionists find much in Huntington's work to endorse their policy prescriptions regarding border security, legal immigration, deportation, detention of undocumented immigrants, separation of children from their parents at the border, and denial of asylum and refugee petitions. Broader trends in the surveillance of immigrant families, efforts to denaturalize immigrants who committed inadvertent errors in their naturalization applications, as well as the occurrence of harassment and hate crime incidents against Hispanics and Mexican Americans in public life and social media all suggest that the racialization of ethno-racial minorities is not just an historical, but an ongoing, threat to constitutional democracy in the United States.

Du Bois was certainly correct when he asserted in 1903 that the problem of the twentieth century would be the color line. The paramount question for the twenty-first century is *Who is American?* American history, since the turn of the twentieth century, has certainly unfolded along multiple trajectories. One pathway, the majoritarian impulse to racialize ethno-racial minorities as somehow not being *of* the United States, has collided against another countervailing pathway: the counter-majoritarian, constitutional norm of ensuring unencumbered participation in the blessings of democracy. The twenty-first century will reveal which pathway emerges ascendant.

Notes

1. Rich and Troudi, 2006, p. 616.
2. Flores, 2017b.
3. Ibid.
4. Ibid.
5. In descending order of population: Mexicans, Puerto Ricans, Salvadorans, Cubans, Dominicans, Guatemalans, Colombians, Hondurans, Spaniards, Ecuadorians, Peruvians, Nicaraguans, Venezuelans, and Argentineans.
6. Flores, 2017a.
7. U.S. Census Bureau, 2010.
8. Ríos, Romero, and Ramirez, 2014, p. 16.
9. Parker et al., 2015.
10. U.S. Census Bureau, 2018.
11. Ibid.

12. It is not uncommon for older Hispanics to still refer to whites as "Americanos."

13. Desilver, 2013.

14. Taylor et al., 2012.

15. Ibid.

16. Ibid.

17. Appiah, 1997, p. 618.

18. Ibid., pp. 619, 625.

19. Fernandez De Castro, 2015.

20. Florido, 2016.

21. Ramos, 2005, p. 2.

22. Parker et al., 2015.

23. Cohen, 2008.

24. United States Constitution.

25. *Dred Scott v. Sandford*, 1856.

26. Little, 2018.

27. *Ozawa v. United States*, 1922.

28. Ibid.

29. *United States v. Bhagat Singh Thind*, 1923.

30. Berard, 2016, p. 137.

31. Ibid.

32. Acosta, "In Re Rodriguez."

33. Molina, 2010, p. 170.

34. Ibid.

35. Alvarez, 1986.

36. Ibid.

37. *Mendez v. Westminster School District*, 1946.

38. *Westminster School District of Orange County v. Mendez*, 1947.

39. Calleros, 2012.

40. Ibid.

41. *Hernandez v. Texas*, 1954.

42. Bradshaw, 2007, p. 352.

43. *Hernandez v. Texas*, 1954.

44. Huntington, 2004, pp. 33–35.

References

Acosta, Teresa Palomo. "In Re Ricardo Rodriguez," *Handbook of Texas Online*, http://www.tshaonline.org/handbook/online/articles/pqitw.

Alvarez, Roberto (1986). "The Lemon Grove Incident," *The Journal of San Diego History* 32, no. 2, https://sandiegohistory.org/journal/1986/april/lemongrove/.

Appiah, Kwame Anthony (1997). "Cosmopolitan Patriots," *Critical Inquiry* 23, no. 3: 617–639.

Berard, Adrienne (2016). *Water Tossing Boulders: How a Family of Chinese Immigrants Led the First Fight to Desegregate Schools in the Jim Crow South*, Boston: Beacon Press.

Bradshaw, Gilbert (2007). "Who's[0][0] Black, Who's Brown, and Who Cares? A Legal Discussion of *Hernandez v. Texas*," *Brigham Young University Education and Law Journal* 2007, no. 2: 351–382.

Calleros, Charles, R. (2012). "*Hernandez v. Texas*: A Milepost on the Road to Civil Rights for Latinos," in *Readings in Persuasion: Briefs that Changed the World*, Linda Edwards, ed., New York: Aspen Publishers.

Cohen, Richard (2008). "Meet 'Juan Crow,'" Southern Poverty Law Center, https://www.splcenter.org/news/2008/06/16/meet-juan-crow.

Desilver, Drew (2013). "How Mexicans in the United States See Their Identity," Pew Research Center, http://www.pewresearch.org/fact-tank/2013/05/03/how-mexicans-in-the-united-states-see-their-identity/.

Dred Scott v. Sandford, 60 U.S. 393 (1856). https://supreme.justia.com/cases/federal/us/60/393/.

Fernandez De Castro, Rafa (2015). "Mexico 'Discovers' 1.4 Million Black Mexicans—They Just Had to Ask," *FUSION*, accessed June 2, 2019, https://fusion.tv/story/245192/mexico-discovers-1-4-million-black-mexicans-they-just-had-to-ask/.

Flores, Antonio (2017a). "How the U.S. Hispanic Population Is Changing," Pew Research Center, http://www.pewresearch.org/fact-tank/2017/09/18/how-the-u-s-hispanic-population-is-changing/.

Flores, Antonio (2017b). "2015, Hispanic Population in the United States Statistical Portrait: Statistical Portrait of Hispanics in the United States," Pew Research Center, https://www.pewresearch.org/hispanic/2017/09/18/2015-statistical-information-on-hispanics-in-united-states/.

Florido, Adrian (2016). An Emerging Entry in America's Multiracial Vocabulary: 'Blaxican,'" *NPR*, https://www.npr.org/sections/codeswitch/2016/03/08/467358961/an-emerging-entry-in-americas-multiracial-vocabulary-blaxican.

Gong Lum v. Rice, 275 U.S. 78 (1927). https://supreme.justia.com/cases/federal/us/275/78/.

Hernandez v. Texas, 347 U.S. 475 (1954). https://supreme.justia.com/cases/federal/us/347/475/.

Huntington, Samuel (2004). "The[0][0] Hispanic Challenge," *Foreign Policy* 141: 30–45.

Little, Becky (2018). "Why Mexican Americans Say 'The Border Crossed Us': How White Settlers Edged Out Mexicans in Their Own Backyard," https://www.history.com/news/texas-mexico-border-history-laws.

Mendez v. Westminster School District, 64 F. Supp. 544 (S.D. Cal. 1946). https://law.justia.com/cases/federal/district-courts/FSupp/64/544/1952972/.

Molina, Natalia (2010). "'In a Race All Their Own': The Quest to Make Mexicans Ineligible for U.S. Citizenship," *Pacific Historical Review* 79, no. 2: 167–201.

Ozawa v. United States, 260 U.S. 178 (1922). https://supreme.justia.com/cases/federal/us/260/178/.

Parker, Kim, Juliana Menasce Horowitz, Rich Morin, and Mark Hugo Lopez (2015). "Multiracial in America: Proud, Diverse, and Growing in Numbers," Pew Research Center, https://www.pewsocialtrends.org/2015/06/11/multiracial-in-america/.

Ramos, Rodrigo (2005). "The Emergence of Movements for Ethnic Revitalization Amongst Chicanos in 1970s and early 1980s," paper presented at Immigration and Ethnicity in the United States since 1870, March 29, 2005, University of Nottingham.

Rich, Sarah, and Salah Troudi (2006). "Hard Times: Arab TESOL Students' Experiences of Racialization and Othering in the United Kingdom," *TESOL Quarterly* 40, no. 3: 615–627.

Ríos, Merarys, Fabián Romero, and Roberto Ramirez (2014). "Race Reporting among Hispanics: 2010," Population Division, U.S. Census Bureau, Working Paper, no. 102: 1–20.

Taylor, Paul, Mark Hugo Lopez, Jessica Martínez, and Gabriel Velasco[0][0] (2012). "When Labels Don't Fit: Hispanics and Their Views of Identity," Pew Research Center, http://www.pewhispanic.org/2012/04/04/when-labels-dont-fit-hispanics-and-their-views-of-identity/.

United States Constitution, Amendment XIV, Section 1[0][0], https://www.archives.gov/founding-docs/amendments-11-27.

United States v. Bhagat Singh Thind, 261 U.S. 204 (1923). https://supreme.justia.com/cases/federal/us/261/204/.

U.S. Census Bureau (2010). "United States Census Questionnaire 2010," https://www.census.gov/2010census/pdf/2010_Questionnaire_Info.pdf.

U.S. Census Bureau (2018). "Quick Facts," https://www.census.gov/quickfacts/fact/table/US/PST045218.

Westminster School District of Orange County v. Mendez, 161 F.2d 774 (9th Cir. 1947). https://law.justia.com/cases/federal/appellate-courts/F2/161/774/1566460/.

CHAPTER FOUR

Puerto Rico: "También Somos Americanos"

My mom, aunts, and cousins are all very insistent. Every time we talk about race, they say, "We are not white!"

—Emma, age 22

Introduction

This chapter examines the experience of Puerto Rican Americans, the second largest Hispanic/Latino group in the United States. Their more than one hundred years of experience as citizens of the United States offers insights into what it means to be "in" but viewed as an "outsider" in a country in which you claim citizenship. The Commonwealth of Puerto Rico has a rich and diverse history, making its residents uniquely different from the other major groups who comprise Hispanic America. Yet, conflicts surrounding race and racial oppression are deeply interwoven into the 500-year history of the modern-day development of Puerto Rico and the descendants of the island.

The Indigenous People

Prior to European colonization, the Ortoiroid, Saladoid, Arawak, and Taino Indians, indigenous tribes to the region, populated the island. During the early part of the sixteenth century, the island was conquered by Spain. Upon the arrival of the Spaniards to the island, the system of *encomiendas* was put into place wherein a Taino was given to a colonizer "in trust" as a slave with the obligation to convert them to Catholicism. This was the beginning of the assault on Puerto Rican identity.[1] Forced into slavery and put to work in the gold mines, the Taino Indians would be among the first victims of racial domination by the Europeans. This pattern of racial discrimination would be repeated throughout the Caribbean islands.

The darker-skinned, wide-eyed Tainos enjoyed a developed culture and community with a stable system of governance. They were not a nomadic tribal group. The Tainos erected permanent structures to house their villages, which were sometimes as large as three thousand members. They were accomplished hunters and gatherers and skilled artisans. The Tainos had an organized system of religious beliefs, which included both male and female deities—a sign of advanced cultural consciousness about gender and equality. And like in most organized societies, conflict with other tribal groups existed. The indigenous Tainos were experienced warriors, having engaged in conflict with the neighboring Carib tribe throughout their history. However, their warring experiences and weaponry were no match for the invading Europeans who controlled the island within a few years of their arrival.[2]

In addition to the Europeans' military might, the onset of infectious diseases brought to the island by the Europeans nearly decimated the entire Taino population and culture. As a result, the emerging Spanish Empire was in desperate need of a labor force. Reportedly, a Spanish religious leader, Friar Bartolomé de las Casas, outraged by the treatment of the Taino Indians, who were facing total elimination, suggested that Africans would be more suitable for the arduous work required in the gold mines.[3] As early as 1515, the island began its repopulation with the forced migration of West Africans during the period later known as the transatlantic slave trade.[4] According to several historical accounts, free African men, known as *libertos*, accompanied the Spanish conquistadors who first invaded the island. However, the overwhelming majority of the black population that would eventually call Puerto Rico their home resulted from the nearly 300-year period of enslavement that is part of the island's history.

A Period of Enslavement

Throughout the sixteenth through the nineteenth centuries, thousands of Africans were taken from the West Coast, the majority of whom were members of the Bantu, Yoruba, and Igbo nations. Africans were branded with a hot iron on their foreheads to show that they were obtained by "legal" means. They were also put to work in the fields to support the emerging sugar industry.[5] The unrestricted freedom of sexual exchange between the powerful European landowners and the less powerful Taino and African female populations produced the first generation of Puerto Ricans of mixed racial heritage.

For the African, enslavement was a way of life in Puerto Rico. However, the enslaved population could gain their freedom in numerous ways. For example, they could be legally freed by decree of the church or the court. A slave who may have been in the position to earn wages resulting from the sale of his or her own craft was also permitted to buy his or her own freedom, if the master was agreeable. In addition, the frequent occurrence of slave children born into slavery but whose parentage was linked to the slave owner often resulted in emancipation at the time of the owner's (father's) death. This stipulation, usually included in the master's will, produced a growing population of free people of color.[6]

Both the Africans and the Tainos resisted enslavement efforts and, as early as 1527, engaged in fights (slave rebellions) for their freedom. These efforts were, for the most part, unsuccessful. However, much like what occurred in the American colonies (Florida, Louisiana, North Carolina, and Virginia) and other Caribbean communities (Cuba, Dominica, the Dominican Republic, Haiti, and Jamaica), "maroon" populations of escaped Africans and Tainos established free communities in mountainous terrain on the island.[7]

While the demand for laborers in the gold mines decreased over time, the expansion of sugar plantations created a need for slave labor that would continue for another three hundred years. Moreover, Puerto Rico was in need of a free working population to help develop and stabilize the island. In 1664, Spain offered freedom and land to African-descended people from non-Spanish colonies.[8] Many free people of color who chose to immigrate to the island were of mixed race, mostly of African and European descent. Once settled on the island, they too adopted the ways of the Spaniards and would later declare themselves as true Puerto Ricans, expanding the racially mixed composition of the island. However, the continued importation of Africans resulted in a significant black presence that would shape and influence the people and the culture of Puerto Rico.

After three hundred years of racial mixing, the official Spanish government's census of Puerto Rico in 1834 found that only a slight majority (54 percent) indicated that they were white or of European descent. (The European population also included those from Ireland, Italy, and Portugal who had made their way to Puerto Rico.) Free people of color represented

35 percent of the population, and the enslaved accounted for 11 percent.[9] The free people of color immersed themselves in the Spanish-dominated culture, again choosing to take on the language, values, and customs of the socially and politically controlling Spaniards. Moreover, the enslaved Africans, who were forcefully stripped of their language, customs, and religious beliefs, bore successive generations of children. They, too, would eventually adopt the social customs of the Spaniards but would add their own unique contributions (food, music, language) to the development of the culture. For example, the unique form of "Puerto Rican Spanish" borrows heavily from words from the African Congo, the bomba and plena style of music are of West African origin, and the traditional festivals and carnivals that celebrate Puerto Rican heritage are infused with African masks, dress, music, and customs. Finally, since its earliest inception, a belief in Catholicism dominated the island, yet Santeria ("the way of the saints") emerged as a popular form of religious practice. Santeria is a religion based on Yoruba beliefs and traditions, with some added elements of Catholicism.[10] The representation of "deities" in the Yoruba religion and "saints" in the Roman Catholic Church aided in the syncretization of these two forms of religious practices.

The rise in antislavery sentiments, strongly felt in the Caribbean after the 1803 liberation of Haiti, was of concern to the governing body of Puerto Rico as well.[11] By mid-century, abolitionist forces were mounting, as many prominent citizens of the island believed it was time to end the system of enslavement. Following four years of a bloody civil war, the United States, one decade shy of marking the hundred-year anniversary of the Declaration of Independence, abolished slavery with the passage of the Thirteenth Amendment in 1865.[12] Forces of change rippled throughout the region; the system of enslavement was doomed. In Puerto Rico, enslavement would eventually be abolished in 1873, but unlike in the United States, former slaves were not emancipated. Rather, the impoverished slaves were required to buy their freedom from their former masters. The law stipulated that a three-year term of service was necessary to compensate their previous owner for their economic loss.[13]

Puerto Rico had remained part of the Spanish Empire for nearly four centuries and served as an important strategic military location during the many wars between Spain and other European powers fighting to control the region. However, by the end of the nineteenth century, Spain would finally lose control of the island to the emerging political and military might north of the island: the United States of America. In April 1898, the United States declared war on Spain. The ten-week Spanish-American War concluded with the signing of the 1898 Treaty of Paris, granting the United States ownership of Puerto Rico. Puerto Rico gained commonwealth status, and in 1917, the Jones Act granted the residents U.S. citizenship.[14]

At the time of its seizure as a possession of the United States, Puerto Rico was, by all measures, a racially diverse and racially mixed island.[15] The conceptualization of race and the implementation of racist practices were embedded in the island's history and remained factors associated with daily living. Those of European descent were granted social privileges advantageous to social and economic uplift; darker-skinned Puerto Ricans would encounter social and economic barriers. The twentieth century would bring challenges to members of the Puerto Rican community as questions about race, culture, and identity would become contentious points of interest on the island and on the mainland.

Puerto Rican Identity—A Sense of Peoplehood and Cultural Nationalism

Some would argue that a Puerto Rican's view of race and ethnic identity differs from the view held by those on the mainland. For islanders, their identity as a Puerto Rican was paramount to that of a racial identity. Racial identities are socially ascribed, based on observable physical characteristics (skin color, hair, eyes, etc.), and genetically transferred from one generation to the next.[16] On the other hand, ethnic identities are tied to a nation state or place of origin.[17] While not a nation in the strictly geopolitical sense, the desire for sovereignty and independence and the insistence upon claiming the unique culture and identity of the people have been part of Puerto Rico's history for more than 150 years. This is when islanders first launched their fight for independence. During the mid-nineteenth century, the Puerto Ricans' right to self-determination was restricted by Spanish rule, yet what emerged was a sense of peoplehood, or a form of cultural nationalism tied to the pride of the people. Now free from Spain, in the twentieth century, Puerto Rico would struggle with the United States around its national identity and status as a commonwealth. Islanders were granted the right to claim U.S. citizenship; however, this did little to squelch their desire to be seen first and foremost as Puerto Ricans.

White supremacy coupled with European imperialism were key factors in the historical development of Puerto Rico. Race and racial identity were and continue to be important social indicators in Puerto Rican society. Europeans and those with whiter skin were viewed as superior to all others, including native Indians, African descendants, and mixed-race populations. Both racism and colorism were in play. Puerto Ricans were, undoubtedly, aware of the advantages and disadvantages of being associated with certain racial categories and understood that white meant might! The desire to be included in the white category was evident by the change in racial identification status among Puerto Ricans in the decade between 1910 and 1920, when there was a dramatic shift in the numbers of people identifying themselves as white.

Mara Loveman and Jeronimo Muniz offer insight into what many would describe as the "whitening" of Puerto Rico.[18] Race, understood to be a socially constructed concept, changed or evolved over time for the people of Puerto Rico. Forced into a strict binary classification of race, given a choice, those with mixed-race heritage were more likely to proclaim their whiteness. This first became evident in the 1920 Census, when the number of individuals who declared themselves as white increased by 25 percent. By the mid-twentieth century, nearly 80 percent of the population indicated that they were white. What is suggested here is that many Puerto Ricans understood the value of whiteness while at the same time understanding and accepting the mixed-race heritage of the island. Stories about a dark-hued grandparent or great grandparent were common among the people. As noted by Richard T. Schaefer, "The most significant difference between the meaning of race in Puerto Rico and on the mainland is that Puerto Rico, like so many other Caribbean societies, has a *color gradient*, a term that describes distinctions based on skin color made on a continuum rather than by sharp categorical separations."[19] Accordingly, those on the island are more sensitive to the mixed-race (*miscegen*) heritage of Puerto Rico and are flexible in their assignment of individuals to different racial categories. "If one thinks highly of a person, then he or she may be seen as a member of a more acceptable racial group. A variety of terms are used in the color gradient to describe people racially: *blanco* (white), *trigueno* (bronze- or wheat-colored), *moreno* (dark-skinned), and *negro* (black) are a few of these." Moreover, there are variations within each of the above categories, with white further being described as *rubio(a)* and *cano(a)*; brown as *indio(a)* or *café con leche*; and black as *grifo(a)* or *prieto(a)*, both of which are viewed as derogatory terms.[20] Again, a form of colorism is evident, wherein intragroup discrimination occurs based on skin color. The view is much different on the mainland, where historically, whiteness ruled supreme and the "one-drop rule" determined that anyone with the slightest hint of known African ancestry was a member of the nonwhite racial group.[21] And, it was the boom in migration from the island to the mainland beginning after World War II that raised new questions among Puerto Ricans about their racial identity.

Out Migration

At the turn of the twentieth century, the United States viewed Puerto Rico as an important strategic military location with opportunities for economic investments. The production of oil and sugar and twentieth-century industrialization fueled the economic advancement of the island. However, the Great Depression of the 1930s would result in an economic downturn. Deteriorating economic and social conditions resulted in the beginning of a migration wave, sending large numbers of islanders to the mainland in search of economic opportunities. "Operation Bootstrap—a series of state-sponsored programs by the U.S. and Puerto Rican governments in the 1940s and 1950s to urbanize, modernize, and industrialize Puerto Rico's economy through investment and job creation by U.S. companies—also encouraged Puerto Rican migration."[22] In the late 1940s and following the end of World War II, Puerto Ricans began to settle on the Northeast coast, with New York City being the most preferred location. Here they created a community known as Spanish Harlem.

Spanish Harlem, which existed in close proximity to Harlem's black community, was located in the East Harlem section of New York City. By the mid- twentieth century, residents of Puerto Rican descent, often referred to as *Nuyoricans*, dominated the neighborhood.[23] (This was not, necessarily, a term of endearment. To be described as a Nuyorican suggests the loss or lack of authenticity in one's Puerto Rican heritage. Islanders describing the return migration of those coming from the mainland also used the term. Second and third generations of Puerto Ricans born on the mainland are described as Nuyoricans, as well.) In this mixed social environment, the realities of race and racial divisions were evident. Puerto Ricans may have chosen to indicate their racial identification as "white" on census forms, and they were permitted to do so; however, they were most often viewed and treated as black or mixed-race people of color. They were, indeed, members of a minority group, denied the white privileges of mainstream American society. They were marked not only by the tan or brown complexion of many of those from the island, but also by their primary language: Spanish. Moreover, the prevalence of race and racial discrimination was clearly visible for the black Puerto Rican, who quickly realized that his or her plight was no different from the mainland-born African American.

Puerto Ricans faced discrimination in employment, housing, education, and entertainment and in cultural, religious, and social organizations. For example, the granting of U.S. citizenship in 1917 permitted Puerto Ricans to enlist—or to be drafted—into the U.S. military. The demand for troops during World War II resulted in many from the island joining military service. The United States operated a segregated army, and those Puerto Ricans who were visibly of African descent were assigned to the all-black segregated units (both on the mainland and in Puerto Rico), where discrimination and racism dominated their tour of duty. Systemic discrimination was also directed at the community's children. Puerto Rican youth were criminalized, viewed as juvenile delinquents. They were overrepresented in the criminal justice system, first as youth and then as young adults. Successful integration into the public school system was a persistent problem; dropout and pushout rates soared for members of the community. Residential discrimination resulted in poor segregated housing, offering limited opportunity for social advancement.[24]

By the end of the war and early into the 1950s, migration to the mainland was less challenging for the Puerto Rican. Affordable air travel significantly increased the number of people leaving the island for the mainland, as they were no longer limited to traveling by boat. Hundreds of thousands of Puerto Ricans arrived and took up residence on the East Coast. While the largest population of Puerto Ricans did, indeed, reside in New York City, sizable Puerto Rican communities were also established in Newark, Chicago, Orlando, Hartford, Cleveland, Springfield, Camden, Boston, and Philadelphia. Puerto Ricans were U.S. citizens, yet many Americans viewed them as immigrants, an undesirable addition to the American melting pot.

The strong migration trend lasted for several decades but began to slow in the 1970s during a period of economic decline. By the end of the century, many established Puerto Rican communities were occupied not by migrants from the island, but by second-generation citizens born on the mainland. However, the close proximity of the island to the mainland and the back and forth traveling patterns of family members helped maintain a strong Puerto Rican identity among second- and third-generation Puerto Ricans throughout the twentieth century. Will that strong sense of identity continue to hold in the twenty-first?

Race, Culture, and Identity

The U.S. government conducts a nationwide census every ten years. As a commonwealth territory, Puerto Rico partakes in this process. How do Puerto Ricans view their racial identity? In the 2010 Census, 75.8 percent of Puerto Ricans identified themselves as white, 12.4 percent as black, 11.1 percent as mixed race or other, and less than 1 percent as Indian or Asian.[25] The 75.8 percent actually represents a slight decrease in the number of islanders who indicated that they are white. In the 2000 census, 80.5 percent of the population racially identified as white.[26] The decrease in the number of white residents may be attributed to two factors: (1) during the past two decades, African immigrants have relocated to the island and now call Puerto Rico their home; and (2) African American citizens have also migrated to the Caribbean island. However, the overwhelming majority of the island's population view themselves as white. Interestingly enough, anyone visiting the island would be overwhelmed by the visible presence of brown people, which would appear to contradict the Puerto Rican claim to whiteness. While estimates do vary, the long history of miscegenation on the island would suggest that a significant number (nearly half) of the Puerto Rican people have African ancestry.[27] Those who identify as black or Afro–Puerto Rican are, for the most part, descendants of the African slave trade and, undoubtedly, willing to identify as such due to obvious physical characteristics, i.e., the darker hue of their skin. Afro–Puerto Ricans are aware of their racial status and the social limitations placed on their communities based on race and color. There is evidence of residential segregation throughout the island. However, there are large black populations in Puerto Rico (Loíza, Arroyo, Maunabo, Vieques, Culebra, Río Grande, and San Juan), where a proud Afro–Puerto Rican culture remains visibly strong and vibrant.[28]

Puerto Ricans living on the mainland are faced with similar challenges. Vacillating between identities as Puerto Ricans, Hispanics, and Latinos, many find the race question to be perplexing and unsettling. While those of Puerto Rican descent are frequently described as "brown" people of color and oftentimes embrace the concept of being members of a minority group victimized by racial discrimination, their racial identity remains ambiguous. For example, question nine on the 2010 census form asks a very specific question: What is the person's race? There are many possibilities, including white, black, African American or Negro, American Indian or Alaska Native, Asian Indian, etc.; however, the "brown" category is missing. The last and fifteenth choice on the form—"some other race"—is the response most frequently selected by members of the Hispanic community.[29] A related study by the Pew Research Center found that most Latinos prefer not to identify as either black or white, and 70 percent of those who check the "some other race" category are Hispanic.[30] However, many Puerto Ricans may choose to identify themselves as white, which would be consistent with the prevailing belief of the majority of those on the island.

Whether one is on the island or the mainland, whiteness is, demonstratively, the most favored or desired category for many members of the

Puerto Rican community. The two-category racial classification system (white or nonwhite) embedded in the American social and cultural history continues to reinforce the ideals of white supremacy.[31] This is certainly a more privileged status for those Puerto Ricans who are primarily of European heritage. The same cannot be said for members of the indigenous, mixed-race, or African-descendant populations.

People of Color?

People of color is a term widely used in the United States to describe nonwhite populations. It includes Africans Americans, Indians, Asians, Latinos, and mixed-race populations. Because of their nonwhite status, people of color are viewed as members of racial minority groups and experience systemic racism, which may result in the denial of social and economic opportunities. The term has been generalized to include all the immigrants crossing the Southern border and members of the Latino community. But is it a term that should be applied to the Puerto Rican community?

Puerto Rican, Hispanic, Latino, and/or person of color are terms now being used interchangeably in the Spanish-speaking community. Many leaders in the Latino and specifically the Puerto Rican community have also embraced the use of the term *people of color.* They, too, sometimes refer to themselves as members of the "brown" community. Newly elected U.S. Representative Alexandria Ocasio-Cortez (NY) described her experience as a "woman of color" who was mistaken for a spouse and an intern when she arrived at the Democratic Members' Luncheon on Capitol Hill in 2018.[32] Ocasio-Cortez has often emphasized her Puerto Rican roots. The Trump administration's slow response to the needs of Puerto Rico following the devastation of Hurricane Maria was often described as a racist attack on "people of color."[33] Leading civil rights advocates refer to the struggles against racism and discrimination faced by young African American and Puerto Rican youth in New York as an ongoing attack against "our brown and black sisters and brothers."[34] *People of color* seems to resonate with the emerging national identity of the Latino community.

According to their website, "Voto Latino is a pioneering civic media organization that seeks to transform America by recognizing Latinos' innate leadership. Through innovative digital campaigns, pop culture, and grassroots voices, we provide culturally relevant programs that engage, educate and empower Latinos to be agents of change. Together, we aim to build a stronger and more inclusive democracy." Maria Teresa

Kumar, president and CEO of Voto Latino and a frequent guest on the MSNBC Sunday morning talk circuit, embraces the notion that Latinos are people of color. In their quest to gain political power through the ballot box, the organization emphasizes that the "Latinx population is projected to be the largest non-white electoral group in 2020."[35]

However, as more and more members of the younger generation of the Puerto Rican community embrace the concept of a Latino identity, it may not maintain its permanence. The Puerto Rican as Latino could possibly be the result of a contemporary, popular cultural trend that will fade over time. As reported in the *Washington Post*, a 2015 study by the Pew Research Center suggests that one's identity as a member of the Hispanic, Latino, or people of color community fades over time.[36] A combination of lower immigration rates, higher rates of interracial marriage, decreased contact with Spanish-speaking relatives, and a decline in celebrations of ethnic culture results in one's identification as Hispanic to diminish. To complicate matters further, an increasing number of young Hispanics, especially those raised in mixed-racial/ethnic families are no longer fluent in the Spanish language. Consistent with existing theories about ethnic identification among second and third generations of immigrant families, younger generations of Hispanics are more likely to view themselves as Americans, rather than Hispanics, Latinos, or Latinx.[37] This would seem to hold true for all members of the diverse Hispanic community, including those of Puerto Rican ancestry. According to the study, "although recent immigrants identify as Hispanic at a rate of almost 90 percent, this number drops to around 50 percent after the fourth generation. Currently, 11 percent of adults with Hispanic ancestry do not identify as such . . . 23 percent of Hispanics most often refer to themselves as 'American.'" This trend in self-identification is likely to impact the overstated census projections of Hispanic growth as the largest "minority" population in America. Increased immigration from designated Hispanic countries is likely to have a greater impact on the growth of the U.S. Hispanic community.

Maintaining one's identity as a member of the Hispanic community has significant social and political implications. As noted by Ed Morales, the multiracial backgrounds of the Latino population make it more likely for many to lose their identification as Hispanics. Moreover, "In the past some have chosen to strive for whiteness through marriage—in Spanish it's an adage called 'mejorar la raza' or 'better the race.' But many Hispanics reject white identity." He further adds:

> Whether we choose to identify ourselves as Hispanic, Latino, or the increasingly popular Latinx, these labels help us find our place in

American society and culture. While there will always be Hispanics who no longer need or want to identify, the forces in society that create "included" and "excluded" groups on the basis of what one's race or ethnicity *appears* to be are not going away. From the early 20th-century activism of W. E. B. Dubois and Marcus Garvey through the civil rights movement, African-Americans have consolidated a powerful notion of identity based on racial solidarity. This approach pushed back against anti-black racism and yielded tangible political results, as well as power and influence in American society. Such leverage will remain elusive to Hispanics if we move away from acknowledging and embracing our "difference."[38]

Puerto Rican Pride

The civil rights and black power movements of the 1960s and 1970s called upon black Americans to embrace and take pride in their cultural and ancestral heritage. During this period, the nation witnessed a resurgence of interest in African and African American history. School districts began to examine their curriculums to determine if the African American perspective was adequately represented. Higher education was forced to establish black studies programs, the first of which was founded at San Francisco State in 1968.[39] The black arts movement flourished, resulting in new forms of creativity and artistic expression by members of the African American community. And James Brown proclaimed, "Say it loud— I'm black and I'm proud!"[40] This message also resonated in the Puerto Rican community, who were already engaged in a consciousness-raising movement of their own. In the mid-1970s, the Puerto Rican community, both on the island and the mainland, launched several new initiatives aimed at the celebration of Puerto Rican heritage and identity. Many of the events were educational in nature but also sought to highlight the unique aspects of Puerto Rican culture.

New York City's Puerto Rican Day Parade, first organized in 1957, gained momentum in the late 1960s. It was formerly known as the Hispanic Day Parade, but the name was changed to focus on the specific cultural expressions of the Puerto Rican community. Over the years, the parades have attracted New York City's political leaders, all of whom recognized the growing significance of the Puerto Rican presence in the city as well as the importance of the Puerto Rican voting bloc. Puerto Rican celebrities have also supported the annual event. In 1995, the name was changed to the National Puerto Rican Day Parade, signaling its unity with Puerto Rican communities throughout the nation. New York is home to the largest Puerto

Rican cultural parade in the United States; however, other cities with large Puerto Rican populations also have annual Puerto Rican parades and festivals, including Aurora, Boston, Chicago, Miami, Montebello, Philadelphia, and Rochester. This may be merely a form of symbolistic identification, where once a year individuals lay claim to their Puerto Rican ancestry. Having the opportunity to do so is especially important to second- and third-generation Puerto Ricans born on the mainland.

Puerto Ricans take pride in the social, cultural, educational, and political achievements of members of their community. For example, the political achievements of New York Bronx council members Rubén Díaz, Jr., and Rubén Díaz, Sr., have been noted, as have those of Robert Garcia, Charles Rangel, Rosie Mendez, and Bonnie Garcia. This list also includes celebrities, such as Jennifer Lopez, Ricky Martin, Angela Bofill, Miguel Piñero, Rubén Santiago-Hudson, Rita Moreno, Irene Cara, Miguel Algarín, Piri Thomas, Sandra María Esteves, Willie Colón, Pedro Pietri, and Giannina Braschi. Famous poets include Willie Perdomo, Flaco Navaja, Nancy Mercado, Emanuel Xavier, Edwin Torres, J. L. Torres, Caridad de la Luz (aka La Bruja), Lemon Andersen, and Bonafide Rojas. Not to be missed are historians Arturo Alfonso Schomburg and Dr. Yosef Alfredo Antonio Ben-Jochannan, professional basketball players Carmelo Anthony and Reginald Martinez Jackson, and world champion boxer Félix Trinidad.

Conclusion

The Puerto Rican community is not monolithic. It is a diverse community with European, African, Taino, and mixed-race heritage. The intensity of ethnic and racial identifications varies. Those on the island are insistent upon maintaining and preserving the unique aspects of Puerto Rican heritage and culture. More than a hundred years since the United States of America gained possession and turned Puerto Rico into an American commonwealth, islanders prefer to be identified as Puerto Ricans; Spanish, not English, is the preferred language. Moreover, the struggles for independence have waged on for the past hundred years as well. Questions about statehood, commonwealth status, and independence have been placed in front of the voters on numerous occasions.[41] While the color gradient is utilized to describe members of the Puerto Rican community, the overwhelming majority of citizens on the island self-identify white as their racial category. Mainlanders have been impacted by the successive generations of Puerto Rican descendants who are identified as the "brown" people of color, treated as members of a racial minority group. Whiteness is not a privilege enjoyed by many, and embracing one's identity as Hispanic, Latino, Latinx, brown, or "a people of color" proves more appealing and beneficial to those who have experienced American racism.

Notes

1. Pico, 2014.
2. Rouse, 1992.
3. Comas, 1971.
4. Franklin and Moss, 2000.
5. Figueroa, 2005.
6. Pico, 2014.
7. Diouf, 2016.
8. Martinez, 2003.
9. Middeldyk, 2016.
10. González-Wippler, 2017.
11. Girard, 2011.
12. Franklin and Moss, 2000.
13. Baralt, 2014.
14. Middeldyk, 2016.
15. Findlay, 1999.
16. Reid-Merritt, 2017.
17. Schaefer, 2011.
18. Loveman and Muniz, 2007.
19. Schaefer, 2011, p. 249.
20. Duany, 2002.
21. Daniel, 2002.
22. DPLA, 2019.
23. Verin-Shapiro, 2000.
24. Korrol and Hernandez, 2010.
25. U.S. Census Bureau, 2010.
26. U.S. Census Bureau, 2000.
27. Kinsbruner, 1996.
28. U.S. Census Bureau, 2010.
29. Duany, 2000.
30. Pew Research Center, 2017.
31. Daniels and Kitano, 1970.
32. Alexandria Ocasio-Cortez (@AOC), November 14, 2018, https://thehill .com/homenews/house/416999-ocasio-cortez-i-was-stopped-because-it-was -assumed-i-was-an-intern.
33. Gibson, 2017; Pitt, 2018; Auber, 2018.
34. West, 2017.

35. Voto Latino, http://votolatino.org.
36. Morales, 2018.
37. Schaefer, 2011.
38. Morales, 2018.
39. Karenga, 2010.
40. Brown and Tucker, 1986.
41. Patterson, 2012.

References

Auber, Tamar (2018). "CNN Commentator Swipes at Toobin: Puerto Rico Is Not Case of Trump 'Ignoring People of Color,'" https://www.mediaite.com/tv /cnn-commentator-swipes-at-toobin-puerto-rico-is-not-case-of-trump -ignoring-people-of-color.

Baralt, Guillermo A. (2014). *Slave Revolts in Puerto Rico: Conspiracies and Uprisings, 1795–1873*, Princeton: Markus Wiener Publishers.

Brown, James, and Bruce Tucker (1986). *James Brown: The Godfather of Soul*, New York: Thunder's Mouth Press.

Comas, Juan (1971). "Historical Reality and the Detractors of Father Las Casas," in *Bartolomé de las Casas in History: Toward an Understanding of the Man and His Work* (Collection Spéciale: CER), Juan Friede and Benjamin Keen, eds., DeKalb: Northern Illinois University Press, 487–539.

Daniel, G. Reginald (2002). *More Than Black? Multiracial Identity and the New Racial Order*, Philadelphia: Temple University Press.

Daniels, Roger, and Harry H. L. Kitano (1970). *American Racism: Exploration of the Nature of Prejudice*, New York: Prentice Hall.

Diouf, Sylviane A. (2016). *Slavery's Exiles: The Story of the American Maroons*, New York: NYU Press.

DPLA (2019). "Puerto Rican Migration to the U.S.," https://dp.la/primary-source -sets/puerto-rican-migration-to-the-us.

Duany, Jorge (2000). "Neither White nor Black: The Politics of Race and Ethnicity among Puerto Ricans on the Island and in the US Mainland," presented at The Meaning of Race and Blackness in the Americas: Contemporary Perspectives, Brown University, Providence, Rhode Island.

Duany, Jorge (2002). *The Puerto Rican Nation on the Move: Identities on the Island and in the United States*, Chapel Hill: University of North Carolina Press.

Figueroa, Luis A. (2005). *Sugar, Slavery and Freedom in Nineteenth-Century Puerto Rico*, Chapel Hill: University of North Carolina Press.

Findlay, Eileen J. Suárez (1999). *Imposing Decency: The Politics of Sexuality and Race in Puerto Rico, 1870–1920*, Durham: Duke University Press.

Franklin, John Hope, and Alfred Moss (2000). *From Slavery to Freedom*, New York: McGraw Hill.

Gibson, Carrie (2017). "How Colonialism and Racism Explain the Inept U.S. Response to Hurricane Maria," *Vox*, https://www.vox.com/the-big-idea /2017/10/5/16426082/colonialism-racism-american-response-puerto -rico-maria.

Girard, Philippe R. (2011). *The Slaves Who Defeated Napoleon: Toussaint Louverture and the Haitian War of Independence, 1801–1804*, Tuscaloosa: University of Alabama Press.

González-Wippler, Migene (2017). *Santeria: African Magic in Latin America*, 2nd rev. ed., New York: Original Publication.

Karenga, Maulana (2010). *Introduction to Black Studies*, 4th ed., Los Angeles: Sankore Press.

Kinsbruner, Jay (1996). *Not of Pure Blood: The Free People of Color and Racial Prejudice in Nineteenth-Century Puerto Rico*, Durham: Duke University Press.

Korrol, Virginia Sánchez, and Pedro Juan Hernández (2010). *Pioneros II: Puerto Ricans in New York City 1948–1998* (Images of America), Charleston: Arcadia Publishing.

Loveman, Mara, and Jeronimo O. Muñiz (2007). "How Puerto Rico Became White: Boundary Dynamics and Intercensus Racial Reclassification," *American Sociological Review* 72: 915–939, https://doi.org/10.1177 /000312240707200604.

Martinez, Robert A. (2003). "African Aspects of the Puerto Rican Personality," http://connection.ebscohost.com/c/articles/11207606/african-aspects -puerto-rican-personality.

Middeldyk, R. A. Van (2016). *The History of Puerto Rico: From the Spanish Discovery to the American Occupation*, North Charleston: CreateSpace Independent Publishing Platform.

Morales, Ed (2018). "A New Report Says Hispanic Identity Is Fading. Is That Really Good for America?" *The Washington Post*, https://edmorales.net /2018/07/01/a-new-report-says-hispanic-identity-is-fading-is-that-really -good-for-america/.

Patterson, David Royston (2012). "Will Puerto Rico Be America's 51st State?" *New York Times*, November 25, https://www.nytimes.com/2012/11/25 /opinion/sunday/will-puerto-rico-be-americas-51st-state.html.

Pew Research Center (2017). "Hispanic America Studies," https://www.pew research.org/fact-tank/2019/09/16/key-facts-about-u-s-hispanics/.

Pico, Fernando (2014). History of Puerto Rico: A Panorama of Its People, 2nd ed., Princeton: Markus Wiener Publishers.

Pitt, William Rivers (2018). "September 11, Puerto Rico and the Racism of Callous Indifference," https://truthout.org/articles/september-11-puerto-rico -and-the-racism-of-callous-indifference.

Reid-Merritt, Patricia, ed. (2017). *Race in America: How a Pseudoscientific Concept Shaped Human Interaction*, Santa Barbara: Praeger.

Rouse, Irving (1992). *The Tainos: Rise and Decline of the People Who Greeted Columbus*, New Haven: Yale University Press.

Schaefer, Richard T. (2011). *Racial and Ethnic Groups*, 12th ed., Boston: Pearson-Prentice Hall.

U.S. Census Bureau (2000). "Puerto Rico," https://www.census.gov/census2000/states/pr.html.

U.S. Census Bureau (2010). "Identification of Hispanic Ethnicity in Census 2000: Analysis of Data Quality for the Question on Hispanic Origin," https://www.census.gov/library/working-papers/2004/demo/POP-twps0075.html.

Verin-Shapiro, Penny (2000). "Why 'Nuyoricans' Are Given the Cold-Shoulder by Other Puerto Ricans," https://eric.ed.gov/?id=ED456178.

West, Cornel (2017). "Cornel West to Activists, Immigrants: Let's Dump the Democratic Party," https://www.colorlines.com/articles/cornel-west-activists-immigrants-lets-dump-democratic-party.

CHAPTER FIVE

Cuban Americano

I remember being taken to a meeting to be introduced to the party officials. They had been informed of my nomination and expressed interest in the fact that I was a Cuban American. But when I walked in the door, one of the party bosses said, "You're a Cuban? You don't look like Bob Menendez!"

Anonymous Afro-Cuban

Introduction

Cuban Americans are the third largest ethnic group of the Hispanic population residing in the United States. While immigrants from Cuba arrived in America as early as the sixteenth century, the significant increase in the Cuban American population that began in the middle of the twentieth century can best be explained from a geopolitical perspective.[1] This chapter focuses on the experience of Cuban Americans whose journey to America has been shaped by a tumultuous political environment complicated by both national and international factors. And as indicated in the quote above, race and color are significant issues that demand further examination in the scholarly discourse on the Cuban American experience.

The History of Cuba

Cuba is a Caribbean island located in the Caribbean Sea just ninety miles off the coast of Florida. The history of the island is similar to that of

others in the region, where exploration by European nations, more specifically Spain, transformed the island's population, character, and culture
over a 400-year period.[2] The indigenous population were Taino Indians,
identified as the Ciboney, Siboney, or Arawakan-speaking Tainos.[3] This
ethnic group was often described as less politically advanced than the
"classic" Tainos who dominated Puerto Rico. The migrating Tainos from
neighboring Hispaniola first overtook the Ciboney or Siboney, and then,
in the latter part of the fifteenth century, colonization by Spain happened.[4]
Under the leadership of Diego Velázquez de Cuéllar, the Spanish conquest
of Cuba was complete in 1511. Almost immediately, the Taino fell victim
to racial discrimination and social oppression. They were forced to work
under a harsh labor system known as encomienda, the same system of
forced enslavement utilized in Puerto Rico by Spanish colonizers.[5] The
unfamiliar form of harsh and brutal labor exacted a heavy toll on the
indigenous people. This, coupled with the exposure to white man's diseases and the destruction of social norms and customs, resulted in a
decline in the native population, which was virtually eliminated by the
end of the century.[6]

Faced with the loss of the native population, the Spaniards would continue to occupy Cuba and eventually developed the island into a major
sugar-producing economy. For labor, the colonizers would rely on the
forced removal of Africans from the West Coast of the continent that was
part of the transatlantic slave trade.[7] The transfer of Africans occurred
throughout the Caribbean during the sixteenth, seventeenth, eighteenth,
and early decades of the nineteenth centuries. Thus, Cuba developed into
a racially mixed island, overwhelmed and dominated by white Europeans
and repopulated by tens of thousands of West Africans, many of whom
were members of the Yoruba and Igbo tribal groups. An early population
census from the mid-eighteenth century indicated that approximately 46
percent of the islanders were white, 37 percent enslaved Africans, and
nearly 17 percent free people of color.[8] (In comparison, nearly a hundred
years later, 39 percent of the population would indicate that they were
free people of color.) A significant portion of the free black population
had acquired their freedom through purchase; this practice was known as
coartacion, or "buying oneself out of slavery." Others gained their freedom
through the legal process of manumission.[9] Hugh Thomas argues that,
like Puerto Rico, Cuban plantation owners were deeply moved by the
1803 Haitian Revolution, an insurgent slave rebellion that resulted in the
island's freedom and independence.[10] With the loss of Haiti, the wealthi-
est of the sugar-producing economies at that time, Cuba sought to position itself as the new "pearl of the Antilles." An estimates 325,000 Africans

were imported to Cuba as slaves between 1790 and 1820, more than quadrupling the estimated 75,000 that had arrived between 1760 and 1790.[11]

The enslaved Africans were an extremely diverse group, coming from different nations with varying ethnic and tribal affiliations. According to Richard Gott, "They came from many tribes and nations along the length of the West African coastline, from Senegal in the north to Angola in the south—and even from Mozambique on Africa's south-east coast. They brought with them different languages, different beliefs, different customs, and different music, and through much of the nineteenth century they preserved these differences in the new Cuban home to which they had been transported."[12]

As was the case with each developing territory in the New World, for moral, religious, and/or social reasons, some members of society were opposed to the system of enslavement, a dehumanizing social system that stripped individuals of all human rights and dignity. And there were anti-slavery sentiments in Cuba, as well as other forms of resistance. For example, Gabino La Rosa Corzo describes the runaway slave settlements (*palenques*) that formed in the mountainous terrain in Cuba from 1737 to 1850.[13] Thousands of former slaves found refuge in these communities. In 1812, José Antonio Aponte was the leader of what later became known as the Aponte Conspiracy, the most successful of the slave rebellions in Cuba.[14]

As the system of enslavement began to disappear in the Caribbean, and with Puerto Rico, the island's closest neighbor, abolishing slavery in 1873, Cuba could not escape the forces of change. The system of enslavement, which denied human dignity and basic human rights to hundreds of thousands of African- and Cuban-born citizens, was doomed. However, efforts at dismantling the institution of slavery proved challenging and were fraught with inconsistencies for those victimized by the system.

> Under the terms of the Pact of Zanjón, which ended the Ten Year War in 1878, slaves who fought on either side of the war were set free, but those who did not fight had to endure almost another decade of slavery.
>
> Two years later the Spanish Cortes approved an abolition law (1880) that provided for an eight-year period of patronato (tutelage) for all slaves liberated according to the law. This only amounted to indentured servitude, as slaves were required to spend those 8 years working for their masters at no charge. On October 7, 1886, slavery was finally abolished in Cuba by a royal decree that also made the patronato illegal.[15]

Emancipation did not bring social equality to black Cubans. The island's development was built on a system of racial exploitation of the

African and native populations, and a belief in white supremacy remained. Moreover, the Spanish colonizers and their descendants did not embrace the freed Africans as wanted members of Cuban society and "warned against the potential 'evils' of a racially mixed society."[16]

Freedom for black Cubans marked the beginning of many major social challenges in the emerging nation. Seeking employment and educational opportunities were the foremost concern. While large numbers of free black Cubans (disproportionately female) were employed in the urban areas, the disproportionately male plantation workers faced a different plight. They were, overwhelmingly, illiterate, having received no formal education. They were "bred" to be slaves, forced to work in the plantation fields until their deaths. Now emancipated, black Cubans were banned from many jobs. Moreover, they were socially segregated in the public sectors and experienced discrimination in housing, transportation, and social support services. However, blacks were permitted to serve in the military, where a few black Cubans were later able to achieve distinguished military careers.[17]

There were attempts to develop the new Cuba into a society free of racial discrimination, leading some to romanticize the history of race relations on the island. For example, racial segregation in public education was to be avoided. An 1880 law stipulated that every community with more than five hundred members had to establish a public school—one for girls and one for boys. These schools, financed by the local municipalities, would be free from racial discrimination. Unfortunately, this was not always the case. According to Aline Helg, "Between 1883 and 1895, the number of schools on the island rose from 535 to 904. However, despite government initiatives, 'many schools refused to accept black children, and some municipalities began to run separate schools for blacks. Others simply refused to enroll blacks, or imposed a special fee that most could not pay.' Furthermore, a system of private schools to serve the needs of rich white families began to emerge."[18] Thus, efforts to develop Cuba into a multicultural society free of racial discrimination were hindered by the racial and class segregation that unfolded at the very beginning of the nation's independence.

Helg further notes that the newly freed black Cuban population was far from being monolithic. They represented different generations: those born in Africa, their first-generation descendants, and third and fourth generations of black Cubans who had assimilated to the culture and viewed the island as their native land. This sentiment was particularly true for Afro-Cubans living in the urban areas. In addition, there were distinctions between the "free" and "enslaved" members of the community. While all were victims of racial discrimination, their experiences with white racism and social oppression were further exaggerated by perceptions of class and color differences. In addition, "no common Afro-Cuban culture or subculture united them against the dominant Spanish-Cuban culture. Rather, African and Spanish traditions blended to produce a continuum of subcultures that can only be crudely sketched."[19]

While the Afro-Cubans struggled to find an acceptable and comfortable space in Cuban society, the nation faced social turmoil and civil disruption from internal and external forces. As an occupied colony, the entire society endured a level of social oppression. The people of Cuba sought freedom and independence from Spain.

Political Turmoil

Cuba presents as an island with a history of social protest. Islanders longed for independence, as was evinced by the prolonged and bloody Ten Years' War against Spain (1868–1878) that further fueled the nation's resentment but did not result in independence. However, social tensions that resurfaced at the very end of the century led to the Cuban Revolution, which began in February 1895. The Cuban insurrection affected the entire island. Cubans not only desired freedom from Spain but also were strongly opposed to American intervention that would likely result in further domination by a foreign power. In the fight for independence, the United States would align itself with the people of Cuba, proving to be a formidable obstacle to continued control and domination by Spain. Such a position promoted the self-interest of the United States, which grew increasingly frustrated with the Spanish presence within the southern region of the Western Hemisphere. Revolutionary efforts on the island contributed to the international conflict between Spain and the United States, which led to the eight-day Spanish-American War. The war officially ended on December 10, 1898, when the United States and Spain signed the Treaty of Paris. Following years of occupation by Spain, Cuba would finally emerge as an independent nation at the end of the nineteenth century. Spain relinquished all claims to the territory. However, Cubans were not free from the United States. At the end of the war, the American flag replaced the Spanish flag flying over Cuba's capital in Havana, and a new political power struggle would begin to unfold.[20]

Reinforced by a military presence, the United States assumed guardianship over Cuban affairs. While efforts at full independence were launched in 1902, Cuba would still be forced to endure interference from the United

States, due in part to the passage of the 1901 Platt Amendment, which stipulated the right of the United States to intervene in Cuba's internal affairs and to lease an area for a U.S. naval base in Cuba. The Platt Amendment was invoked on serval occasions, leading to military intervention in 1906–1909, 1917, and 1921.

The economic and political might of the United States hampered Cuba's social and economic development, producing an unwanted dependency on foreign support. A declining global economy, coupled with political corruption, greed, and ineffective governing, resulted in attempts at another social revolution in the 1930s. President Gerardo Machado y Morales, who served from 1925 to 1933, was forced to resign and soon flee the country. Carlos Manuel de Céspedes assumed power. Sergeant Fulgencio Batista y Zaldívar, with the support of radical students and intellectuals, overthrew the U.S.-backed regime of Carlos Manuel de Céspedes. Batista emerged as the self-appointed chief of the armed forces. Cuba emerged as a nation whose political powers were placed in the hands of the military. Batista would be elected president, serving from 1940 to 1944, and would fill the role as dictator from 1952 to 1959.[21]

The Castro Revolution

Disappointed with the promises made but left unfulfilled during the Batista regime, Cuba was again primed for another social revolution. Civil war, social strife, economic decline, and the destruction of valued social institutions attributed to the rise of Fidel Castro Ruz, described as a charismatic, anti-U.S. revolutionary leader, who seized power on January 1, 1959, and overthrew the U.S.-backed Batista government. The United States was no longer in a position to control or dictate Cuban politics. Castro seized U.S. properties and investments and began to convert Cuba into a one-party Communist system. Powerless and stripped of all internal influence, within a year, the United States imposed an embargo on Cuba and broke off diplomatic relations. An attempt to support Cuban exiles who opposed the Castro regime led to the planned Central Intelligence Agency–sponsored invasion of Cuba.[22] The 1962 Bay of Pigs incident resulted in a humiliating loss for the United States. It was a catastrophic failure. The Castro regime successfully defended the island, destroyed the underground resistance, and took bragging rights for its success in defeating the "Damn Yankees."

Castro, whose revolutionary army was dominated by middle-class white men, would make many promises to the Cuban people, one of which was ending the race problem by creating a society free of racial discrimination and other forms of social oppression.[23] This would prove to be an elusive, unobtainable goal.

Cuban Exodus

The success of the Castro-led Cuban revolution triggered the modern-day Cuban exodus to the United States, nearly a hundred years after the first Cuban exodus of 1869. During this era in the mid-nineteenth century, large numbers of Cubans, many of whom were businessmen and workers linked to the tobacco industry, settled in Florida. Some took up permanent residency; others would later return to Cuba to aid in the nation's fight for independence. However, those who fled the island following Castro's emergence in the mid-twentieth century often viewed themselves as Cuban exiles and vowed not to return as long as Castro was in power.

The expansion of the Cuban population in the United States during the latter half of the twentieth century is linked to three distinctive periods or "Cuban waves." The Cuban elite, well-educated, upper- and middle-class citizens, who were accustomed to many social privileges on the island, dominated the first wave. As would later be observed, this population was disproportionately "fair-skinned" and, perhaps, viewed themselves as the European-descended, white Cubans.[24] This privileged class also hastily arranged to have their children removed from the island. During the first two years following the revolution, Operation Peter Pan sent nearly fourteen thousand children to the United States. This planned exodus of Cuban children resulted from their parents' fears that they would be forced into a new educational system informed by Communist rhetoric and philosophy. Arriving without their parents, these children were connected to friends and relatives living in the United States. Those lacking familial ties were placed with nonprofit charitable organizations, which arranged for temporary placement in foster care, orphanages, or boarding schools. As the Cuban American community again began to take hold in Florida, the Miami-Dade area would gain the moniker Little Havana. Ironically, large numbers of Cubans would also make their way to Union City in New Jersey, which later would be referenced as the Havana on the Hudson.

In 1965, the start of the Freedom Flights resulted from an agreement between the United State and Cuba permitting special charter flights from Havana to Miami with Cuban refugees. The program lasted until 1973. An estimated 340,000 were resettled in the United States, most of whom remained in the Miami-Dade area.[25]

Nearly two decades after the Castro revolution, the Mariel boatlifts provided a pathway for the third wave of Cuban immigrants. Many were those who wanted to escape the Communist regime; however, Castro reportedly included an estimated twenty thousand criminals and mentally ill persons, viewed as Cuba's undesirables. They were of a decidedly different hue and class from the earlier wave and were not greeted with open arms from the established Cuban America community. Given the racial divisions established in Cuba over time, it is not difficult to speculate that this new group of immigrants, which included large numbers of the Afro-Cubans, were not among the society's privileged class. Cuban Americans referred to this latest group of immigrants as *Marielitos*. According to Richard Schaefer, "The word, which implied that these refugees were undesirable, refers to Mariel, the fishing port west of Havana from which the boats departed and where Cuban authorities herded people into boats. The term Marielitos remains a stigma in the media and in Florida."[26]

Toward the end of the twentieth century, Cubans continued to seek entry into the United States, primarily by way of Florida. Under the rules of the U.S. immigration policy system, the wet foot, dry foot policy allowed all Cubans to enter the United States as political refugees. This was a controversial policy, which critics contended offered special status and privilege to asylum seekers from the island. The policy, created by President Bill Clinton in 1995, allowed Cubans able to touch dry soil in the United States to remain in the country; however, those caught at sea would be returned to Cuba. The policy also triggered a change in immigration patterns, as many Cubans would first travel to Mexico and then cross over the Texas-Mexico border. This population, coined *dusty footers*, settled in the Houston, Texas, area, contributing to an expansion of the Cuban American community. President Barack Obama would end the controversial policy in 2017.[27] Today, the United States is home to the largest population of Cuban-born citizens outside of Cuba.

Cuban American Identity

Ethnic identification is what sets the Cuban American population apart from other members of the Hispanic community. They are first, second, and third generations of Cubans who now call the United States their home. While large numbers of Cuban Americans do reside in or near some of America's largest urban areas (New York, North Jersey, Los Angeles, Tampa, and Orlando), the influence of the Cuban presence has been most deeply felt in Florida, especially in the Miami-Dade County area, where the heavy concentration of Cuban immigrants has allowed them unprecedented freedom of cultural expression. This enclave has created many opportunities to reinforce Cuban culture; most embrace the use of the Spanish language and desire to maintain ties with family and relatives who remain on the island. However, the intensity of their connection to the island fades with every new generation born and raised in America. As a group, Cuban Americans (68 percent of whom still live in Florida) have successfully assimilated into American culture, but a pattern of acculturation also exists. An example of their success can be found in Dade County, where, at the end of the twentieth century, Cuban Americans occupied almost every top elected and administrative post and held the offices of mayor and city manager in Miami and Metropolitan Dade County. Cuban Americans also held the positions of "county school superintendent and Metro police chief as well as the presidencies of Florida International University and Miami-Dade Community College."[28] They were in fact the minority group who became the ethnic majority but remained decidedly Cuban. Cuban Americans tend to achieve higher levels of educational achievement, occupational status, income, wealth, and political power than other Spanish-speaking groups. This may account for some of the backlash that Cuban Americans face when staking their interest in programs for minority Americans. The following scenario (shared confidentially) may prove instructive:

> At an ivy-league institution in the northeast, "Black and Brown" students gathered to discuss the need to increase the school's minority population. A special scholarship fund had been established to help alleviate the financial burden of an ivy-league education. Following much discussion about which groups should be targeted, it was agreed that the institution should step up its recruitment of African American and Hispanic students. "But not the Cubans," one Spanish-speaking student added. "They already have received everything! If we're really looking to increase Hispanic enrollments, we should be looking at other Spanish-speaking groups."

Finally, Cuban Americans have also advanced in American politics. Consider, for example, U.S. Senator Bob Menendez (D-NJ), U.S. Senator Ted Cruz (R-Texas), U.S. Representative Mario Díaz-Balart (R-Florida), U.S. Senator Marco Rubio (R-Florida); and Congressman Albio Sires (D-NJ). It is important to note that these political representatives and members of the Cuban American community tend to be of the lighter hue. Within their own communities, they are often referred to as the "white Cubans." There are noted differences regarding levels of achievement within the group, with the more recent arrivals still struggling to achieve the American Dream. However, the older generation of immigrants has assimilated to Anglo American culture. And while many, particularly the younger generation, are willing to embrace the new identity concept of being a Latino American, identifying oneself as a member of a particular racial group remains somewhat of a challenge.

On the island, the racial identity of the Cuban people has indeed fluctuated over time. In 1800, approximately 54 percent self-reported as being white; one hundred years later, that number had increased to 68 percent. In 2000, 55 percent would indicate that they were white. Ten years later, the number of white Cubans would increase to 64 percent. The nonwhite category included Africans, Blacks, Mulatto/Mestizo, and Indians.[29]

The racial diversity that exists on the island is evident: according to the 2012 Cuban Census, the island population was 64.12 percent white, 26.62 percent mulatto, 9.26 percent black, and 0.1 percent Asian. And an earlier study (1995 on the population of Pinar del Rio) "found that 50% of the Mt-DNA lineages (female lineages) could be traced back to Europeans, 46% to Africans and 4% to Native Americans." Others would argue that the racial composition is closer to two-thirds black and mixed race or even as high as 72 percent.[30] A visit to the island provides prima facie evidence that Cuba is indeed populated by people of color.

Racial identity for Cuban Americans paints a different picture. According to the 2010 U.S. Census Report, when asked to self-identify, 85 percent of the Cubans who immigrated to the United States from Cuba identified as being white.[31] These findings could also suggest that a disproportionately large percentage of the Cuban immigrants were, in fact, the more privileged middle- to upper-class white population.

The resettlement of Cubans in Florida must be viewed against the backdrop of America's racist social history. The founding of this country was based on white supremacy beliefs. The native populations were systematically diminished and, like in Cuba, hundreds of thousands of Africans were forcefully transferred here and endured centuries of enslavement under harsh and brutal conditions. Florida is in the Deep South, once part of the Confederacy, with a history of Jim Crow laws designed to limit freedom and civil rights and liberties of both its indigenous and African-descended citizens.[32] During the modern-day Cuban exodus, the historical patterns of racial discrimination were present throughout the state: a large percentage of the Seminole Indians occupied the reservations; the African Americans, the urban ghettos. The majority white population enjoyed white privileges in education, housing, employment, transportation, and other public amenities.

Cuban Americans were aware of the racial divide that existed in America; racism was also part of the heritage and legacy of Cuba. One would not intentionally seek to be identified as part of one of America's racial minority communities. Evelio Grillo's powerful book, *Black Cuban, Black American: A Memoir*, discusses his experiences growing up both black and Cuban.[33] Grillo was raised in in the early 1900s in Ybor City, Florida, an area later renamed as Tampa. He was painfully aware of the racial, class, and color differences that existed in the Cuban American community. Grillo recalls a de facto type of segregation that existed on the island. Discrimination was prevalent, and one came to understand his position in society as a black Cuban. The social separation of the two races was pronounced. There were, more often than not, separate neighborhoods, school systems, and social institutions. The social deprivations that existed in Cuba for its black citizens were further reinforced in America, where he witnessed the preferential treatment afforded to white Cubans. Equality was granted by law but did not reflect the social reality. In addition to the obstacles and stigma placed upon him in the Cuban community resulting from his blackness, his social circumstances were further exacerbated by his identification as a black American. Here, the one-drop rule, a social and legal principle developed and fine-tuned during the earlier part of the twentieth century, deemed anyone with a hint of color as a black American.[34] The one-drop rule was utilized to enforce segregation in education, housing, employment, and property inheritance and, most importantly, to maintain the notion of white purity and white supremacy. The South was the nation's prominent poster child for denying basic human and civil rights on the basis of skin color. The successive waves of Cubans who arrived in America in the latter half of the twentieth century were undoubtedly familiar with the concept of white privilege, and any acknowledgement of African or Native American heritage would be left behind.

The Latino Revolution

Embracing a Latino (Latinx) identity has become popular among many ethnic Spanish-speaking communities. Many Cuban Americans also proudly describe themselves as members of the Latino community (Gloria Estefan, Andy García, Cristina Saralegui, etc.). However, the public perception of *Latino* being synonymous with *people of color* is a bit of a misconception. Journalist Angelo Falcon highlights the problems resulting from the misperception of Latinos as people of color. In "Latinos and the 'Of Color' Problem," he writes:

"People of color," "minorities," "communities of color," and "African descendent" are all terms in common use when referring to non-whites in general. These are aspirational umbrella terms for what is seen as the unification of Blacks, African-Americans, Latinos, and Asians as the "other" in American society. They represent attempts to emphasize the commonalities shared by these groups and the potential power of the aggregation of their numbers. To some, it is the expression of the expansion of a core African-American civil rights struggle within the United States to a broader multi-cultural constituency. To others, this is the logical expression of a dominant process of the racialization of these groups.[35]

However, Latinos are not a racial group, and any effort to categorize this multiethnic and multiracial group into a singular racial category is misguided. Latinos are often referred to as the "brown" people. Indeed, the frequently used expression *our brown sisters and brothers* places emphasis on the mixed-race heritage of many members of the Latino community. But do Latinos view themselves as communities of color? And as members of the Latino community, do Cuban Americans consider themselves to be people of color? Cuban Americans overwhelmingly and disproportionately view themselves as white Americans. While there is no denying the presence of the Afro-Cuban community, they are left struggling to declare their right to self-identify as both black and Latino. However, as indicated in multiple research studies, ethnic identity fades over time.[36] Successive generations, especially those who have never had contact with the island, are least likely to identify themselves as Cuban. Locating oneself in a racial category will be the primary identifying factor. And for Cuban Americans, the preferred group appears to be white American.

Notes

1. Chomsky, Carr, and Smorkaloff, 2004.
2. Thomas, 2010; Staten, 2005.
3. Levinson and Knight, 2018.
4. Granberry and Vescelius, 1992; Rouse, 1992.
5. Yeager, 1995.
6. Saunders, 2005.
7. Franklin and Moss, 2000.
8. Scheina, 2003.
9. Klein, 1967.
10. Thomas, 2010; Girard, 2011.
11. Ferrer, 2014.
12. Gott, 2005, p. 115.

13. Corzo, 2003.
14. Childs, 1970.
15. Historyofcuba.com.
16. Ibid.
17. Helg, 1967.
18. Ibid., 28.
19. Ibid., 30.
20. O'Toole, 1986.
21. Nations Online Project.
22. Kornbluh, 1998.
23. Cooke, 2015.
24. Ibid.
25. Schaefer, 2015.
26. Ibid., p. 216.
27. Gomez, 2017.
28. Clary, 1997.
29. National Office of Statistics of Cuba. "Censos en Cuba".
30. Cooke, 2015.
31. Cubanos por el Mundo, 2010.
32. See Florida, Reid-Merritt, 2018.
33. Grillo, 2000.
34. Higginbotham, 1978.
35. Falcon, 2018.
36. Pew Research Center, 2017.

References

Childs, Matt D. (1970). *The 1812 Aponte Rebellion in Cuba and the Struggle against Atlantic Slavery*, Chapel Hill: University of North Carolina Press.

Chomsky, Aviva, Barry Carr, and Pamela Maria Smorkaloff, eds. (2004). *The Cuba Reader: History, Culture, Politics*, Durham: Duke University Press.

Clary, Mike (1997). "Black, Cuban Racial Chasm Splits Miami," *The Los Angeles Times*, https://www.latimes.com/archives/la-xpm-1997-03-23-mn-41392 -story.html.

Cooke, Julia (2015). "Among Sweeping Changes in U.S. Relations: Cuba's Race Problem Persists," http://america.aljazeera.com/articles/2015/8/13/amid -sweeping-changes-in-us-relations-cubas-race-problem-persists.html.

Corzo, Gabino La Rosa (2003). *Runaway Slave Settlements in Cuba: Resistance and Repression*, Chapel Hill: The University of North Carolina Press.

Cubanos por el Mundo (2010). "U.S. Census Bureau 2010: Facts about Cuban Americans," https://cubanosporelmundo.com/2013/01/14/u-s-census -bureau-2010-facts-about-cuban-americans/.

Falcon, Angelo (2018). "Latinos and the 'Of Color' Problem," *Al Día*, April 3, https://aldianews.com/articles/opinion/latinos-and-color-problem/52221.

Ferrer, Ada (2014). *Freedom's Mirror: Cuba and Haiti in the Age of Revolution*, New York: Cambridge University Press.

Franklin, John Hope, and Alfred Moss (2000). *From Slavery to Freedom*, New York: McGraw Hill.

Girard, Phillippe R. (2011). *The Slaves Who Defeated Napoleon: Toussaint Louverture and the Haitian War of Independence, 1801–1804*, Tuscaloosa: University of Alabama Press.

Gomez, Alan (2017). "Obama Ends 'Wet Foot, Dry Foot' Policy for Cubans," *USA TODAY*, January 12, https://www.usatoday.com/story/news/world/2017/01/12/obama-ends-wet-foot-dry-foot-policy-cubans/96505172/.

Gott, Richard (2005). *Cuba: A New History*, New Haven: Yale University Press.

Granberry, Julian, and Gary Vescelius (1992). *Languages of the Pre-Columbian Antilles*, Tuscaloosa: University of Alabama Press.

Grillo, Evelio (2000). *Black Cuban, Black American: A Memoir*, Houston: Arte Público Press.

Helg, Aline (1967). *Our Rightful Share: The Afro-Cuban Struggle for Equality, 1886–1912*, Chapel Hill: University of North Carolina Press.

Higginbotham, A. L. (1978). *In the Matter of Color: Race, and the American Legal Process*, New York: Oxford University Press.

HistoryofCuba.com. "End of Slavery in Cuba," http://www.historyofcuba.com/history/race/EndSlave.htm.

Klein, Herbert S. (1967). *Slavery in the Americas: A Comparative Study of Virginia and Cuba*, Chicago: University of Chicago Press.

Kornbluh, Peter (1998). *Bay of Pigs Declassified: The Secret CIA Report on the Invasion of Cuba* (National Security Archive Documents), New York: W.W. Norton & Company.

Levinson, Sarah H., and Franklin W. Knight (2018). "Cuba," https://www.britannica.com/place/Cuba.

National Office of Statistics of Cuba. "Censos en Cuba" (Spanish version), http://www.one.cu/loscensos.htm.

Nations Online Project. "History of Cuba," https://www.nationsonline.org/oneworld/History/Cuba-history.htm.

O'Toole, G. (1986). *The Spanish War: An American Epic 1898*, New York: W. W. Norton & Company.

Pew Research Center (2017). "Hispanic America Studies," https://www.pewresearch.org/fact-tank/2019/09/16/key-facts-about-u-s-hispanics/

Reid-Merritt, Patricia, ed. (2018). *A State-by-State History of Race and Racism in the United States*, Santa Barbara: Greenwood Press.

Rouse, Irving (1992). *The Tainos: Rise and Decline of the People Who Greeted Columbus*, New Haven: Yale University Press.

Saunders, Nicholas J. (2005). *The Peoples of the Caribbean: An Encyclopedia of Archeology and Traditional Culture*, Santa Barbara: ABC-CLIO.

Schaefer, Richard T. (2015). *Racial and Ethnic Groups*, 14th ed., Boston: Pearson-Prentice Hall.

Scheina, Robert L. (2003). *Latin America's Wars, Volume I: The Age of the Caudillo, 1791–1899*, Dulles: Brassey's.

Staten, Clifford L. (2005). *The History of Cuba* (Palgrave Essential Histories Series), New York: St. Martin's Press.

Thomas, Hugh (2010). *Cuba: A History*, New York: Penguin Books.

Yeager, Timothy (1995). "Encomienda or Slavery? The Spanish Crown's Choice of Labor Organization in Sixteenth-Century Spanish America," *The Journal of Economic History* 55: 842–859, accessed July 19, 2013, http://www.latinamericanstudies.org/colonial/encomienda-slavery.pdf.

CHAPTER SIX

Dominican and American

I was fourteen when I came here from my country. That is precisely when everyone started calling me black. I thought I was white. I have straight hair. In my country, everybody with straight hair is white.

—Samuel, age 26

Introduction

Samuel's experience is reflective of the many different ways in which Hispanic communities socially construct race. While skin color is the primary factor in determining which racial category one is assigned based on the binary black/white schema, other factors, such as hair texture, social status, wealth, and heritage can also be utilized to assert one's membership in a particular racial group. For the people of the Dominican Republic, their history and heritage as children of Spain appear to take precedence over all other defining social characteristics. The extent to which they embrace their ethnicity as Dominicans and heritage as Spanish-speaking people is well documented in Henry Louis Gates's *Black in Latin America*.[1] Noting that his observations of the people in the capital town of Santo Domingo would suggest that, in America, they would be described as black, he is informed by his scholarly guide, "But not here!" In the Dominican Republic, the strong identification with Spanish culture results in most insisting that they are, in fact, members of the white or mixed-race community but not the black community. This current perception of the people runs diametrically opposed to the history of the island that Silvio Torres-Saillant describes as "the cradle of blackness in the Americas."[2] This chapter examines the race and identity question for members of the Dominican American community. As with other groups, it is important that we understand the unique heritage and journey of Dominican Americans, whose numbers in the United States have grown substantially over the years.

A Caribbean Island

The Dominican Republic is located in the Caribbean Sea on the island of Hispaniola. The island is home to two nations—the Dominican Republic and Haiti. Haiti is situated on the eastern half of the island, and the Dominican Republic is on the west. Like many other Caribbean islands, it shares a history of colonial domination and control by the Spanish Empire. (Its sister nation, Haiti, was first dominated by Spain but later colonized by France.)[3] Spain laid claim to the island, first called Santo Domingo, in the early sixteenth century, quickly decimating the indigenous Taino Indian population.[4] European settlers and Africans, who were forcibly removed during the period of the transatlantic slave trade, repopulated the island as the conquerors continued to build a Spanish-inspired culture in the New World.[5] There was an undeniably large African presence on the island. During the early colonial period, blacks outnumbered whites. The black presence on the island is of historical significance. In Torres-Saillant's groundbreaking work, *Introduction to Dominican Blackness*, he notes that the island of "Hispaniola received the first blacks ever to arrive on the western hemisphere. It inaugurated both the colonial plantation and New World Africa slavery. On this island in 1503 black maroons first rose their subversive heads, and there too the hemisphere's first black slave insurrection took place on December 27, 1522."[6] Spanish domination and the ideology of white supremacy are also embedded in the island's history, coupled with ongoing periods of dehumanizing blackness. However, miscegenation is a major factor in the island's social, cultural, and political history as well. While there are white Europeans, black Africans, and Native Indians, the majority of the population are mixed-race. According to the latest Dominican census, 73 percent of the population identify as mixed race.[7]

Historically, the Dominican Republic was among the least desirable New World colonies. For nearly two centuries, the island struggled to be competitive with neighboring sugar-producing islands in the Caribbean, including Barbados, Cuba, Puerto Rico, and Haiti.[8] However, by the early nineteenth century, Haiti emerged as the first independent nation in the

Western Hemisphere.[9] The successful revolution of formerly held enslaved Africans and their descendants reverberated throughout the region. The former French colony, now a free black nation, invaded Santo Domingo in 1822, unifying the island under one rule. Haiti continued to occupy the Spanish half of the island for two decades. Santo Domingo finally gained its freedom from Haiti in 1844. The liberation of Santo Domingo, which later would be renamed the Dominican Republic, was achieved by dissolving its ties to a former colony, a nation founded by the revolutionary force of ex-slaves. Unfortunately, the island's emergence as an independent nation was brief. In 1861, it *voluntarily* rejoined the Spanish Crown (described by some as having resulted from the political ambitions of the unpatriotic European-descended elites). However, within a few years, the nation reclaimed its independence. Its founders envisioned a multiracial nation, free of racist ideology and notions of white supremacy. Addressing the practice of human enslavement was a priority. Slavery was eliminated; those engaging in the trafficking of human beings would be punished. As a result, Santo Domingo was a refuge for those enslaved on other colonies in the Caribbean, including Cuba and Puerto Rico. An enslaved individual who set foot on Santo Domingo soil was suddenly free.[10]

By the end of the nineteenth century, the Dominican Republic experienced an economic surge, due largely to its thriving sugar-producing industry. Immigration from Europe, North America, and the surrounding Caribbean islands increased, adding to the nation's diverse population.[11] The social and political turmoil resulting from the decline of Spanish control over territories in the Western Hemisphere would also have an impact on the Dominican Republic. The 1898 eight-day Spanish-American War finally eliminated the colonized status of both Cuba and Puerto Rico, the Dominican's close neighbors.[12] And just as the United States had found it necessary to meddle in the affairs of both of these newly independent nations, so too did it take an interest in the social conditions, economic fortunes, and politically strategic location of the Dominican Republic.

An Independent Nation

The emergence of any newly independent nation brings many social challenges. Developing nations often look to the established countries to assist or aid in their social, economic, and political progress. The United States established political and economic ties with the Dominican Republic during the early stages of its independence. Among other political and economic factors, formal international ties with the United States resulted in loan grants to the Dominican Republic. And the United States had high expectations that all debts would be paid.

With concern over political and economic instability (which would affect debt repayment to the United States), in 1916, the United States invaded the Dominican Republic.[13] There were other motivating factors, as well. Efforts to influence the development and future direction of the island were also a reflection of America's racist views toward Haiti, the independent black nation in the Caribbean. America's antipathy toward its black citizens was well known. The nation was built on a solid foundation of white supremacist beliefs, with the Native Americans among its first victims, followed by more than two centuries of African enslavement. Slavery was abolished in 1865; a brief period of reconstruction followed.[14] However, by the end of the nineteenth century, the U.S. Supreme Court's decision in *Plessy v. Ferguson* (1896) signaled a period of Jim Crow segregation that reinforced the view of blacks as inferior to America's dominant white population.[15] Haiti was a symbol of black freedom; it spoke to the powerful influence of an African-based culture. It was a black nation; it existed in the Western Hemisphere, where efforts to restore African humanity and equality were unquestioned. The Dominican Republic was expected to develop into a European-inspired culture, de-emphasizing all elements of its African heritage. These racist, anti-African sentiments were described by the progressive members of the society as Negrophobia, which ran rampant among the European-dominated elite class.[16]

While the 1916 U.S. Marines–backed invasion was met with resentment by the people of the republic, it is credited with the restoration of social order, including the balancing of the country's budget, a reduction in the national debt, the rebuilding of the country's infrastructure projects, and the stimulation of economic growth. "A professional military organization, the Dominican Constabulary Guard, replaced the partisan forces that had waged a seemingly endless struggle for power."[17] The U.S. occupation ended in 1924.

From 1930 to 1961, the island was under the leadership of military ruler Rafael Leónidas Trujillo Molina; the period was known to the Dominicans as the Trujillo Era. Molina served two terms as the elected president—the first from 1930 to 1938, and the second from 1942 to 1952. History records this era as a dark and bloody period in which the Trujillo rule was responsible for the death of more than fifty thousand people, including twenty to thirty thousand Haitians during the Parsley Massacre.[18] Trujillo opposed the Haitians on many levels, one of which was purely racial. Haiti embraced itself as a black nation, taking great pride in its African heritage. The Dominican Republic did not, and great efforts were made to erase the African influence on Dominican culture.[19] During his first presidency, Trujillo demanded that no more Haitians enter the Dominican Republic; rather, he encouraged European immigration. It was his hope that the Europeans would marry the Dominicans, further aiding in the "lightening" of the population and the Europeanization of the culture. Trujillo ceded the presidency to his younger brother in 1952 but continued to use military force to serve as the unofficial dictator of the country. There were many revolutionary forces in opposition to Trujillo. Moreover, members of the international community voiced concern over his ironfisted dictatorship. However, it was his fellow countrymen who so vehemently objected to his brutal regime that they reportedly assassinated Trujillo in 1961; his death drew worldwide attention.[20]

Civil unrest and political instability rocked the country for the next several years. The U.S. government intervened again in 1965.[21] Under the guise of "halting the advance of Communism," President Lyndon B. Johnson made the controversial decision to send more than twenty-two thousand U.S. troops to the island. After restoring order, the troops were charged with overseeing the democratic election of Joaquin Balaguer to the presidency. However, the people of the Dominican, wary of the past and still uncertain about the future, sought opportunities outside of the nation's borders. Aided by the change in U.S. immigration policy resulting from the Immigration and Nationality Act of 1965 (often referred to as the Immigration Reform Act), large numbers of Dominican emigrants joined the new wave of Hispanics immigrants to the United States. According to Rueben Rumbaut, immigration of Dominicans to the United States began as a trickle but by the 1980s rose to unprecedented levels.[22] "The number of Dominicans legally entering the United States between 1981 and 1990 was far greater than the number of Cubans: indeed, more Dominicans entered the United States in the last decade than any other Western Hemisphere national group except migrants from Mexico."[23] Thus, by the end of the century, there were sizable numbers of Dominican American communities existing in the United States. And they carried with them an understanding of race and race relations based on the unique history and heritage of the Dominican culture.

Dominican Americans

According to the U.S. Census, less than one percent of the population, or roughly two million individuals, identify themselves as Dominican Americans.[24] This is a much smaller number than other Spanish-speaking groups; however, their concentration in specific regions of the country helps to raise their profile as a distinctively unique Hispanic population. While New York City is home to the nation's largest population of Dominican Americans, Massachusetts, Connecticut, Pennsylvania, Florida, and Rhode Island also have residential areas with highly concentrated Dominican populations. They are the fifth largest Spanish-speaking group in America, following those from Mexico, Puerto Rico, Cuba, and Guatemala.

As the Dominicans began arriving in the United States, they, like other Hispanic immigrants, were faced with the race question: To what race do you belong? Unlike the Indian-looking Mexican or the light-hued first wave of Cubans, the Dominicans appeared to be brown. They are, in fact, the brownest of the Spanish-speaking groups and may rightfully be described as "the people of color." Others were undeniably black, their phenotypical, genetically inherited characteristics profoundly obvious. As indicated above, the Dominican Republic has a strong history of miscegenation. While many may have been permitted to socially construct themselves as white or mixed race on the island, their experience in the United States proved to be quite different. Dominicans were, more often than not, viewed and treated as black Americans, leaving some to feel resentful of their newly assigned racial status.[25] As noted by Sean Buffington, "The mixed Afro-Hispanic heritage of many Dominicans has led them to be categorized as black by white Americans; they have encountered the same racial prejudice that African Americans have experienced for centuries."[26] Decades of anti-African and Negrophobic propaganda, coupled with the intragroup practice of colorism, have left many Dominicans feeling ashamed or embarrassed about their African heritage. As a community, they are not known for outward displays of African pride. In fact, some would argue that Dominicans are encouraged to hide their blackness. And there has been a bevy of discussion in popular culture about the use of skin lighteners among the Dominican people. (Recall how Sammy Sosa's complexion lightened over time.) However, scholars caution that the Dominicans' views on race and racial identity cannot be viewed from the prism of the American race experience. While acknowledging the multiracial aspects of the Dominican people, Dominican Americans do not feel it necessary "to wear their racial identity on one's sleeve."[27] Torres-Saillant argues that this lack of affinity toward one's African roots is due more to ignorance than denial of the obvious phenotypic connection to African people. They have been exposed to a process of deracialization. Moreover, the Dominican people are products of an educational and social system that has consciously, and very deliberately, attempted to diminish the island's African past, including the many contributions that African-descended people have made to the Dominican culture.[28]

The United States conducts its census survey of all Americans every ten years. The collection of data is important in determining political representation, distribution of federal and state dollars, and trends in consumer consumption. However, it also provides a snapshot of America, asking specific questions about race and ethnic identity. According to the 2010 U.S. Census, the majority of Dominican Americans chose to indicate their racial category as *other*; 29.6 percent responded that they were white, with 12.9 percent indicating that they were black. The *other* category reflects the insistence among many Dominicans to rightfully claim and acknowledge their mixed racial heritage. They are, in fact, *miscegan*, a term recently coined by Reid-Merritt to describe the racially blended characteristics of primarily Latino populations who, after successive generations of intermingling, can no longer separate the European from the African or indigenous characteristics of their genetic heritage.[29]

Like other Spanish-speaking groups, Dominican Americans can self-identify as Hispanic, Latino, Afro-Latino, American, or Dominican. According to the 2013 Pew Research Center Report, the majority (66 percent) indicated their preference to identify themselves as Dominican.[30] While other terms were utilized, it is clear that ethnic identification is strong in the Dominican American community.

As indicated above, Dominican Americans are the fifth largest Hispanic/Latino group in America; however, research on the Dominican American experience has not matched the level of study of the three largest groups: Mexicans, Puerto Ricans, and Cubans. A concerted effort to study the Dominican American experience got underway with the establishment of the City University of New York's (CUNY) Dominican Studies Institute in 1992. The CUNY Dominican Studies Institute houses the largest collection of scholarly research on the Dominican American experience.[31] The institute offers a wealth of information on social, economic, and political concerns facing Dominican Americans, both here and on the island. In addition, research generated at the institute explores the various ways in which Dominicans attempt to maintain their culture in their new host country, the United States of America. For example, Daisy Cocco De Filippis's *Documents of Dissidence: Selected Writings by Dominican Women* (2000) offers a collection of varying views on Dominican feminism;[32] Ramona Hernandez and Francisco Rivera-Batiz provide a statistical analysis of Dominican Americans living in the United States;[33] Sarah Aponte's work offers an extensive annotated bibliography focusing on the Dominican migration;[34] and Torres-Saillant tells the story of Dominican blackness.[35] This institute investigates a plethora of social interests and concerns. The institute's website proudly claims, "A Dominican was the first Latino to arrive in North America."[36]

The concentration of Dominican American families in certain areas allows their presence to be felt and aids in the reinforcement of Dominican cultural values. The Caribbean cultural base of Dominican Americans is similar to that of Puerto Ricans and Cubans. They are a gifted, creative, Spanish-speaking community with unique forms of cultural expression in daily ways of living, including food, music, dance, and religious worship. While they are primarily Catholic, elements of traditional African religion are also part of the culture. Dominicans are family-oriented, with strong connections to extended family members, which is important if one recognizes the primacy of the nuclear family in American culture.

The Dominican community has been known to boast about their athletic prowess, especially considering the modern-day success of Dominican players in the field of baseball. Baseball is the most popular sport among the Dominican people, both here and abroad.[37] Professional major league baseball players have emerged as superstars in American culture, including Pedro Martinez, Vladimir Guerrero, Juan Marichal, Robinson Cano, Manny Ramirez, David Ortiz, and Sammy Sosa. However, the reinforcement of cultural practices and traditions is dependent not only on the day-to-day living activities of the community, but also on the need for successive generations of Dominicans to embrace their history and cultural heritage. As noted in previous chapters, identification with one's ethnic heritage among children born in the United States decreases over time. This trend has held steady throughout America's immigration history.[38] The decrease in ethnic identification among the next generation of American-born citizens is true for the Hispanic populations, as well.[39] Furthermore, complications about one's ethnic or racial identity occur when one engages in exogamy, or marriage outside of the group. For example, the Dominican Americans have very high intermarriage and procreation rates with Puerto Ricans. "The intermarriage of Dominicans with partners of other ethnicities sometimes creates circumstances that, depending on the dominant ethnic presence in the environment surrounding the family, may lead the children to identify with the ancestry of one of their parents rather than the other."[40]

Dominican American Pride

There is evidence of Dominican American pride in many forms. As the number of Dominicans in America grew, organizations and special events to celebrate Dominican culture emerged. For example, in August 1981, the first Dominican Day Parade was held in New York City. This annual event has grown from a small festival confined to one avenue in the Washington Heights section of the city to a major citywide affair. The parade and associated activities are described as the "most important Dominican community event in the U.S."[41] In addition to highlighting traditional music, dance, food, and customs, the parade organizers have turned the celebration into an ongoing educational, cultural, and fundraising event. Each year the organization awards hundreds of thousands of scholarship dollars to students of Dominican heritage from all over the nation.[42] The many activities that have been incorporated into the annual event bring together the Dominican American community and its many supporters. It has become a necessary stop for local politicians seeking the support of the Dominican community.

Transnational Connections

The close proximity of the Dominican Republic to the United States and other Caribbean nations allows for ongoing contact with members of the Dominican community. The ability to return or visit the homeland helps to reinforce cultural values, traditions, and one's identity as a Dominican. However, Dominicans who return home often face accusations that they assimilated into American culture. Other Hispanic groups have faced a similar dilemma. Puerto Ricans born or residing on the mainland, or more specifically New York City, are sometimes described as *Nuyorican*, which is often viewed as a pejorative term. Nuyoricans are accused of emerging themselves into American culture and possessing only a superficial, symbolic attachment to the Puerto Rican culture. The Dominican American, too, may be viewed with suspicion. Dominicans who return home face accusations that they have assimilated into American culture and only embrace Dominican culture as a matter of convenience. Moreover, second- and third-generation Dominicans may also struggle with coming to grips with a transnational identity, meaning they may wish to identity as Dominican even though they were born and reared in the United States. However, "Dominicans have tended to be seen by Americans as especially resistant to assimilation and committed to their country, culture, and language of origin."[43]

The Dominican community continues to discover new ways to integrate themselves into the American lifestyle. Being comfortable in their own skin is part of that process. America's visual perception of the Dominican people is one that recognized this Hispanic/Latino population as "people of color." As members of the larger ethno-racial group of Hispanics, the Dominican American community must understand how the conceptualization of race and the practice of racism shape every aspect of American culture. Gaining clarity on the importance of understanding one's racial identity maximizes one's ability to successfully navigate the social, political, and economic environment in the United States of America. Race, whether perceived, assigned, or self-described, is a major factor in shaping one's future and destiny in twenty-first century America.

Notes

1. Gates, 2011.
2. Torres-Saillant, 2010.
3. Girard, 2010.
4. Moya Pon, 2010.
5. Franklin and Moss, 2000.
6. Torres-Saillant, 2010.
7. DominicanRepublic.com.
8. Moya Pon, 2010.
9. Girard, 2010.
10. Torres-Saillant, 2010.
11. Middeldyk, 2016.
12. World History Project.
13. Reid-Merritt, 2017.
14. Franklin and Moss, 2000.
15. Torres-Saillant, 2010.
16. World History Project.
17. History.com, 2019a.
18. Torres-Saillant, 2010.
19. Saneaux and Hernández, 2013.
20. History.com, 2019b; Minster, 2019.
21. Immigration to the United States.
22. Rumbaut, 1992, p. 288.
23. Ennis, Ríos-Vargas, Albert, 2010.
24. Flores, 2017.
25. Buffington, 2019.
26. Williams, 2017.
27. Torres-Saillant, 2010.
28. Ennis, Ríos-Vargas, Albert, 2010.
29. Reid-Merritt, 2018.
30. López, 2015.
31. The City College of New York, 2019.
32. Cocco De Filippis, 2000.

33. Hernández and Rivera-Batiz, 2003.
34. Aponte, 1999.
35. Torres-Saillant, 2010.
36. The City College of New York, 2019.
37. Jessop, 2013.
38. Schaefer, 2015.
39. Rosentiel, 2012.
40. Buffington, 2019, p. 4.
41. *New York Latin Culture Magazine*, 2019b.
42. *New York Latin Culture Magazine*, 2019a.
43. Buffington, 2019, p. 4.

References

Aponte, Sarah (1999). *Dominican Migrations to the United States: 1970–1997*, New York: CUNY Academic Works.

Buffington, Sean (2019). "Dominican Americans," Countries and Their Culture, https://www.everyculture.com/multi/Bu-Dr/Dominican-Americans.html #ixzz5nubZufEU.

The City College of New York (2019). "CUNY Dominican Studies Institute," https://www.ccny.cuny.edu/dsi/.

Cocco De Filippis, Daisy (2000). *Documents of Dissidence: Selected Writings by Dominican Women*, New York: CUNY Academic Works.

DominicanRepublic.com (2019). "Demographics," https://www.dominicanrepub lic.com/demographics/.

Ennis, Sharon R., Merarys Ríos-Vargas, and Nora G. Albert (2010). "The Hispanic Population: 2010," U.S. Census Bureau, https://www.census.gov /prod/cen2010/briefs/c2010br-04.pdf.

Flores, Antonio (2017). "2015, Hispanic Population in the United States Statistical Portrait: Statistical Portrait of Hispanics in the United States," Pew Research Center, https://www.pewresearch.org/hispanic/2017/09/18/2015 -statistical-information-on-hispanics-in-united-states/.

Franklin, John Hope, and Alfred Moss (2000). *From Slavery to Freedom*, New York: McGraw Hill.

Gates, Henry Louis (2011). "Black in Latin America" (episode 1), PBS, https:// www.pbs.org/video/black-in-latin-america-black-in-latin-americas -henry-louis-gates/.

Girard, Phillippe (2010). *Haiti: The Tumultuous History—From Pearl of the Caribbean to Broken Nation*, New York: St. Martin's Griffin.

Hernández, Ramona and Francisco Rivera-Batiz (2003). *Dominicans in the United States: A Socioeconomic Profile 2000*, New York: CUNY Academic Works.

History.com. (2019a). "Rafael Trujillo," https://www.history.com/topics/1960s /rafael-trujillo.

History.com. (2019b). "U.S. Troops Land in Dominican Republic," https://www
.history.com/this-day-in-history/u-s-troops-land-in-the-dominican-republic.

Immigration to the United States. "Immigration and Naturalization Act of 1965,"
http://immigrationtounitedstates.org/594-immigration-and-nationality
-act-of-1965.html.

Jessop, Alicia (2013). "The Secrets behind the Dominican Republic's Success in
the World Baseball Classic and MLB," *Forbes*, March 19, https://www
.forbes.com/sites/aliciajessop/2013/03/19/the-secrets-behind-the
-dominican-republics-success-in-the-world-baseball-classic-and-mlb
/#58f25716285f.

López, Gustavo (2015). "Hispanics of Dominican Origin in the United States,
2013: Statistical Profile," Pew Research Center, https://www.pewhispanic
.org/2015/09/15/hispanics-of-dominican-origin-in-the-united-states
-2013/.

Middeldyk, R. A. Van (2016). *The History of Puerto Rico: From the Spanish Discovery to the American Occupation*, North Charleston: CreateSpace Independent Publishing Platform.

Minster, Christopher (2019). "The U.S. Occupation of the Dominican Republic,"
ThoughtCo, https://www.thoughtco.com/us-occupation-of-the-dominican
-republic-2136380.

Moya Pon, Frank (2010). *The Dominican Republic: A National History*, 3rd ed.,
Princeton: Markus Wiener Publishing Inc.

New York Latin Culture Magazine (2019a). "Dominican Day Parade Announces
$200,000 in Scholarships," https://www.newyorklatinculture.com/dominican
-day-parade-2019-scholarship-winners/.

New York Latin Culture Magazine (2019b). "Dominican Day Parade 2019 ¡Quisqu-
eya!" https://www.newyorklatinculture.com/dominican-day-parade/.

Reid-Merritt, Patricia, ed. (2017). *Race in America: How a Pseudoscientific Concept
Shaped Human Interaction*, Santa Barbara: Praeger.

Reid-Merritt, Patricia, ed. (2018). *A State-by-State History of Race and Racism in the
United States*, Santa Barbara: Greenwood Press.

Rosentiel, Tom (2012). "Latino? Hispanic Neither? A Conversation on Identity,"
Pew Research Center, https://www.pewresearch.org/2012/05/30/latino
-hispanic-neither-a-conversation-on-identity/.

Rumbaut, Ruben G. (1992). "The Americans: Latin American and Caribbean
Peoples in the United States," in *Americas: New Interpretive Essays*, Alfred
Stepan, ed., Oxford: Oxford University Press, 275–307.

Saneaux, Sully, and Ramona Hernández (2013). *La República Dominicana y la
prensa extranjera: Mayo 1961—Septiembre 1963* (Desde la desaparición de
Trujillo hasta Juan Bosch), New York: CUNY Academic Works.

Schaefer, Richard T. (2015). *Racial and Ethnic Groups*, 14th ed., Boston: Pearson-
Prentice Hall.

Torres-Saillant, Silvio (2010). *Introduction to Dominican Blackness*, New York:
CUNY Academic Works.

Williams, Janice (2017). "From Black to White: Why Sammy Sosa and Others Are Bleaching Their Skin," *Newsweek*, https://www.newsweek.com/sammy -sosa-skin-bleaching-lightening-636516.
World History Project. "1916 United States Occupation of the Dominican Republic," https://worldhistoryproject.org/1916/1916-united-states-occupation -of-the-dominican-republic.

CHAPTER SEVEN

Costa Ricans and Racial Exceptionalism

I am a black American. While visiting Orlando, Florida, I decided to attend the annual Hispanic Festival Parade. I watched from the sides as various Latino groups passed by. I took special notice of the Costa Rican group marching down the street, playing drums and wearing afro wigs. They looked at me and hollered, "We are you! We are you!"

—Christina, age 38

Introduction

As previously indicated, Hispanic Americans now constitute the largest ethno-racial minority group in the United States. This new demographic reality has profound implications for the meaning of national identity in the United States. An opportune moment also exists to reevaluate, more specifically, how the nation thinks about matters of ethno-racial identity, particularly for Hispanic America. This chapter further supports the underlying assumption about race discourse in the United States, namely that a basic feature of how we think about race in this country is a distinction between the *Racial Other* and the *Exceptional Other*. This framework of analysis is utilized here to examine the experience of the Costa Rican American. The chapter contends that features of the Racial Other are ascribed to the ethno-racial identity of Hispanics generally, while the Exceptional Other is reserved for Costa Rican identity.

Costa Rican Americans

The U.S. Census Bureau estimates that 58.8 million Hispanic Americans resided in the United States in 2017, a 4.2 percent increase from the 2015 Hispanic population of 56.5 million.[1] Though the diversity of the Hispanic population in the United States is drawn from the length and breadth of the Western Hemisphere, in terms of national origin, the Pew Research Center estimates that Hispanic Americans are predominantly comprised (72.8 percent) of just two Hispanic nationalities—people of Mexican descent and Puerto Ricans. Central Americans account for only 9.25 percent of all Hispanics in 2015, and the overwhelming majority (85.5 percent) traced their lineage to the three countries in Central America referred to as the Northern Triangle (El Salvador, Guatemala, and Honduras). Only 2.8 percent of all Central Americans in the United States were of Costa Rican descent in 2015, and they made up only a fourth of a percent of all Hispanics in the country. The Pew Research Center (PEW) estimates that, based on tabulations from the annual American Community Survey, there were 145,711 self-identified persons of Costa Rican descent in the United States in 2015, a 14.2 percent increase from the 2010 figure of 127,575.[2] Among the seven Central American countries, only Belize has fewer nationals in the United States than Costa Rica. Despite their small numbers, the United States remains the preferred destination for most Costa Rican expatriates.[3] PEW disaggregates the entire U.S. Hispanic population into twenty specific nationalities and three "other" categories of Hispanics for purposes of demographic analysis.[4,5] The only Hispanic nationalities with less U.S. residents than Costa Ricans are Bolivians, Uruguayans, and Paraguayans.[6]

Costa Rican Americans have a discernible presence in the New York metropolitan area, especially in the north central counties of New Jersey (Essex, Passaic, Somerset, and Union). Costa Ricans are also located in New York City and the metropolitan areas of Los Angeles and South Florida, as well as the counties of Suffolk (NY), Fairfield (CT), and Lincoln (NC). The presence of Costa Ricans in the United States differs from that of other Hispanic immigrant groups. Costa Rican immigration to the United States is not driven by the same "push" factors that are salient in other countries of Central America (especially El Salvador, Guatemala, and Honduras), such as political and social instability and violence or the lack of domestic economic opportunity. Costa Ricans tend to immigrate to the United States not as political or economic migrants, but for personal/familial motivations and to secure professional and educational opportunities. The minimal level of immigration from Costa Rica to the

United States means that population growth for Costa Rican Americans will continue to rely more on U.S.-born Costa Ricans than on immigrants. The lack of large enclaves of Costa Rican communities in the United States, the low rate of immigration from Costa Rica, and the geographic dispersal of Costa Ricans in the United States suggest that levels of assimilation into mainstream U.S. popular culture and acculturation with other Hispanic groups are higher for Costa Ricans than other Hispanic groups in the United States.[7] In the public imagination, representations of Costa Ricans refer more to individuals of Costa Rican descent, like the scientist and NASA astronaut Franklin Chang-Diaz, than to Costa Ricans as a Hispanic group. Despite the nominal level of immigration to the United States, a vibrant network of business, trade, and tourism collaborations exist between Costa Rica and the United States.

Despite the common misconception in the United States that Hispanic groups are mostly foreign-born, virtually two-thirds (65.6 percent) of the Hispanic population in the United States is native-born. The balance between U.S.- and foreign-born Costa Rican Americans is approximately equal. Slightly more than half (50.9 percent) of Costa Rican Americans are foreign-born, but two-thirds of that group are above the age of eighteen. Growth in the Costa Rican American population will be shaped mostly by U.S. births, rather than immigration and naturalization. Data from the Department of Homeland Security (DHS) confirms this demographic trend; among the seven Central American nationalities, only Belizeans and Panamanians had less naturalizations than Costa Ricans from 2015 to 2017: 5,215 for Costa Ricans, 4,136 for Panamanians, and 2,531 for Belizeans.[8] In contrast, the same data indicates that the Central American country with the most naturalizations was El Salvador, at 51,084.

The small presence of Costa Ricans in the United States is not a salient feature of the highly polarized and vitriolic national discourse on race and immigration. However, we argue that the self- and other-defined aspects of Costa Rican national identity reinforce the paradoxical character of that discourse. Some Hispanic nationalities, especially Mexicans and Central Americans from the Northern Triangle, are racialized as threats to the nation (the *Racial Other*) whereas Costa Ricans are exoticized as categorically distinct and exceptional among Hispanic nationalities (the *Exceptional Other*). This chapter challenges this racialized construction and concludes that the racial and political exceptionalism of Costa Rica is largely a contrivance. In important respects, Costa Rican national identity differs more in degree than in kind compared to the country's Central and South American neighbors.

Costa Ricans as the Exceptional Other

A previous chapter reimagines the question "How does it feel to be *in* but not *of* this country?" as a contemporary version of W. E. B. Du Bois's poignant query, "How does it feel to be a problem?" Both questions contain a set of central, and still unresolved, challenges to ethno-racial identity in the United States: the dilemma of double consciousness for African Americans and the *problematic of mere presence* for Hispanic Americans. That chapter also distinguished between the self- and other-defined aspects of ethno-racial identity. Whereas the dilemma of double consciousness corresponds to the self-defined dimension of African American identity, the problematic of mere presence underlies the other-defined aspect of Hispanic identity, i.e., how the ethno-racial majority (whites) constructs its perceptions of an ethno-racial minority (Hispanics). The problematic is the other-defined perception that the mere presence of Hispanics in the United States is a threat to the nation's culture (non-assimilation), sovereignty (open borders), economy ("taking *our* jobs!"), and constitutional order (exploiting birthright citizenship).

The problematic of mere presence reveals two insights about how Hispanics are perceived by the ethno-racial majority. The first is that the perception of threat is attached to the collective (other-defined) identity of Hispanics in the United States, regardless of national origin, citizenship status, English proficiency, phenotypical differences, and degree of assimilation. The ethno-racial majority recognizes Hispanic identity mostly through the prism of its own standpoint, not that of Hispanics. What is paramount for whites is how *they* define Hispanic identity, not how Hispanics in the United States define it for themselves. The second insight is that whites impose an implicit burden of proof on Hispanics to overcome the presumption that the latter's mere presence in the country is not a threat to the nation's culture, sovereignty, economy, and constitutional order. A corollary to the second insight is that the ethno-racial majority reserves for itself the prerogative, indeed the exclusive authority, of deciding whether that presumption is ever met, which can remain constantly elusive by simply moving the metaphoric goalposts.

Framing the problematic of mere presence in terms of threat is a mode of racialization that structures how the ethno-racial majority generally defines Hispanic identity, a frame that renders Hispanics as the Racial Other. The converse of this mode of racialization occurs when the mere presence (or its lack thereof) of an ethno-racial minority is defined not as a threat but as an example of racial exceptionalism. A group can be perceived as the Exceptional Other in multiple ways. First, an ethno-racial minority's presence within the country may be so minimal that it poses no perceived threat to the majority. However, as its presence increases, a corresponding rise in the perception of threat may ensue if the elements of threat are still ascribed to the ethno-racial minority. This places the ethno-racial minority in the precarious position of being defined as either the Exceptional or Racial Other, depending on the group's level of presence and the corresponding perception of threat. Second, a group can be other-defined as an Exceptional Other when it emulates the culture of the dominant group, but with two important caveats. The first is that the emulation is not reciprocal but unidirectional, from a socially subordinate minority to the dominant majority. The second qualification is that "hyphenated" Americans (e.g., Costa Rican Americans) must anchor their national allegiance to the right of their hyphenated identity.

Third, the moniker of the Exceptional Other is bestowed on an ethno-racial minority when it becomes the tableau upon which an ethno-racial majority projects its exoticized (and racialized) fantasies about the identity of the minority group. Costa Ricans occupy this third variant of the Exceptional Other. Despite their small numbers in the United States, the other-defined identity of Costa Ricans reinforces the bifurcated structure of race discourse in the United States between the Racial Other and the Exceptional Other. The Exceptional Other appears at first glance to be categorically distinct from the Racial Other because the former is embraced while the latter is perceived as a threat to society. Both designations, however, share the underlying assumption that their primary referent is not the self-definition of an ethno-racial minority but the (other-defined) perceptions of the majority. Additionally, the majority assumes it is just (i.e., right and proper) for it to serve as the final arbiter in naming an ethno-racial minority as either the Racial Other or the Exceptional Other. That a group's identity is rightly based on the (other-defined) perception of the majority is not a truism. Indeed, as the political philosopher Charles Taylor suggests, recognition of an ethno-racial minority's identity should be primarily (though not exclusively) from the standpoint of that group. To do otherwise is unjust because it fails to respect a group's moral dignity and right to self-definition. Consequently, real harm is inflicted on minority groups when the majority refuses to recognize or even *mis*-recognizes them.[9]

The idea of racial exceptionalism has a deep and long-standing resonance in the United States; jarring phrases like "model minority," a "credit to his/her race," or "she's pretty for a dark girl" are quite familiar to the lexicon of race thinking (i.e., racialism) in the United States. Individuals who transcend the (perceived) problematic character of their own racial group and emulate the (putatively more virtuous) nature of another are judged to be racial exceptions. Instances of racial exceptionalism abound, from everyday interpersonal conversations to presidential politics. An example of the former is the author's childhood memory of a well-intentioned white landowner in rural Texas who conferred the distinction of racial exceptionalism on a local Mexican American farmer to whom he leased land. The privilege was predicated on the landowner's judgment that the farmer did not embody the problematic characteristics he ascribed to Mexicans generally. Instead, the farmer exhibited attributes the landowner assumed belong to whiteness (e.g., hard work and an entrepreneurial spirit). The landowner observed to the farmer: "Sal, you're a good Mexican."[10] In the 2008 presidential primary, Senator Joe Biden extended a similar (racially encoded) compliment to candidate Barack Obama, who, as Biden observed with apparent surprise, was "articulate and bright and clean."[11] Such moments reveal the power dynamics embedded in race thinking. The landowner and Senator Biden both presumed that the authority to designate individuals as racially exceptional is the exclusive prerogative of whites—the racially dominant group. A corollary of that prerogative is the implied implausibility that Sal or Obama held the same license to compliment the racial exceptionalism of the landowner or Senator Biden, if indeed they could be described as exceptional.

Donald Trump launched his presidential campaign on June 16, 2015, by demonstrating how the idea of racial exceptionalism can also encompass nationality. He disparaged Mexicans as a people with problems who send their drug dealers, criminals, and rapists to the United States, but also speculated that some might be exceptional Mexicans by entertaining the possibility that "some, I assume, are good people."[12] As president, Donald Trump again broadened the scope of racial exceptionalism—to the nation's immigration discourse. While meeting with U.S. senators to deliberate immigration policy, the President asked, "Why are we having all these people from *shithole* [italics added] countries come here?" and "Why couldn't we just take in immigrants from, say, Norway?" President Trump generalized the problems he ascribed to Mexicans beyond their nation's southern border by insisting, "It's coming from all over South and Latin America."[13]

President Trump's racialization of Hispanic immigrants as the Racial Other, with a few Exceptional Others, mirrors the bifurcated framework of immigration discourse in the United States. One strain of the discourse (the Racial Other) consists in part of sensationalized media images of immigrant caravans trudging northward to the U.S. border, on foot or on trains dubbed *the beast*, purportedly teeming with diseased individuals, unaccompanied minors, drug and human traffickers, violent youth gangs (MS-13), and asylum seekers. Partisan and anti-immigrant diatribes portray these immigrants as actual embodiments of threat (i.e., invasion, contamination, and violence); they also serve as a potent racial mnemonic for ascribing threat more broadly to Hispanics. Segments of the ethnoracial majority invoke this mode of race thinking to render most Hispanics as the Racial Other by framing their mere presence in the United States as being synonymous with actual or imagined threat.

The nominal presence of Costa Ricans in the United States only partially explains why their other-defined identity is not viewed through the prism of the Racial Other, but instead through the third variant of the Exceptional Other. Costa Rican identity is constructed through the exoticized fantasy that the nation is categorically distinct among Central American countries, as somehow *in* but not *of* Central America. The fantasy that Costa Rica is more European than Latin America—the "Switzerland" of Latin America—is based on the formative myth that it is a global exemplar of political stability (democratization), peace (demilitarization), and environmental sustainability (ecotourism and decarbonization) and is devoid of social and racial problems (racial homogeneity). A formative myth, as distinguished from a founding myth, is an ongoing narrative framework for constructing a country's national identity. A formative myth is shaped through the meaning attached to salient features of a nation's character or critical (historical) junctures that create a new trajectory for political and social development. Formative myths are especially potent when a general alignment exists between the self- and other-definitions of an ethno-racial group's identity. Such an alignment contributes to the formative myth that Costa Rican identity is categorically distinct from that of other Central and South American countries. That alignment also explains why Costa Rican Americans are not racialized in the same manner as other Hispanic nationalities.

A key point of reference in constructing the other-defined perception of Central American identity in the United States is not Costa Rica, but the region's Northern Triangle (Guatemala, El Salvador, and Honduras), i.e., countries that are mostly associated in the public mind with immigrant caravans, civil war, political persecution, and natural disaster. This myopic frame has two important implications for the other-defined aspect of Costa Rican identity. First, it obscures the fact that the region also consists of Belize, Nicaragua, Costa Rica, and Panama, thereby enabling perceptions of the Northern Triangle to be generalized to the region more broadly. Second, Costa Rican exceptionalism appears even more anomalous because it stands in such seemingly stark contrast to these perceptions. The construction of (other-defined) Central American identity in the United States therefore has a certain Janus-faced quality: The proxy for the Racial Other is the threat immigrants from the Northern Triangle embody, while the Exceptional Other is represented by the uniqueness (racial purity, political stability, eco-consciousness) of Costa Rican national identity. On the one hand, Central American immigrants from the Northern Triangle are the racialized immigrants du jour. On the other, millions of Americans and Europeans extol the national exceptionalism of Costa Rica, which is widely perceived as a model for countries aspiring to transition from developing to a middle-income status. The country welcomes foreign investment; provides the type of vacation amenities North American and European tourists expect; creates a robust study abroad program for university faculty and students; encourages expatriation (approximately 120,000 American citizens, including many retirees, reside in Costa Rica);[14] invests in quality-of-life indicators (the Gini index for income inequality in Central American countries); and aggressively pursues renewable energy policies (complete decarbonization by 2050).[15] The country is a travel destination for millions from high-income nations, including approximately one million American tourists annually who find the country's climate, ecotourism, and large number of English-speaking expatriates especially alluring. The mystique of Costa Rica is reinforced by its ranking among the happiest countries in the world—thirteenth, compared to eighteenth for the United States.[16]

The Formative Myth of Costa Rican Exceptionalism

Costa Rica has constructed a formative myth of exceptionalism that it is unique among Central and Latin America for its whiteness, Europeanness, political stability, and egalitarianism (in contradistinction to other Latin American countries). As noted previously, a formative myth is not synonymous with a founding myth, though the former may well be an extension of the latter. A founding myth of the United States is that Providence has left it to this country to decide, as Alexander Hamilton prophesized in the Federalist Papers, whether humanity can govern itself according to principles of reason. In contrast, a formative myth of the United States is that it is an immigrant nation, that its vitality, cultural renewal, spirit of innovation, and embrace of diversity are all a function of the constant global influx of immigrants. Myths, of course, are hardly representative of empirical reality, but they provide a narrative framework within which a nation understands itself and projects that understanding to the rest of the world. Costa Rican national identity entails a remarkable alignment between how the country defines itself and how it is defined externally.

The alignment between self- and other-defined narratives of Costa Rican identity turns on the formative myth that the country is an egalitarian, pacific, and white nation in a predominantly nonwhite region dominated by high inequality, violence, and instability.[17] A generally shared characterization of Costa Rica is that it is "a small, middle-income country, traditionally outstanding for having economic and political stability and social cohesion well above the usual levels in the Central American and Caribbean region."[18] Costa Rica certainly occupies a seemingly enviable position in relation to other Central American countries in terms of various quality-of-life measures. However, a little more than a cursory glimpse at these measures suggests that although Costa Rica is better situated than its neighbors on some measures, it is not categorically exceptional. Life expectancy at birth illustrates the point well. Costa Rica's global ranking (fifty-fifth) at 78.9 years is the highest in Central America; the United States ranks forty-fifth at 80.10 years. Panama ranks fifty-eighth but is precisely tied with Costa Rica at 78.9 years. Costa Rica receives international acclaim for its commendable effort to provide universal access to education, health care, clean water, sanitation, and electricity; the country devotes 20 percent of Gross Domestic Product (GDP) to its vaunted social welfare system.[19] Costa Rica certainly has the highest proportion in Central America of GDP (9.3 percent) devoted to health care and is ranked thirty-third globally. The United States is ranked second, with 17.1 percent of its GDP directed to health care. However, Costa Rica is not categorically distinct among its Central American, Caribbean, and Latin American neighbors in this regard. Cuba (twelfth) and Paraguay (twenty-sixth) both rank higher than Costa Rica—11.1 percent and 9.8 percent of GDP for health care, respectively. Five Central or South American countries are within a percentage point of Costa Rica's level of GDP, health-care expenditures: Ecuador (9.2 percent), Nicaragua (9 percent), Honduras (8.7 percent), Uruguay (8.6 percent), and Brazil (8.3 percent).[20]

A similar picture emerges with education. Costa Rica ranks eleventh globally for education expenditures, as a percentage of GDP—the highest in Central America. However, that figure is significantly below Cuba's top global ranking—12.8 percent of GDP toward education. Central and South Americans within a percentage point of Costa Rica's level of educational expenditures include Bolivia (ranked twelfth with 7.3 percent of GDP in education), Belize (ranked fourteenth with 7.1 percent of GDP in education), and Venezuela (ranked eighteenth with 6.9 percent of GDP in education).

While Costa Rica's reputation for egalitarianism is not without merit, its Gini index for income distribution (or, inequality) places it among the twenty-five countries with the most income inequality; it ranks twenty-second with a Gini index of 48.5. Though six Central and South American countries have higher levels of inequality, Costa Rica's Gini index is not unique among regional countries.[21] Indeed, its Gini Score (48.5) is more similar to levels of income inequality in other Central and South American countries than in the United States (45)—countries such as Mexico (48.2), Nicaragua (47.1), Honduras (47.1), and Bolivia (47.0).[22] In the last decade of the twentieth century, the trend line for Costa Rica was not favorable in terms of income inequality. Thomas Gindling and Juan Trejos note that in around 1990,[23] Costa Rica had inequality well below that of Guatemala, Honduras, Nicaragua, and El Salvador. In 2005, Costa Rica was ranked as having the second lowest Gini inequality among seventeen Latin American and Caribbean countries (only above Uruguay); two Central American countries, Honduras and Nicaragua, were among the most unequal globally.[24] However, more recent estimates now rank Nicaragua and Honduras as having somewhat less income inequality than Costa Rica, and El Salvador has significantly less income inequality than Costa Rica; the Gini index for El Salvador is 36.0.[25] Current trends indicate that Costa Rica is becoming increasingly more similar to its regional neighbors than to the United States in terms of income inequality.

Costa Rica's international reputation for egalitarianism and an extensive social welfare system is certainly warranted in large measure. However, even a cursory comparative analysis suggests that Costa Rica is not in a class of its own; differences in quality of life indices are matters of degrees, not differences in kind, in comparison to its Central and South American neighbors. The same conclusion generally holds true in terms of Costa Rica's ethno-racial identity and history.

Costa Rica as the Exceptional Other: The Formative Myth of Race

Slavery is euphemistically referred to as the "peculiar institution" of the United States. That long-standing and unfortunate phrasing has obscured the central role slavery played in the country's nascent economy, constitutional design (especially federalism, congressional apportionment, and electoral college), and social structure. The "original sin"[26] or "birth defect"[27] of slavery is slowly but increasingly understood in public and academic discourse as a founding, organizing principle of the United States. What is not fully conveyed in the curricula of elementary and secondary public education is that the country's peculiar institution was certainly not unique to the United States. The African slave trade and the brutally dehumanizing institution of slavery were hemispheric in scope and breadth. Many undergraduate students are surprised to learn that the overwhelming majority of Africans forcibly transported to the Western Hemisphere disembarked in the Caribbean and South America, rather than in the British colonies that later became the United States.[28] After the importation of slaves was prohibited, slavery in the United States increased substantially, mostly through the domestic slave trade and natural reproduction of the enslaved population.

Despite the increased academic attention to slavery's historical significance, the United States has failed to officially apologize for the atrocities of enslavement and the aftermath of violence and de jure subordination of African Americans. The closest the nation has come to a modicum of atonement for slavery is President Bill Clinton's expression of "regret" for the country's involvement in the Atlantic slave trade and two largely symbolic congressional resolutions that were not enacted—nor were they ever intended to be enacted—into law.[29] The first (H. Res. 194, 110th Congress) passed as a "simple resolution," which applies only to the House of Representatives and is not considered in the Senate, nor does it have the force of law.[30] The second was a concurrent resolution (S. Con. Res. 26, 111th Congress) that had died in a previous congressional session. The resolution merely expressed the sentiment of the Senate without having the force of law and declared that nothing therein authorized, supported, or served as a settlement for any claim against the United States.[31] A key challenge for the twenty-first century is whether the country's national identity can remain unreconciled with the history and legacy of human bondage in the United States. The challenge is certainly not unique to the United States. Indeed, Latin American countries from Mexico to Peru are undergoing serious reexaminations of their roles in the Atlantic slave trade as well as the impact of Afro-descendants on their history, culture, and national identity.

Although African slaves came to Costa Rica with the earliest Spanish colonizers, slavery was not as extensive in Costa Rica as in other parts of New Spain. Costa Rica did not require, nor could it maintain, significant levels of enslaved labor. When slavery was abolished in Costa Rica (1824), it was already an institution in decline. Nonetheless, the abolition of slavery led to thousands of Afro-Caribbeans (primarily Jamaicans) entering the country from the second half of the nineteenth century to the 1920s as free laborers to work on railroad construction and banana and cocoa plantations.[32] Puerto Limon became an Afro-Caribbean enclave that was differentiated racially, linguistically (English not Spanish), and religiously

(Protestant not Catholic) from the predominantly Spanish-speaking, Catholic, and white/mestizo majority. The marginalization, discrimination, and political disenfranchisement that were quite prevalent before the revolution of 1948 placed Afro-Caribbeans in a liminal position of being treated as the Racial Other. Their presence in, and contributions to, Costa Rica's economy and society were virtually excluded from the prevailing narrative that Costa Rica was essentially an Anglo-European nation juxtaposed against the mestizo populations of other Central American countries.[33]

Costa Rica is undergoing a similar process of (self-) redefinition of its ethno-racial identity into a more inclusive posture. The 2011 Census establishes a clearer profile of the nation's ethnic and racial diversity by asking respondents to self-identify racially and whether they are indigenous. The race options are black or Afro-descendent, mulatto, Chinese, white or mestizo, other, and none.[34] Three questions specifically address the nation's indigeneity, in terms of self-identity, membership in a tribe, and proficiency in an indigenous language.

The 2011 Census has separate categories for black/Afro-descendent and mulatto, whereas white and mestizo are aggregated into a single category. The conflation of white and mestizo complicates the self-defined, ethno-racial identity of Costa Ricans. Census data suggests that 83.6 percent of Costa Ricans considered themselves white or mestizo in 2011.[35] However, the census question fails to adequately distinguish Costa Ricans who are predominantly of Euro-Iberian descent from Costa Ricans who are mixed-race mestizos through miscegenation of indigenous and Euro-Iberian ancestors. What is unclear is whether the vast majority of Costa Ricans who identified as white or mestizo are predominantly of indigenous or Euro-Iberian descent. The census data seemingly reinforces the formative myth that the country is racially homogenous—i.e., a nation that is overwhelmingly white—but the ambiguity inherent in the white/mestizo category undermines the veracity of that myth. If most respondents who chose the white/mestizo category are predominantly mestizo, can the country claim to be as white as it purports? Moreover, a country that almost exclusively privileges a specific ethno-racial group in terms of national identity, even if that group is numerically the majority, renders the ethno-racial minorities as the Racial Other (being *in* but not *of* the country). The 2011 Census reveals that 11.3 percent of Costa Ricans self-identified as mulatto, indigenous, black/Afro-descendent, or other. An additional 5.1 percent of respondents checked no racial category, or they refrained from specifying one. Thus, 16.4 percent of Costa Ricans identified as nonwhite/mestizo—not an insignificant portion of the national population.

Costa Rica stood steadfast for decades in constructing a (self-defined) national identity as a white nation, seemingly more European than Latin American. An October 1939 article in *The Geographical Review* described Costa Rica as a "native-born white population of small farmers." The author attributed Costa Rica's racial exceptionalism to a causal link between the nation's whiteness and the low salience of social and economic differences in the country, a link that distinguished Costa Rica from other Latin American countries. The author described the nation as being "virtually free" of racial problems and observed, without any hint of irony, that racial solidarity was predicated on the physical and ideological separation of the white and nonwhite populations. The former separation corresponded to the geographical distance between nonwhites in the lowlands of the Atlantic Coast and whites who predominated in the central highlands of the country, where San Jose, the nation's capital city, is located. The latter was reflected in the racialized assumption the author embraced that nonwhites were present *in* Costa Rica but were clearly not *of* the country. He attributed the country's economic progress and high intellectual life exclusively to white Costa Ricans.[36] The author did not consider Costa Rican nonwhites as inconsequential. Indeed, he characterized their mere presence as an inherent threat to national solidarity; racial strife arose wherever some mestizos and large numbers of Afro-descendants lived. Apparently, the problem, in the author's estimation, was the mere presence of nonwhites.

The 2011 Census and the long-standing narrative that Costa Rica is predominantly a white (European) nation reveal the paradoxical character of Costa Rican national identity. On the one hand, the racial profile of the country has been understood as consisting mainly of three ethno-racial groups—Europeans, Afro-descendants, and indigenous people. The implication was that each community represented a distinct lineage within the national population, with Europeans being the predominant group. Indeed, the myth of Costa Rican racial exceptionalism is that the nation could be differentiated from the racial profiles of other Central and Latin American countries. On the other hand, as in the rest of Latin America, miscegenation created a large population of mixed races, such as mestizos and mulattoes, but the framing of the 2011 Census form precludes a more precise count of how many Costa Ricans are predominantly European, mestizo, or mulatto. Thus, while a majority of Costa Ricans may in fact be mestizos (Spanish and indigenous in terms of bloodline descent), they also consider themselves to be more racially white than other Central Americans. The paradox is resolved in part by downplaying the salience of race as a social category in the media and the political and educational systems—an inclination that is more commonly a Latin American phenomenon than a uniquely Costa Rican disposition.

Another means Costa Ricans have employed to reconcile the paradox is to nationalize elements of the nation's Afro–Costa Rican culture. Afro–Costa Rican Week was established in 1980,[37] during the presidency of Rodrigo Carazo Odio (1978–1982),[38] to celebrate the African roots of Costa Rica and to repudiate ethnic prejudice, racism, social discrimination, and xenophobia.[39] The appropriation of La Negrita (La Virgen de los Angeles) as the patron saint of Costa Rica is another instance in which the country's identity nationalized what was originally Afro–Costa Rican in origin. National (transracial) devotion to La Negrita underlies Costa Rica's self-identity as an egalitarian democracy while simultaneously obscuring the centrality of La Virgen to Costa Ricans of African descent.[40] Appropriating La Negrita as a symbol of racial homogeneity and equality for Costa Rica's national identity conceals the country's history of racial discrimination against, and disenfranchisement of, its Afro-descendent population. La Negrita has served the formative myth that Costa Rican racial exceptionalism, as a racially tolerant nation, distinguishes the nation from other Central and South American countries.[41]

Costa Rica as the Exceptional Other: The Formative Myth of Unique Politics

The formative myth of Costa Rica as politically stable—much like a European country—is a myth built on a myth; European history is hardly the paragon of social tranquility and political stability, unless the relative stability of post–World War II Europe is projected back in time. As noted at the outset, a formative myth is an ongoing narrative about the emerging character of a nation—i.e., a narrative that is shaped through certain critical, historical junctures. The formative myth of political exceptionalism has become an element of Costa Rica's national identity as a pacific, egalitarian, and racially tolerant democracy. The myth is predicated on the critical juncture of the revolution of 1948. However, that episode of political upheaval is understood conventionally as an aberrant moment in an otherwise stable polity, unlike the political turbulence associated, somewhat stereotypically, with Central and South American countries. An episode of political convulsion—however brief—is not an historical outlier if it produces a new trajectory for political and social development. The revolution of 1948 was indeed a transformative moment for Costa Rica. Its aftermath resulted in constitutional reform, demilitarization, full enfranchisement and political empowerment for Afro–Costa Ricans, and the dismantling of policies that previously disadvantaged Afro–Costa

Ricans (e.g., employment bans on blacks in the Pacific zone). Pre-1948 statutory restrictions on domestic migration and relocation confined Afro–Costa Ricans to the Atlantic Coast generally and Limon more specifically—the functional equivalent of a racial quarantine.

The revolution of 1948 is framed as incongruent with the course of normal politics in modern Costa Rican history, but it was not an inconsequential or aberrant historical moment. The revolution was a critical juncture for the country's ethno-racial identity. Statutory enactments and a new constitution formally recognized Afro–Costa Ricans as full citizens for the first time in the nation's history. Black, native-born Costa Ricans had been previously rendered as less than full citizens, while full citizenship rights had been extended to white foreigners of Costa Rican descent. The Costa Rican revolution of 1948, and the statutory and constitutional reforms it precipitated, made the country—at least formally—a full political democracy. The historical import of the period parallels a similar era of full democratization in the United States, when statutory and constitutional reforms in the latter half of the twentieth century formally dismantled the de jure strictures of the apartheid-like racial system of the American South.

The revolution of 1948 was precipitated by a disputed presidential election in which Otilio Ulate won an upset victory over Rafael Calderon. The defeated candidate aligned with the communist Vanguard Party and the incumbent president (Teodoro Picardo) to overturn Ulate's surprise victory. Jose Figueres led a victorious armed revolt against the Picardo government's army and ruled temporarily before stepping aside to allow Ulate to assume the presidency he was denied.[42]

The Costa Rican revolution of 1948 belies the country's exceptionalism in another important respect; the country has not been immune to the military and covert interventions the United States has prosecuted throughout Latin America and the Caribbean under the ideological aegis of the Monroe Doctrine and twentieth-century anti-Communism (Mexico, Puerto Rico, Nicaragua, El Salvador, Guatemala, Honduras, Brazil, Chile, Cuba, Dominican Republic, Grenada, Colombia, and Panama are among the most familiar). Indeed, the political intervention of the United States in the Costa Rican revolution inaugurated a decades-long campaign of military and covert interventions to thwart perceived, though mostly imagined, Communist threats in the Western Hemisphere. The U.S. State Department directly and indirectly supported the armed revolt against the incumbent president (Teodoro Picardo), who was perceived as an ally of Costa Rican Communists. The Truman administration pressured Picardo to resign, hampered the Costa Rican government from procuring arms to combat the armed rebels, blocked the Nicaraguan regime from providing military assistance to Picardo's government, and did not block military supplies from Guatemala to Figueres's armed revolt.[43]

More recently, the scourge of human trafficking that plagues the region more generally also challenges Costa Rica's self-defined national identity as the Exceptional Other among its Central and South American neighbors. Notwithstanding ameliorative efforts, Costa Rica is presently designated as a Tier 2 nation by the U.S. Department of State in terms of human trafficking. The designation means a country does not meet, but is increasingly making significant efforts to meet, the minimum standards outlined in the Trafficking Victims Protection Act.[44] The State Department's annual Human Trafficking Report (2018) noted that Costa Rica devotes insufficient government-funded resources for victim protection services, referral mechanisms are ineffective, and prosecutions of human traffickers have been inadequate. Costa Rica is seeking to align domestic anti-trafficking legislation with international law, increase prosecution of traffickers, and improve training and funding for law enforcement and judicial officials, as well as for civil society advocates for trafficking victims. Despite these improvements, the country remains an important source, point of transit, and destination for sex trafficking (particularly sex tourists from the United States and Europe) and forced labor for men, women, and children. Members of the LGBTI (lesbian, gay, bisexual, transgender, and intersex) and migrant communities remain particularly vulnerable as victims of human trafficking. The country also serves as a transit for illegal drugs from South America, particularly cocaine and heroin. Domestic consumption of crack cocaine and other controlled substances is also rising, as are the consequences of the illicit drug trade like cash smuggling.[45]

Pathways to Assimilation

The migration and residential patterns of Costa Ricans appear to be similar to those of both Puerto Rican and Dominicans. While a disproportionately large percentage of Costa Rican Americans reside in the New York/Northern New Jersey metropolitan area, sizable communities also exist in California, Florida, and Texas. However, due to their very small numbers, members of the community are more likely to be readily identified as Hispanic/Latino rather than more specifically as Costa Ricans.[46] This pattern of assimilation can be attributed to the relatively small number of Costa Ricans in both Hispanic and Anglo-majority communities. The rapid integration into generic Hispanic or Latino communities reduces strong ethnic identification for second- and third-generation

Costa Ricans. As a first-generation, Northern New Jersey PhD-holder states: "I was born in Costa Rica but raised here in New Jersey. I am bilingual and continued to speak Spanish at home and especially when I'm with my parents and other relatives. I view myself as an American. My race is Latino. I was not aware of my status as a minority person until a young boy told me that I talked funny. It's the language that makes me different."

As indicated earlier, Costa Rican immigration to the United States was fueled by economic opportunity rather than war, political disruptions, or social and economic turmoil in their homeland. Given their higher education and skill levels, the transition to the United States was less problematic. Thus, the social pressures associated with acculturation to a new environment were lessened for Costa Ricans, most of whom arrived possessing marketable skills that exceeded those of other Central American immigrants. Upward mobility was obtainable for some but not all members of the Costa Rican community. Questions about the existence of problems with illegal immigration have been part of the discourse about the Costa Rican experience. Most notably, President Trump's attack on immigration led to an investigative report by the *Washington Post* that detailed the connection between illegal immigrants from Costa Rica and workers at his estate in Bedminster, New Jersey.[47]

There is pride in the Costa Rican American community, and efforts to promote the unique aspects of Costa Rican culture can be seen throughout the United States. The willingness to share the fruits of their success can be measured, in part, by the "migrating dollars" that Costa Rican Americans send back to their families on the island, estimated to be about $650 million per year.[48] When the opportunity presents itself, members of the Costa Rican community are willing participants in celebrations of Hispanic heritage (parades, festivals, educational forums, etc.).[49] Massachusetts Senator Sonia Chang-Díaz, actors Jean Brooks and Heather Hemmens, and professional athletes Ringo Cantillo, Ricky Garbanzo, and Rosa Mendes are a few of the notable success stories in America that claim Costa Rican heritage.

Conclusion: The Racialism of the Exceptional Other

Earlier in the chapter, race thinking was referred to as *racialism*. Racialism is distinguished from *racism*, which is an ideological belief that race is a natural—not merely a socially constructed—phenomenon that is ordered hierarchically from inferior to superior races. A corollary to this belief is that races have a biologically embedded essence that is causally connected to their behavior, moral worth, and even native intelligence. The psychological dimension of racism is manifested through animus and hatred toward groups considered inferior (even less than human) that are triggered by markers of inferiority such as phenotype, cultural practices, language, or perceived threat. While racialism is a predicate to racism, it is not reducible to it; individuals may engage in race thinking without activating racism's ideological and psychological dimensions. However, racialism is evident in the underlying assumptions of race discourse. The two underlying assumptions of race discourse, particularly in the United States, are the contrasting notions of the Racial Other and the Exceptional Other. These assumptions inform the self- and other-defined aspects of ethnoracial identity. The key association with the former (the Racial Other) is the perceived threat an ethno-racial majority projects onto an ethno-racial minority, like Hispanic Americans. The latter (the Exceptional Other) also entails projection, but typically it takes the form of an exoticized fantasy about the exceptionalism of an ethno-racial minority. To varying degrees of intensity, the Racial Other is ascribed to Hispanics in general, particularly within the hyper-partisan context of immigration politics in the United States. In contrast, the Exceptional Other is reserved for individuals, groups, or nations that are regarded as categorically distinct from the Racial Other. Instead of being viewed through the prism of threat, the individuals, groups, or nations that are designated the Exceptional Other are extolled for embodying the (other-defined) identity—fantasy, to be more precise— that is projected onto them. This chapter has argued that the Exceptional Other is projected onto Costa Rican national identity (especially in the United States and Europe) but also aligns with the self-definition of Costa Ricans. And given the country's history of exceptionalism, Costa Rican Americans are more likely to racially identify as white Americans. However, there is a racially identifiable black presence in Costa Rica and the Costa Rican American community, and they, too, insist that their voices be heard.

The Racial Other and the Exceptional Other that are respectively ascribed to Hispanics in general and Costa Ricans more specifically are both based on the central fallacy of racialism—i.e., contrived fears and exoticized fantasies that are empirically ungrounded. Hispanics are not the existential threat to the United States that many nativists fear, nor are Costa Ricans the global exemplars of social utopianism.

Notes

1. Noe-Bustamante, 2019; Flores, López, and Radford, 2017.
2. Flores, López, and Radford, 2017.

3. Central Intelligence Agency, 2019a.

4. From most to least populous: Mexican, Puerto Rican, Salvadoran, Cuban, Dominican, Guatemalan, Colombian, Honduran, Spaniard, Ecuadoran, Peruvian, Nicaraguan, Argentinean, Panamanian, Chilean, Costa Rican, Bolivian, Uruguayan, and Paraguayan.

5. All other Spanish/Hispanic/Latino, Other Central American, and Other South American.

6. Belize is categorized as Other Central American in Pew's analysis.

7. Chase, "Costa Rican Americans."

8. Department of Homeland Security, 2017.

9. Taylor, "The Politics of Recognition," pp. 25–26.

10. The actual enunciation at the time was closer to *Mescan*.

11. Joyner, 2007.

12. Lee, 2015.

13. Moreno, 2015.

14. U.S. Department of State, 2018.

15. United Nations, 2019.

16. Helliwell, Layard, and Sachs, 2018.

17. Gradin, 2013, p.1.

18. Ibid.

19. Central Intelligence Agency, 2019a.

20. Ibid., 2019c.

21. Guatemala (53.0), Paraguay (51.7), Colombia (51.1), Panama (50.7), Chile (50.5), and Brazil (49.0).

22. Central Intelligence Agency, 2019b.

23. Gradin, 2013, p. 1.

24. Ibid.

25. Central Intelligence Agency, 2019b.

26. Gordon-Reed, 2017.

27. Reyner, 2017.

28. Mintz, "Historical Context."

29. Seelye, 1998.

30. H. Res. 194 (110th), 2008.

31. S. Con. Res. 26 (111th), 2009.

32. Gradin, 2013, p. 5.

33. Sharman, 2001, p. 48.

34. Censo, 2011.

35. Central Intelligence Agency, 2019a.

36. Waibel, 1939, p. 529.

37. The annual celebration occurs on August 31; while decreed by President Rodrigo Carazo Odio, the celebration was initiated by a teachers'union, the Sindicato de Educadores Costarricenses (SEC).

38. *Encyclopaedia Britannica*, "Rodrigo Carazo Odio, President of Costa Rica."

39. TCRN Staff, 2018.

40. Loshe, 2013, p. 323.
41. Ibid.
42. Longley, 1993, p. 149.
43. Ibid.
44. Victims of Trafficking, 2000.
45. Central Intelligence Agency, 2019a.
46. Chase, "Costa Rican Americans."
47. Partlow, 2019.
48. Luxner, 2015.
49. Chase, "Costa Rican Americans."

References

Censo (2011). "X National Population Census and VI Housing Census, Costa Rica" (English version), https://unstats.un.org/unsd/demographic/sources/census/quest/CRI2011en.pdf.

Central Intelligence Agency (2019a). "Central America: Costa Rica," *The World Factbook*, https://www.cia.gov/-library/publications/the-world-factbook/geos/cs.html[0][0].

Central Intelligence Agency (2019b). "Country Comparison: Distribution of Family Income—Gini Index," *The World Factbook*, https://www.cia.gov/library/publications/the-world-factbook/rankorder/2172rank.html.

Central Intelligence Agency (2019c). "Country Comparison: Health Expenditures," *The World Factbook*, https://www.cia.gov/-library/publications/the-world-factbook/fields/358rank.html#CS.

Chase, Cida S. "Costa Rican Americans," https://www.everyculture.com/multi/Bu-Dr/Costa-Rican-Americans.html.

Department of Homeland Security (2017). "Persons Naturalized by Region and Country of Birth: Fiscal Years 2015–2017," https://www.dhs.gov/immigration-statistics/yearbook/2017/table21.

Encyclopaedia Britannica. "Rodrigo Carazo Odio, President of Costa Rica," https://www.britannica.com/biography/Rodrigo-Carazo-Odio.

Flores, Antonio, Gustavo López, and Jynnah Radford (2017)[0][0]. "2015, Hispanic Population in the United States Statistical Portrait: Statistical Portrait of Hispanics in the United States," Pew Research Center, https://www.pewresearch.org/hispanic/2017/09/18/2015-statistical-information-on-hispanics-in-united-states-current-data/.

Gordon-Reed, Annette (2017). "America's Original Sin: Slavery and the Legacy of White Supremacy," *Foreign Affairs*, https://www.foreignaffairs.com/articles/united-states/2017-12-12/americas-original-sin.

Gradin, Carlos (2013). "Race, Ethnicity and Living Conditions in Costa Rica," paper presented for the IARW-IBGE Conference on Income, Wealth, and Well-Being in Latin America, Rio de Janeiro, Brazil, September 11–14: 1–27.

Helliwell, John, Richard Layard, and Jeffrey Sachs (2018). "World Happiness Report 2018," accessed May 3, 2019, https://s3.amazonaws.com/happiness -report/2018/WHR_web.pdf.

H. Res. 194 (110th) (2008). "Apologizing for the Enslavement and Racial Segregation of African-Americans," GovTrack.us, https://www.govtrack.us/congress /bills/110/hres194.

Joyner, James (2007). "Biden: Obama Clean, Articulate, Bright African American," *Outside the Beltway*, https://www.outsidethebeltway.com/biden _obama_clean_articulate_bright_african-american/.

Lee, Michelle Ye Hee (2015). "Donald Trump's False Comments Connecting Mexican Immigrants and Crime," *The Washington Post*, https://www .washingtonpost.com/news/fact-checker/wp/2015/07/08/donald-trumps -false-comments-connecting-mexican-immigrants-and-crime/?utm _term=.e36deafd4c21.

Longley, Kyle (1993). "Peaceful Costa Rica, the First Battleground: The United States and the Costa Rican Revolution of 1948," *The Americas* 50, no. 2: 149–175.

Loshe, Russell (2013). "'La Negrita' Queen of the Ticos: The Black Roots of Costa Rica's Patron Saint," *The Americas* 69, no. 3: 323–355.

Luxner, Larry (2015). "Welcome to Bound Brook, New Jersey, Ground Zero of Costa Rican Migration to the U.S.," *The Tico Times Costa Rica*, December 22, https://ticotimes.net/2015/12/22/welcome-to-bound-brook-new -jersey-ground-zero-of-costa-rican-migration-to-the-us.

Mintz, Steven. "Historical Context: Facts about the Slave Trade & Slavery," *History Now*, https://www.gilderlehrman.org/content/historical-context -facts-about-slave-trade-and-slavery.

Moreno, Christina (2015). "9 Outrageous Things Donald Trump Has Said about Latinos," *The Huffington Post*, https://www.huffingtonpost.com/entry/9 -outrageous-things-donald-trump-has-said-about-latinos_us_55e483 a1e4b0c818f618904b.

Noe-Bustamante, Luis (2019). "Key Facts about U.S. Hispanics and Their Diverse Heritage," Pew Research Center, https://www.pewresearch.org/fact-tank /2019/09/16/key-facts-about-u-s-hispanics/.

Partlow, Joshua (2019). "'My Whole Town Practically Lived There': From Costa Rica to New Jersey, a Pipeline of Illegal Workers for Trump Goes Back Years," *The Washington Post*, February 8, https://www.washingtonpost .com/politics/my-whole-town-practically-lived-there-from-costa-rica-to -new-jersey-a-pipeline-of-illegal-workers-for-trump-goes-back-years /2019/02/08/8cdbc1dc-2971-11e9-97b3-ae59fbae7960_story.html.

Reyner, Solange (2017). "Rice: America Born with a Birth Defect, 'Slavery,'" *Newsmax*, https://www.newsmax.com/US/condoleezza-rice-slavery -america-cbs/2017/05/07/id/788639/.

S. Con. Res. 26 (111th). (2009). "A Concurrent Resolution Apologizing for the Enslavement and Racial Segregation of African Americans," GovTrack.

us, accessed May 11, 2019, https://www.govtrack.us/congress/bills/111
        /sconres26.
Seelye, Catherine (1998). "Clinton Comment on Slavery Draws a Republican's
        Ire," *New York Times*, March 28, https://www.nytimes.com/1998/03/28
        /us/clinton-comment-on-slavery-draws-a-republican-s-ire.html.
Sharman, Russell Leigh (2001). "The Caribbean Carretera: Race, Space and
        Social Liminality in Costa Rica," *Bulletin of Latin American Research* 20,
        no. 1: 46–62.
Taylor, Charles. "The Politics of Recognition," accessed September 14, 2019,
        http://www.elplandehiram.org/documentos/JoustingNYC/Politics_of
        _Recognition.pdf.
TCRN Staff (2018). "Costa Rica Celebrates Black and Afro-Costa Rican Culture
        Day on August 31st," *The Costa Rica News*, August 31, accessed May 12,
        2019, https://thecostaricanews.com/costa-rica-celebrates-black-and-afro
        -costa-rican-culture-day-on-august-31st/.
United Nations (2019). "Costa Rica Commits to Fully Decarbonize by 2050,"
        https://unfccc.int/news/costa-rica-commits-to-fully-decarbonize-by
        -2050.
U.S. Department of State (2018). "U.S. Relations with Costa Rica: Bilateral Rela-
        tions Fact Sheet," https://www.state.gov/u-s-relations-with-costa-rica/.
Victims of Trafficking and Violence Protection Act (2000). Public Law 106–386,
        114 Stat. 1464.
Waibel, Leo (1939). "White Settlement in Costa Rica," *The Geographical Review*
        29, no. 4: 529–560.

CHAPTER EIGHT

Ethno-Racial Identity and the Colombian Experience of *Mestizaje*

My mother is from Guatemala; my father is from Colombia. I remember getting ready to go to school and my mother telling me, "If anyone asks, say you are white!" I didn't feel conflicted until I took this class.

—David, age 23

Introduction

The other-defined aspect of Hispanic (ethno-racial) identity in the United States is hampered by the myopic tendency to define Hispanics through the prism of the two largest Hispanic groups—Mexican Americans and Puerto Ricans. An unfortunate consequence is the possibility that a more hemispheric framework for understanding the Hispanic presence in the United States is diminished. Though South American immigration to the United States predates World War II, most foreign-born South Americans arrived in the United States after 1960, particularly after the enactment of the Immigration and Nationality Act of 1965. The Act eliminated the national quota system for immigration—a serious limitation on entry to the United States from non-European countries, though Mexico and Central and South American countries were exempted from the quota system. Research on the presence of South Americans in the United States prior to 1960 is hampered because the U.S. Census did not specifically ask country of origin for South Americans until that year.[1] Colombian Americans provide an interesting case in point. They began arriving in the United States before World War II and have represented the largest South American immigrant population in the United States for decades.[2] South Americans, however, represent a smaller share of Hispanic Americans than U.S. citizens/residents of Mexican and Central American ancestry. The Migration Policy Institute estimates that in 2017, slightly less than one-fourth (24.4 percent) of all South American immigrants in the United States were Colombian.[3] The next largest group was Peruvians, who accounted for only 14.3 percent of South Americans. Despite their decades-long presence in the United States, Colombian Americans have not been the focus of academic studies until relatively recently.[4]

A more nuanced perspective on Hispanics in the United States necessarily entails differentiating among the various Hispanic groups—like Colombian Americans—from Hispanics more generally in terms of demography, patterns of immigration, and how the national identity of sending countries informs the ethno-racial identity of Hispanic Americans. This chapter explores these dimensions of Colombian history and the experience of Colombian Americans and proposes a reconceptualization of the role *mestizaje* (Spanish for miscegenation) plays in the ethno-racial identity formation of Colombians and Colombian Americans. The next section coins the term *mezcegenation*, a fusion of the terms *mestizaje* and *mezcla* (intermixing), to describe ethno-racial intermixing that avoids privileging and excluding certain groups from the process of national identity formation.

Historical Antecedents

Like other Latin American countries, Colombia has a complex history and a complicated relationship with the United States. There are presently several hundred U.S. military and contract personnel deployed in Colombia, and the United States played a pivotal role in the partition of Colombia that led to the establishment of Panama and the Panama Canal. Colombia's ethno-racial profile is equally multifaceted. Although Colombians define their national identity in terms of being a white and mestizo nation, the country has the second largest population of Afro-descendants in South America. This is a consequence of Colombia's unique history; the country was home to the second largest enslaved population before abolition in the mid-nineteenth century. The only countries in the Western Hemisphere that currently have more Afro-descendants than Colombia are Brazil, Haiti, and the United States.

As the gateway to Central America, Colombia is situated in the north-western portion of South America and is the only South American country with both a Pacific and Caribbean coastline. Its territorial jurisdiction even extends into Central America; the country possesses the San Andrés y Providencia archipelago, though it is geographically closer to Nicaragua than Colombia. In 2019, the country's population was slightly below fifty million, and its land mass is slightly smaller than twice the size of Texas.[5] The Spanish conquest of Colombia began approximately three decades after Christopher Columbus (after whom the country is named) began Spanish incursions into the Western Hemisphere. The forced importation of enslaved Africans into Colombia began as the Spanish organized the areas of present-day Colombia, Panama, and Venezuela into the Kingdom of New Granada (Nuevo Reino de Granada). The founding of what is now Colombia occurred at the intersections of conquest, colonialism, enslavement, and miscegenation among Spaniards, indigenous populations, and Africans.

From *Mestizaje* to *Mezcegenation*

One God, One Race, One Tongue[6]

This inscription on the façade of the Spanish Language Academy in Bogotá is a stark reminder that the organizing principle of Colombia's national identity is the idea of *mestizaje*, but this has been understood historically in the nation as mono-ethnicity, not multiethnicity. *Mestizaje* has both a generic and a specific meaning. The former refers generally to miscegenation among distinct ethno-racial groups; the latter refers to the specific intermixing of Spanish (or Europeans) and Amerindians (indigenous peoples of the Americas). Colombia's *mestizaje* is an important dimension of its national identity project; it has been employed historically in the service of becoming white (*blanqueamiento*) and more recently in the country's recognition of its indigeneity (*reindigenización*).[7] However, mere recognition—along with politico-cultural rights—of Colombia's indigenous population will not suffice to achieve a more thoroughgoing cosmopolitan and multiracial democracy unless two ideological commitments of traditional *mestizaje* are reconceptualized. The first is the directionality of *mestizaje*. Though mestizos greatly outnumber whites, the pathway for national (and racial) improvement through *mestizaje* was understood as proceeding from the former to the latter to achieve a broader whitening (*blanqueamiento*) of the population.[8]

The second ideological commitment of Colombian *mestizaje* is nonrecognition of Afro-Colombians, at least until the constitutional reforms of 1991.[9] As noted, all but three of the national censuses between 1905 and 2005 excluded questions that identified the county's Afro-Colombian population, despite the fact that Colombia has the second largest number of Afro-descendants (behind Brazil) in South America and served as a major port of entry for over one million enslaved Africans through Cartagena de Las Indias. Indeed, the enslavement of Africans by the Spanish was the cornerstone of establishing Colombia. Though the mythical city of El Dorado remained an elusive imperial fantasy to Spanish conquistadores, they established some of the earliest South American settlements in present-day Colombia that extended into the broader northwestern region of South America. The region has held a variety names throughout its colonial and postcolonial history: the New Kingdom of Granada (Nuevo Reino de Granada);[10] the Spanish Viceroyalty of New Granada (known colloquially as "Nueva Granada"), which became the Republic of Colombia (but was referred to as "La Gran Colombia"[11]) between 1819 and 1821, after Simón Bolívar led a successful war of independence against Spain. La Gran Colombia consisted of Colombia, Venezuela, Panama, and Ecuador but was partitioned after the secession of Venezuela and Ecuador. Historians prefer the moniker of La Gran Colombia for the 1819–1831 period to distinguish it from the contemporary Republic of Colombia. Panama was lost in 1903–1904, due, in no small measure, to the imperial machinations of the United States in securing a canal from the Atlantic to the Pacific oceans.

Colonial Spaniards seized command of Colombia's natural ports and navigable rivers to serve as vital conduits for the large-scale extraction and exportation of gold and other minerals from the New to the Old World. The imperative to finance further incursions into the Western Hemisphere compelled the colonial Spanish in Colombia to reinforce a pattern begun in Mexico. The decimation of indigenous populations through military conquest, viral infestation, and enslavement led to the forced migration of enslaved Africans to replace the depleted native peoples, thereby establishing one of the largest slave populations in South America.

Though the country began emancipating some slaves in the early 1820s, abolition was not achieved formally until 1852; however, forms of virtual enslavement persisted for decades, a phenomenon not unfamiliar to post-Reconstruction conditions in the United States, especially through convict labor. Not all Afro-Colombians descended from the Spanish slave trade. Like Costa Rica, Colombia has Afro-descendants with traditions rooted in Protestantism and creolized English; the Raizal people of the Archipiélago de San Andrés, Providencia y Santa Catalina established a settlement as a result of the British slave trade before being incorporated into the Spanish New World.[12]

Colombia's current multicultural embrace of its diversity and ethnicity is based on greater politico-cultural recognition and collective property rights for the country's indigenous and Afro-Colombian communities.[13] The 1991 constitutional reforms may partially ameliorate the long-standing effects of African enslavement, decimation of indigenous populations, dispossession of communal property, and official discrimination and nonrecognition. However, what remains uncertain is whether recognition and politico-cultural guarantees will decouple the ideological commitments to traditional notions of *mestizaje* from Colombian national identity. The post-1991 Colombian understanding of *mestizaje* may remain limited to a mere "celebratory multiculturalism" if whites and mestizos are still overwhelmingly privileged in Colombia's national identity.[14] That privilege juxtaposed the "nonethnic" white and mestizo core of Colombian national identity against the "ethnic" indigenous and Afro-Colombian peoples, thereby marginalizing the latter as the *Ethnic Other.* Before the constitutional reforms of 1991, Afro-Colombians were rendered virtually invisible, even as an *Ethnic Other.* However, in August 2018, Colombian President Juan Manuel Santos officiated at a ceremony in which the portrait of Colombia's only president who descended from African slaves, Juan Jose Nieto, was returned to the presidential gallery. The portrait had been removed, and the countenance of President Nieto underwent a whitening procedure in Europe. President Santos apologized for his country's racist distortion of history and the delay in restoring President Nieto's place in Colombia's history and national identity.[15]

The restoration of President Nieto's portrait and memory serves as a poignant reminder that Colombia's historical understanding of *mestizaje* is tethered to the social phenomenon of whitening (*blanqueamiento*). The term *mestizaje* literally means miscegenation. The generic use of the term *mestizaje*, noted at the outset of this section, refers generally to miscegenation among distinct ethno-racial groups. However, miscegenation also connotes a form of racial magical thinking, i.e., the fantasy that racial purity, or essence, exists biologically and is threatened by dilution through the sexual union among members of racially discrete groups. The racist dimension of this thinking is the ideological view that racial purity is organized hierarchically in nature and that such unions are therefore

unnatural and subvert the social and political order of a racially organized society (e.g., slave, Jim Crow, and apartheid societies). The term
also harkens back to a shameful and repugnant use of state power
throughout much of the United States, not just in Southern states, to
criminalize interracial marriage and sex between African Americans and
whites in state laws and some state constitutions. The United States
Supreme Court even affirmed the constitutionality of such laws in 1883
(*Pace v. Alabama*, 106 U.S. 583).[16] The slow process of repealing such
expressly racist laws began before the turn of the twentieth century but
accelerated during the post–World War II civil rights movement, culmi-
nating with the wholesale invalidation of such laws by the Supreme Court
in 1967 in *Loving v. Virginia* (388 U.S. 1).[17]

Anti-miscegenation laws were also colloquially known as miscegenation laws, an unfortunate conflation that still attaches negative racial con-
notations to the term miscegenation. In the era of scientific racism, the
confluence of anti-miscegenation ideology and social Darwinism encouraged the United States and some South American countries, like Colombia, to bar non-European immigrants who were perceived as being racially
incompatible with Colombian national identity and development.[18] The
preoccupation with whitening (*blanqueamiento*) in Colombia is a legacy of
that confluence.

As noted earlier, the specific use of the term *mestizaje* refers to racial
and cultural intermixing among persons of Spanish and Amerindian lineage, i.e., mestizos. However, the use of *mestizaje* to achieve *blanqueamiento* suggests Colombian national identity has relied on both the
specific and generic (magical thinking) uses of the term. Consequently,
other forms of ethno-racial intermixing have been effectively excluded
from Colombian national identity (e.g., between whites/mestizos and
Afro-Colombians and between indigenous and Afro-Colombian people).
Indeed, the link between *mestizaje* and *blanqueamiento* depended on
excluding other forms of ethno-racial intermixing from Colombian
national identity.

The post-1991 rebranding of Colombia into a cosmopolitan, multiracial democracy can be facilitated by severing the link between *mestizaje*
and *blanqueamiento* from its national identity. The term *mestizaje* also carries the discredited racial essentialism of José Vasconcelos's highly problematic idea of *raza cosmica* (the cosmic race), which he developed in his
famous essay "Mestizaje." Vasconcelos prophesized that triracial miscegenation (European, indigenous, and African) throughout Latin America
would produce a fifth (and superior) race that would dominate humanity.[19] The central problematic of *mestizaje* is the notion of a racial teleology,

namely that certain forms of miscegenation are naturally oriented to achieving the highest forms of human development through *blanqueamiento* or the ascendancy of the cosmic race.

De-linking Colombian national identity from the problematic associations with miscegenation can be facilitated through a notion of ethno-racial intermixing that avoids privileging or exclusion (i.e., nonrecognition) of certain groups. The straightforward and racially unencumbered term of *mezcla* (Spanish for intermixing) denotes the kind of intermixing among a country's ethno-racial communities that befits a cosmopolitan and multiracial democracy. Indeed, the prefix of *mezcla* (*mez*) can replace the prefix of miscegenation (*mis*) to coin a new term—*mezcegenation*—that rejects the racial teleology of *blanqueamiento* and *raza cosmica*. A derivative term from *mezcegenation*, *mezcegen*, can serve as a descriptor for the progeny of ethno-racial intermixing, i.e., multicultural individuals with multiple and overlapping ethno-racial lineages. To extend the etymology even further, the term *mezopolitan* can refer to individuals whose worldview is anchored in exploring, engaging, and embracing the multiple intersections of ethno-racial identities they, and others, inhabit. *Mezcegenation* can provide the conceptual framework for severing the link between *mestizaje* and *blanqueamiento* and offer the organizing principle for a truly multiracial national identity in Colombia.

Colombian Immigration to the United States

Colombians were among the first South American immigrants in the United States and are the largest immigrant group from that region of the Western Hemisphere. Scholars generally agree that Colombian immigration to the United States has proceeded through three successive waves, though disagreement exists on the precise time frame of each wave.[20] One approach distinguishes each wave by the type of emigrant leaving Colombia for other South American countries and the United States: traditional emigrants (1918–1948, pre–Colombian civil war), political migrants (1948–1962), and post-1962 economic migrants.[21] Another approach marks the first discernible wave of Colombian immigrants as beginning in the 1950s and extending to the end of the 1970s; the second wave is bookmarked from the late 1970s to the mid-1990s; and the third is from the mid-1990s to the present. Cándida Madrigal notes that yet another framework marks the beginning and end of each wave with quite specific temporal markers: 1945–1965, 1966–1990, and 1991–2008.[22]

Despite differences in time frames, an underlying consensus exists on the two overriding push factors behind Colombian immigration to the

United States: (1) employment opportunities for professional, semiskilled, and unskilled Colombians (post–World War II through the 1980s); and (2) political violence and social upheaval associated with narco-trafficking and domestic insurrection spearheaded most notably by the Revolutionary Armed Forces of Colombia (FARC) from the 1980s through the 1990s. Because Colombian immigrants in this latter period of immigration are unjustifiably stigmatized as responsible for the drug trade, their reception was more discriminatory than it was for the first generation of post–World War II Colombian immigrants. Generally, benign associations were attributed to the earlier generation of immigrants because the expanding manufacturing economy of the Northeast needed professionals and skilled workers. The pull factor of economic opportunity for Colombian immigrants expanded beyond the professional classes (first wave of immigrants) to include an increased demand for unskilled, blue-collar, and service workers in the United States, though members of the professional classes also continued to emigrate from Colombia.

Since the 1980s, the push factors of narco-violence, political instability, and economic distress have combined to also increase the number of undocumented Colombian immigrants in the United States—estimated at approximately 140,000,[23] making Colombia the largest source for undocumented immigrants from Latin America, behind Mexico and Central America, in overall numbers of undocumented immigrants. The push factors behind legal and undocumented immigration from Colombia to the United States parallel those for Central America more than Mexico. Mexican immigrants to the United States, in contrast, are primarily economic migrants, except for during the tumultuous period of the Mexican Revolution, when thousands of Mexicans were externally displaced by political violence and instability. However, the push factors in Colombian society have brought a broader cross section of its citizens to the United States than is the case for Central Americans (i.e., artists, intellectuals, medical professionals, entrepreneurs, blue-collar workers, and even some drug traffickers).

Colombian immigrants generally fall between the higher and lower strata of economic opportunity for Latin American immigrant groups. They do not occupy managerial and professional occupations to the same extent as Venezuelans, Argentines, and Chileans, but they are also not as overly concentrated in lower-skilled jobs as Mexicans and many Central American and Caribbean groups.[24] Helen Marrow notes that in addition to their economic diversity, Colombians who emigrate to the United States are also racially (white/mestizo, Afro-Caribbean, and indigenous) and regionally diverse, coming from rural areas and the large urban centers of Bogota, Cali, and Medellín.[25]

The predicate to understanding the Colombian American experience is the array of sociopolitical factors in Colombia that compel emigration to the United States. Similarly, domestic changes in Colombia, particularly since the constitutional reforms of 1991, provide the broader context for understanding the ethno-racial identity of Americans of Colombian descent.

The Colombian Presence in the United States

The sizable number of undocumented immigrants in the United States complicates precise data gathering on the number of Colombians residing in the United States. As previously indicated, Colombians are the third largest ethnic group from Latin America, behind Mexicans and Central Americans. The U.S. Census estimated there were 1.9 million Colombian Americans in 2015, or 1.9 percent of all Hispanic Americans. The Colombian American population remains demographically vibrant as the seventh largest Hispanic group in the US.[26] The Colombian American population tripled between 1990 and 2013, in part due to sustained immigration but increasingly through growth in the U.S.-born population. The latter fact is reflected in the differential between the overall proportion of Colombian Americans who are foreign-born (61 percent)[27] and the percentage of adult Colombian Americans not born in the United States (74.6 percent).[28]

Certain dimensions of the demographic profile of Colombian Americans mirror the characteristics of Hispanic Americans and the U.S. population more generally, while others are notably different. The proportion of foreign-born Colombian Americans, for instance, is significantly higher than for Hispanic Americans generally, 61 percent and 34.4 percent, respectively. Slightly more than half of Colombian Americans are U.S. citizens, whereas an overwhelming proportion of all Hispanic Americans are citizens (77.6 percent) through birthright citizenship or naturalization.[29] Immigrants from Colombia in the United States are markedly older than U.S.-born Colombians; the median age for immigrants is forty-five, and seventeen for the latter. The median age for the United States is thirty-seven, for Colombians is thirty-four, and for Hispanics is twenty-eight. Among the fourteen largest Hispanic groups in the United States, only Cubans (forty), Argentineans (thirty-seven), and Peruvians (thirty-six) have a higher median age than Colombians. Mexicans are the largest Hispanic group and the youngest, with a median age of twenty-six.[30]

The geographical distribution of U.S.- and foreign-born Colombians is not national; 83 percent of all Colombian Americans live in two regions of the country—the South and Northeast. One-third of those in the former region prefer Florida, while one-fourth of those residing in the Northeast live in New York and New Jersey. California also has a notable presence of Colombians; in 2011, the state ranked fourth in the number of residents of Colombian descent but still ranked significantly behind Florida, New York, and New Jersey.[31] The specific points of destination for Colombian immigrants determine their geographic distribution of residential settlement. For example, in 2000, 30.6 percent of Colombian immigrants settled primarily in Miami-Dade and Broward counties of Florida, whereas 21.4 percent settled in New York (primarily in Queens, the site of "Little Colombia"), 13.3 percent in New Jersey, 7.2 percent in California, and 4.3 percent in Texas.[32]

A 2013 snapshot of the economic and educational status of Colombian Americans revealed a socioeconomic position that was stronger than Hispanics generally but weaker than Americans as a whole, though not in all respects. Colombian Americans earned more than Hispanics as a group, but less than Americans generally. In 2013, the median income for Colombian Americans ($50,000) was approximately $9,000 higher than for Hispanics and only $2,000 less than the median income for all Americans. Though the poverty rate for Colombian Americans was the same as all Americans (16 percent) it was lower than the rate for Hispanic poverty overall (25 percent). In terms of employment, Hispanics were more likely in 2013 than the general population to be unemployed, but U.S.-born Colombians fared only slightly better than foreign-born Colombians— 8 percent and 7.7 percent, respectively.[33]

Educational attainment is a notable mark of distinction for Colombian Americans. They are more educated than the U.S. Hispanic population and even slightly above the general population. Colombian Americans are more than twice as likely than all Hispanic Americans to have at least a bachelor's degree and even slightly more likely than all Americans to have an undergraduate degree. U.S.-born Colombians also fare better than foreign-born Colombians by this metric—42 percent and 30 percent, respectively.[34] Before implementation of the Affordable Care Act (aka Obamacare), and despite having a higher median income, Colombian Americans were less likely to have health insurance than Hispanics in general—25 percent and 29 percent, respectively. In terms of achieving the American Dream of homeownership, Colombian Americans are as likely as all Hispanics to own their homes (45 percent). Both groups, however, are significantly less likely than Americans in general (64 percent) to be homeowners. Another indicator of socioeconomic stability, marital status, shows that Colombian Americans have relative parity with

Americans in being married—49 percent and 50 percent, respectively. A stark difference exists between foreign-born and U.S.-born Colombians in this regard; foreign-born Colombians are far more likely than U.S.-born Colombians (ages eighteen and above) to be married—55 percent and 31 percent, respectively. This metric suggests that in addition to having a lower median age than foreign-born Colombians, U.S.-born Colombians are deferring marriage to later years—a trend that holds for the general population.[35]

Colombians and Ethno-Racial Identity

The chapter on Costa Rican Americans notes that racial mnemonics are often an element in the (other-defined) ethno-racial identities of minority or immigrant groups. Some racial mnemonics are positive (though involving a degree of myth making), like the racial exceptionalism of Costa Ricans. A negative mnemonic for Colombian Americans is the (empirically ungrounded) association of Colombian Americans with drug trafficking. The vitriolic politics of immigration and the human devastation of the opiate crisis in the United States have broadened the narrative frame of the narco-crisis beyond Colombia to include undocumented immigration from Mexico and Central America. Nonetheless, elements of threat ascribed to the Racial Other are also extended to Colombian Americans, though very few are involved in the drug trade and they have a stronger socioeconomic profile than Hispanics in general. Thus, an important aspect of the other-defined ethno-racial identity of Colombian Americans is not informed by the empirical reality of Colombians in the United States but by how perceptions of Colombia fuel the public imagination in the United States.

Revisiting Race and Ethnic Identity in Colombia

Another perception of Colombia that will inform the other-defined aspect of Colombian American identity is the rebranding Colombia has undertaken since constitutional reforms in 1991 toward a multiracial democracy. International and national efforts to rehabilitate Colombia's image abroad as a diverse, multicultural nation are predicated on successfully marketing the cosmopolitanism of Bogotá, the nation's capital—particularly its modern, urban spaces like the Zona Rosa.[36] Cosmopolitanism, however, is not the mere recognition of a country's diverse elements; that is little more than a thin form of multiculturalism. Instead, a cosmopolitan ethos forges a new national identity from substantive engagement across those elements of difference without privileging a country's majority and marginalizing its minority groups. Rebranding Colombian national identity as a cosmopolitan, multiracial democracy is a formidable challenge, given the country's history of enslavement of Africans, decimation of indigenous populations, and the privileging of whites/mestizos in the project of national identity formation.

Colombia certainly warrants acknowledgement by demographers for being among the most diverse nations in the Western Hemisphere, with eighty-five ethnic groups. However, the country had a long-standing reticence to align its national identity with the breadth of its ethno-racial diversity. A Library of Congress study, commissioned by the U.S. Department of Defense, described Colombia's population as having descended from three racial groups—Amerindians, blacks, and whites.[37] Official government policy consolidated the country's vast ethnic diversity into just three ethnic minority groups: Afro-Colombian, indigenous, and gypsy (Rom, or Romany). Afro-Colombians are comprised of blacks, mulattoes, and zambos (colonial term for persons of Amerindian and black ancestry).[38] This peculiar construction of the nation's ethnic profile explains why the 2005 census reported that 86 percent of Colombia's people belong to the country's "nonethnic population" of whites (37 percent) and mestizos (49 percent).[39] The study suggested that the actual proportion of Euro-descendants (whites) is closer to 20 percent, making the nation's mestizo population account for approximately two-thirds of all Colombians. The study attributes this discrepancy to the tendency among some Colombians to self-identify as white though their family lineage suggests that mestizo would be the more accurate designation.

Interestingly, the 2005 Census questionnaire did not ask respondents to identify themselves as white or mestizo; questions 33 and 34 focused only on the indigenous, black, and Rom populations and whether members of these groups speak their native language. Question 33 specifically asked Colombians if they are: (1) indigenous, (2) Rom, (3) Raizal, (4) Palenquero, (5) Black, mulatto, Afro-Colombian, or African ancestry, and (6) None of the above. The portion of the population that checked "None of the above" were presumably, by a peculiar process of elimination, the mestizo and white population of Colombia in 2005.

The same census placed the Afro-Colombian population at approximately 10.6 percent, but estimates are that the population is closer to 20 percent.[40] Uncertainty surrounds the accuracy of census estimates of the Afro-Colombian population, but even the lower estimate means that only Brazil has a larger Afro-descendant population in South America. However, the government's own revised estimates projected the Afro-Colombian population to be 26 percent, which suggests a serious undercount in the 2005 Census. Critics of the government's method of counting the Afro-Colombian population argue the country's black population is in fact between 36 and 49 percent.[41] The Colombian Embassy in Washington, D.C., compounds the uncertainty about the country's demographic profile by describing the country's population as being 60 percent mestizo, 20 percent of European descent, 5 percent Afro-Colombian, 14 percent mixed African and Indian, and 1 percent Native Indian,[42] in contrast to the results of the 2005 Census and subsequent projections by the Colombian government. However, combining the embassy's figures for Afro-Colombian and mixed African and Indian percentages approximates the 20 percent level of black Colombians advanced by critics of the 2005 Census.

The 2005 Census describes the population of Colombia as being 86 percent "nonethnic," consisting primarily of whites (Euro-descendants) and mestizos (Amerindian and European).[43] The characterization is a peculiar construction. What does it mean for 86 percent of Colombians to be without ethnicity? That is obviously not the conclusion intended to be conveyed by the 2005 Colombian census. In addition to its flawed methodology for ascertaining a precise picture of the country's ethno-racial profile, Colombia has a long-standing practice excluding questions about Afro-Colombians from its national census. A report by the Colombian Department for National Statistics (DANE),[44] the nation's census bureau, notes that the government administered eleven censuses from 1905 to 2005. The current uncertainty regarding a precise count of the Afro-Colombian population is rooted in a long history of inadequate census questionnaires throughout this period. While census questionnaires included questions about the indigenous population in all but two years (1905 and 1928), they included questions about Afro-Colombians in only three (1912, 1993, 2005).[45] The Rom category appeared for the first time in the 2005 census. Moreover, the criterion for identification in the earlier period of the national census was the surveyor's assessment of the phenotypical, linguistic, or cultural characteristics of the respondents. Self-identification was employed by the census for the first time in 1985. None of the eleven censuses asked whites (Spanish and Euro-descendants) or mestizos to identify themselves accordingly. As noted earlier, the 2011 census did not include a "white or mestizo" category. The 2018 census involved extensive consultations with indigenous and ethnic groups to construct a more inclusive and accurate count of the ethno-racial profile of the country. However, public releases of the preliminary results of the 2018 census did not reveal the demographic profile of Colombians in terms of race and ethnicity.[46]

Different constructions of census questionnaires underscore the inherent fluidity and ambiguity of ethno-racial categories. In the U.S. Census, all Americans are asked to identify themselves ethnically as either Hispanic or non-Hispanic. Although the census question is about ethnicity, the options for respondents are framed in terms of nationality, i.e., being Mexican, Puerto Rican, Cuban, Colombian, etc. Americans are then asked to self-identify racially, with the proviso that Hispanic origin is not considered a racial category.[47] In the United States, at least officially, the term *Hispanic* is an ethnic category that is coupled with nationality but decoupled from race. In contrast, as noted in chapter 7, the underlying logic of the Costa Rican 2011 census questionnaire is that white and mestizo are conflated into one racial category that is distinct from the other racial categories respondents are asked to consider for purposes of self-definition: (1) black, mulatto, Afro-descendant; (2) indigenous; and (3) Chinese. The 2005 Colombian Census decouples race from ethnicity for whites and mestizos, regarding them as the "nonethnic population," but conflates race and ethnicity for Colombians of indigenous, Rom, Raizal, Palenquero, or African descent.

An important finding of the 2005 Colombian Census that is not obscured by uncertainty is that Afro-Colombians are disproportionately disadvantaged; 74 percent of Afro-Colombians earned less than the minimum wage and were concentrated in areas of the country with the lowest per capita expenditures on education, health, and infrastructure and some of the highest levels of political violence.[48] Afro-Colombians have not been granted their share of redistributive justice from the constitutional reforms of 1991. Though Afro-Colombians are more numerous than indigenous groups, they have not received similar levels of benefits of collective property rights, culturally relevant education, linguistic freedom, social services, and greater self-governing autonomy.

Prior to the 1991 constitutional reforms, Colombian society pursued integration, in contrast to the de jure segregation of the U.S. South, by promoting ethno-racial tolerance.[49] The underlying logic of integration was assimilation into the dominant (white/mestizo) culture of Colombia to achieve national unity. However, coupling integration with assimilation led to cultural nonrecognition and loss of land rights. Integration concealed the demographic, cultural, and historical presence of indigenous and Afro-Colombian populations. The ideology underlying official policy presented Colombia as a nonblack country; terms like *negro* or *pardo* were not used in official government documents.[50]

The Constitution of 1991 mandated the preservation and protection of the country's racial and cultural diversity as an alternative to integration.

The grant of collective land, property, and cultural rights alone will not reverse the long-standing practice of nonrecognition of indigenous and Afro-Colombian groups in Colombian national identity. That possibility rests with a reconceptualization of Colombia's national identity as a white/mestizo nation.

Conclusion

The pan-ethnic term *Hispanic* has assumed broad usage in the United States. The term has a certain undeniable utility in bureaucratic and demographic contexts, but its value as a signifier of (pan-) ethno-racial identity for all Hispanic Americans is uncertain, at best. The Hispanic origin question in the U.S. Census underscores the terminological difficulty of conflating ethnicity with nationality. The conflation invariably tends to associate the ethnicity of a country with the largest or most powerful ethno-racial group of a nation. That form of privileging also excludes smaller, less powerful groups in the formation of (national) ethno-racial identity, as the case of Colombia illustrates. A similar phenomenon occurs in the United States by privileging the largest Hispanic groups (Mexicans and Puerto Ricans) in the formation of Hispanic identity. Additionally, the term *Hispanic* is used almost exclusively within the United States; its resonance throughout Latin America is virtually nonexistent. A reconceptualization of the term *Hispanic* that focuses less on pan-ethnicity in the United States and more on ethno-racial intermixing throughout Latin America may provide a more inclusive basis for ethno-racial identity for Hispanics. The post-1991 reconceptualization of Colombian national identity explored in this chapter provides instructive guideposts for Hispanics in the United States and throughout the Western Hemisphere. Ultimately, whether the self-defined racial identity of Colombian Americans is white, black, brown, or person of color, their other-definition may well continue to be mediated through a myopic racial discourse in the United States that homogenizes all Hispanic American groups into a singular, ethno-racial identity.

Notes

1. *Gale Encyclopedia of Multicultural America*, 2019.
2. The U.S. Census uses the terms *immigrant* and *foreign-born* interchangeably but also includes individuals who were born abroad but are now naturalized U.S. citizens.
3. Zong and Batalova, 2018.

4. Madrigal, 2013, p. 28.

5. NationMaster, 2019.

6. Arocha, 1998, p. 71.

7. Chaves and Zambrano, 2006, p. 5.

8. Ibid.

9. Ibid., pp. 8, 15.

10. Nuevo Reino de Granada, "Los nombres de Colombia," 2010.

11. "Los nombres de Colombia," 2010.

12. Hudson, 2010, p. 88.

13. Chaves and Zambrano, 2006, p. 8.

14. Ibid., p. 17.

15. Alsema, 2018.

16. *Pace v. Alabama*, 106 U.S. 583 (1883).

17. *Loving v. Virginia*, 388 U.S. 1 (1967).

18. Chaves and Zambrano, 2006, p. 7.

19. Manrique, 2016.

20. Madrigal, 2013, p. 28.

21. Marrow, 2005.

22. Madrigal, 2013, p. 30.

23. Marrow, 2005.

24. Ibid.

25. Ibid.

26. Flores, López, and Radford, 2017.

27. Lopez, 2015.

28. Flores et al., 2017.

29. Lopez and Patten, 2015.

30. Ibid.

31. Marrow, 2005.

32. Lopez, 2015.

33. Ibid.

34. Ibid.

35. Madrigal, 2013, p. 28.

36. Castro, 2013, p. 106.

37. Hudson, 2010, p. 86.

38. Ibid., p. 87.

39. Ibid., p. 86.

40. Aguero, 2016.

41. "Afro-Colombians: Profile."

42. Embassy of Colombia.

43. World Population Review, 2019.

44. Departamento Administrativo Nacional De Estatística; see Romer, 2005, p. 12.

45. Romer, 2005, p. 12.

46. "Resultados Preliminares."

47. U.S. Census Bureau, 2010.
48. Hudson, 2010, p. 90.
49. Arocha, 1998, pp. 70–72.
50. Ibid., p. 71.

References

"Afro-Colombians: Profile," Minority Rights International Group, https://minorityrights.org/minorities/afro-colombians/.

Aguero, Felipe (2016). "How More Accurate Census Data Can Shape Social Justice in Colombia and Peru," The Ford Foundation, https://www.fordfoundation.org/ideas/equals-change-blog/posts/how-more-accurate-census-data-can-shape-social-justice-in-colombia-and-peru/.

Alsema, Adriaan (2018). "Portrait of Colombia's Only Black President Returns to Presidential Gallery," *Colombia Reports*, August 2, https://colombiareports.com/portrait-of-colombias-only-black-president-returns-to-presidential-gallery/.

Arocha, Jaime (1998). "Inclusion of Afro-Colombians: Unreachable National Goal?" *Latin American Perspective* 25, no. 3: 70–89.

Castro, Fatimah Williams (2013). "Afro-Colombians and the Cosmopolitan City: New Negotiations of Race and Space in Bogotá, Colombia," *Latin American Perspectives* 40, no. 2: 105–117.

Chaves, Margarita, and Marta Zambrano (2006). "From Blanqueamiento to Reindigenización: Paradoxes of Mestizaje and Multiculturalism in Contemporary Colombia," *European Review of Latin American and Caribbean Studies/Revista Europea de Estudies Latinoamericanos y del Caribe*, no. 80: 5–23.

Embassy of Colombia, Washington, D.C. http://colombiaemb.org/overview.

Flores, Antonio, Gustavo López, and Jynnah Radford (2017). "2015, Hispanic Population in the United States Statistical Portrait: Statistical Portrait of Hispanics in the United States," Pew Research Center, https://www.pewresearch.org/hispanic/2017/09/18/2015-statistical-information-on-hispanics-in-united-states-current-data/.

Gale Encyclopedia of Multicultural America (2019). "Colombian Americans," https://search.credoreference.com/content/entry/galegale/colombian_americans/0.

Hudson, Rex (2010). "Colombia: A Country Study," Federal Research Division, Library of Congress., U.S. Government Printing Office, 1–364, https://cdn.loc.gov/master/frd/frdcstdy/co/colombiacountrys00huds/colombiacountrys00huds.pdf.

Lopez, Gustavo (2015). "Hispanics of Colombian Origin in the United States, 2013: Statistical Profile," Pew Research Center, https://www.pewhispanic.org/2015/09/15/hispanics-of-colombian-origin-in-the-united-states-2013/.

Lopez, Gustavo, and Eileen Patten (2015). "Impact of Slowing Immigration: Foreign-Born Share Falls among 14 Largest U.S. Hispanic Origin Groups, Appendix: Additional Tables and Charts," Pew Research Center, https://www.pewhispanic.org/2015/09/15/appendix-additional-tables-and-charts/.

"Los nombres de Colombia" (2010). *Alta Consejería de la Independencia*, accessed May 20, 2019, http://www.bicentenarioindependencia.gov.co/Es/Contexto/Especiales/Paginas/NombredeColombia.aspx.

Loving v. Virginia, 388 U.S. 1 (1967). JUSTIA U.S. Supreme Court, accessed May 23, 2019, https://supreme.justia.com/cases/federal/us/388/1/.

Madrigal, Cándida (2013). "Colombians in the United States: A Study of Their Well-Being," *Advances in Social Work* 14, no. 1: 26–48.

Manrique, Linnete (2016). "Dreaming of a Cosmic Race: José Vasconcelos and the Politics of Race in Mexico, 1920s–1930s," *Cogent Arts & Humanities*, https://www.tandfonline.com/doi/pdf/10.1080/23311983.2016.1218316?needAccess=true.

Marrow, Helen (2005). "Colombian Americans," in the *Encyclopedia Latina: History, Culture, Society*, Ilan Stavans, ed., New York: Grolier. http://helenmarrow.com/wp-content/uploads/2011/10/Marrow_2005_EL_ColombianAmers.pdf.

NationMaster (2019). "Colombia Geography Stats," https://www.nationmaster.com/country-info/profiles/Colombia/Geography.

Pace v. Alabama, 106 U.S. 583 (1883). JUSTIA U.S. Supreme Court, accessed May 23, 2019, https://supreme.justia.com/cases/federal/us/106/583/.

"Resultados Preliminares: Censo Nacional de Población y Vivienda 2018," http://geoapps.esri.co/censo2018/index.html.

Romer, Astrid Hernández (2005). "La visibilización estadística de los grupos etnicos colombianos," *DANE*, https://www.dane.gov.co/files/censo2005/etnia/sys/visibilidad_estadistica_etnicos.pdf.

U.S. Census Bureau (2010). "United States Census Questionnaire 2010," https://www.census.gov/2010census/pdf/2010_Questionnaire_Info.pdf.

World Population Review (2019). "Colombia Population 2019," http://worldpopulationreview.com/countries/colombia-population/.

Zong, Jie, and Jeanne Batalova (2018). "South American Immigrants in the United States," Migration Policy Institute, https://www.migrationpolicy.org/article/south-american-immigrants-united-states#EnglishProficiency.

CHAPTER NINE

Guatemalan Americans

I was actually born in Guatemala but raised in the U.S. I came here when I was three. I am an American citizen. There were many of my fellow countrymen in our community, but when I went to school, most of the people were white. I married a blonde girl and we have a ten-year-old daughter. I don't think she thinks of herself as a Guatemalan American. She has dark hair like me, but other than that, she's a little white girl.

—Guillermo, age 29

Introduction: Proximity of the *Familiar Other:* Guatemala

Guatemala illustrates how the idea of *proximity* frames the presence of specific Hispanic American groups in the United States. This chapter recognizes three forms of proximity in this context—geographic, historical, and metaphorical (i.e., geopolitical). Some Hispanic American groups, like Mexican Americans, Puerto Rican Americans, and even Dominican Americans, have national-origin affinities to Latin American countries (or a nation, in the case of Puerto Ricans) that have a close geographic proximity to the United States. Other Hispanic American groups, particularly from (Spanish-speaking) countries of Central and South America do not have geographic contiguity to the United States but have a complex historical proximity to the exercise of American hegemony in the Western Hemisphere. That proximity is often compounded by the frequency of political and military interventions into the internal affairs of a single nation. At a metaphorical level, interventions by a hegemonic power necessarily tear at the cultural and institutional sinews of the targeted nation whose sovereignty is being violated and invariably create a peculiar form of mutual familiarity between the aggressor power and the targeted nation. At a macro level, they become embroiled in a process that self- and other-defines their respective national identities through the scope, violence, and legacy of such foreign entanglements to invoke a phrase imprecisely attributed to President George Washington. At a more micro level, the process of self- and other-definition also occurs at the level of how the ethno-racial identity of members from the targeted nation is shaped as they migrate and integrate themselves into the mainstream culture of the hegemonic power.

The (geopolitical) familiarity that is born of hegemonic entanglements is not typically expressed as mutual affinity but more often as open or suppressed enmity, especially by the nation subjected to a hegemon's intervention. The essential point is that foreign interventions generate a complicated familiarity that informs how each nation self-defines its national identity and other-defines the identity of the other nation. The hegemon's enmity toward the targeted nation is typically expressed through a racialization (or othering) of the latter as insufficiently developed or civilized to properly govern itself or as a threat to the political and economic "sunk costs" the hegemon has incurred in the targeted nation. Conversely, from the standpoint of the targeted nation, the hegemonic power has also incurred moral and political obligations to the nation it has disrupted. The weight of those obligations is enlarged when migrants and asylum seekers from the former seek entry into the latter.

The metaphorical (or geopolitical) proximity of the hegemon to the targeted nation derives from the direct or indirect projection of power onto a sovereign nation. The disruption of intervention and incurrence of costs and obligations of foreign entanglements all drive the deep and troubled familiarity both nations develop in relation to each other. The confrontation at a hegemon's border between caravans of migrants and asylum seekers on one side of the border and the quasi-militarized border control forces on the other side is also a metaphorical standoff between nations with a deep historical familiarity wrought of intervention and forced migration. Migrants and asylum seekers from a targeted nation are subjected to the trauma and turmoil of arrest, detention, and family separation at the hands of a hegemon's border agents. That experience carries a metaphorical familiarity to the trauma and turmoil a targeted nation experienced through the intervention of the hegemon. Metaphorically, the present-day border crisis is a confrontation not among strangers, but between nations with a keen familiarity of each other.

A targeted nation's presence within a hegemon's sphere of influence renders the former the *Familiar Other* in the eyes of the latter. This seemingly paradoxical position has two structural features. First, the asymmetry of power between a hegemon and a targeted nation is compounded by the racialization (as the Foreign Other) of the latter by the former. Second, the breadth and depth of entanglement between the two nations produces a deep, mutual familiarity that informs their respective processes of (national) identity formation. The chapter suggests that the historical and metaphorical proximity of Guatemala to the United States, particularly since the 1954 (U.S.-orchestrated) overthrow of the democratically elected government of Jacobo Arbenz Guzman, is an instructive case study of the Familiar Other. This chapter explores the implications of this conceptual frame for understanding: (1) the (ethno-racial) identity formation of the 1.4 million Guatemalan Americans in the United States; (2) the thousands of Guatemalans, along with thousands from Central America (primarily from El Salvador and Honduras), who seek entry into the United States either as unauthorized immigrants, legal immigrants, or asylum seekers; and (3) the (national) identity formation of the United States as a hegemonic power in the Western Hemisphere.

Identity Formation

The process of ethno-racial identity formation of individuals and groups proceeds through parallel processes of self- and other-definition. This distinction provided the conceptual framework for chapter 3, which focused on Mexican Americans. What is true for individuals and ethno-racial groups is also true for nation-states. Their identity (or national character) is the result of an iterative process between a country's self-definition and how it is other-defined by countries with which it has geographical, historical, and metaphorical proximity. This process of national identity formation is immensely complex for regional and/or global hegemonic powers. On the one hand, the self-definition of a hegemon's national identity is in part a function of how it projects and exercises power when it intervenes in the internal affairs of countries within its sphere of influence. Conversely, the conditions that precipitate foreign interventions and their relative degree of success or failure shapes a hegemon's other-definition of the nation it has disrupted. On the other side of this equation, how a country responds to the often-repeated violations of its sovereignty also informs its other-definition of the hegemon and invariably contributes to how it self-defines its own national identity.

The Familiar Other in the United States: Guatemalan Americans

In chapter 2, we noted that the "hyphenated" descriptor for specific Hispanic American groups (e.g., Dominican Americans) is used in this book to refer to national-origin groups who reside in the United States, irrespective of immigration status, citizenship, English-language proficiency, or level of acculturation and assimilation. These descriptors are the actual terms members of the various Hispanic groups may use to name their own ethno-racial identity. Mexican Americans may use a variety of terms, including *Mexicano*, *Tejano*, or *Chicano*. Puerto Rican Americans may use the terms *Puertorriqueño*, *Boricua*, or even *Nuyorican* for mainland Puerto Ricans living in New York. Similarly, Guatemalan Americans may refer to themselves as *Guatemaltecos* (or even the colloquial term *Chapin* or *Chapina*). The "hyphenated" moniker for Hispanic American groups is therefore simply a descriptor; it is generally not a term Hispanic groups use for self-defining their respective ethno-racial identities.

What is true for Hispanic groups generally holds as well for Guatemalan Americans; they are also geographically dispersed throughout the United States. They reside in each state but are heavily concentrated in the Northeastern region of the country and in Southern California. The states with the heaviest concentrations of Guatemalan Americans are California, Texas, Illinois (primarily in Chicago), New York (mostly in the metropolitan region of New York City), Florida (southern), Louisiana (New Orleans), Arizona (Phoenix/Tucson), and North Carolina.[1] Guatemalan immigrants, particularly those with unauthorized status, tend to settle in communities in the United States that have well-established Hispanic communities, like the Pico-Union District of Los Angeles. The community was initially overwhelmingly Mexican American but gradually became predominantly Central American.[2]

The Pew Research Center gathers and analyzes census data on the fourteen largest Hispanic American groups in the United States; in 2015, they were (in order of population size): Mexicans, Puerto Ricans, Salvadorans, Cubans, Dominicans, Guatemalans, Colombians, Hondurans, Spaniards, Ecuadorians, Peruvians, Nicaraguans, Venezuelans, and Argentines.[3] (These numbers differ slightly from those from the 2010 U.S. Census, which indicate that Cuban Americans are the second largest Hispanic group.) Guatemalan Americans are among the least integrated and most economically marginalized of these Hispanic American groups. The long-term import of their current demographic profile is underscored by the fact that they are the sixth largest Hispanic group, with approximately 1.4 million Guatemalans in the United States, and that they are among the youngest Hispanic American groups, with a median age of twenty-eight.[4] They also have one of the highest rates (61 percent) of foreign-born persons among U.S. Hispanics, ranking fourth, and one of the lowest levels of U.S. citizenship by virtue of birthright citizenship or naturalization (53 percent), and are among the least English-proficient among Hispanic groups, ranking thirteenth, which translates into less than half (46 percent) with English-language proficiency. Their low level of formal education will have long-term consequences for their integration into the American economic mainstream. In 2015, Guatemalans ranked eleventh for having a high school diploma (23 percent) and ranked last among the fourteen largest Hispanic groups in terms of holding a four-year college degree (9 percent).[5]

The correlation between educational attainment and income holds true for Guatemalan Americans. They rank twelfth in terms of median household income ($40,200) and consequently rank quite high (third) for individuals living in poverty (26 percent). Income and levels of poverty are also associated with other markers of socioeconomic stability, such as having health insurance and homeownership. Guatemalans fare much worse than other Hispanic groups by these metrics as well. They have the second-highest proportion of individuals without health insurance among the fourteen largest Hispanic groups (34 percent)—only Hondurans have a higher percentage of uninsured (37 percent)—and rank twelfth in homeownership; less than a third (31 percent) currently have the capacity to build financial stability through home equity.[6]

The backdrop for the relative socioeconomic marginalization of Guatemalan Americans is a confluence of factors that are associated with the thirty-six-year civil war in Guatemala—the longest and most violent in Central America—as well as the post-conflict economic and natural crises (e.g., the 1976 earthquake). First, the 1996 peace accord between the government and the Guatemalan National Revolutionary Unity (URNG) did not transform a country ravaged by genocidal civil war into a politically stable democratic nation with a reinvigorated civil society. The salient feature of post-conflict Guatemala was the inability of civil authority to enforce and protect public order and safety. Organized criminal organizations and street gangs stepped into the void and imposed rule through extortion, harassment, and murder. The decimation of Guatemala's institutional capacity for effective governance had regional and international implications by continuing the increasing out-migration of Guatemalans to Mexico, the United States, and Canada.

Second, Guatemala has the largest population and economy in Central America, as well as the largest indigenous population, and is the most

ethnically and linguistically diverse in the region. Additionally, a disproportionate share, indeed the vast majority, of the civil war's victims were
Mayas (approximately 150,000 of the war's 200,000 were killed or disappeared).[7] The level of internal and external displacement was particularly
devastating for the rural Mayan population of Guatemala; over one million were internally displaced and another 200,000 were forcibly displaced beyond the borders of the country into Mexico, the United States,
and Canada.[8] The country's indigenous (primarily Mayan) population
bore a vastly disproportionate impact of the war's devastation and its
post-conflict legacy. Post-conflict migrants from Guatemala to the United
States are generally referred to as economic migrants, not political refugees. However, the factors that forced them to abandon their homeland in
the post-conflict period derive from the same conditions that forced Guatemalan migrants to flee during the height of the thirty-six-year civil war.
During the latter stages of the civil war, counterinsurgency campaigns
focused overwhelmingly on predominantly Mayan communities and
other indigenous villages in the country's highlands. Even within their
own country, these indigenous communities were viewed as the less
desirable, racialized others.

Third, despite a liberalization of asylum policy in the United States
during the presidency of Jimmy Carter,[9] the Reagan administration effectively foreclosed asylum for Central American immigrants fleeing war and
civil unrest in Central America—specifically El Salvador and Guatemala—
while simultaneously granting asylum applications from Iranians and
Afghans escaping the Iranian Revolution and the Soviet invasion of
Afghanistan, respectively.[10] Asylum policy during the Reagan administration was largely determined by the geopolitical calculus of the Cold War.
Asylum seekers from countries with governments the United States
favored, particularly those that projected an ardently anti-Communist
posture, were generally denied. In contrast, applications from countries
with a government the United States opposed had a high probability of
being approved. The virtual impossibility that Guatemalan migrants
would even be permitted the opportunity of applying for asylum in the
United States meant that many had little effective recourse but to enter the
country without authorization. The conditions under which immigrants
enter a country (i.e., authorized or unauthorized) largely delimit the range
of possibilities for successful integration into their adopted country. The
integration of Guatemalan immigrants into American society is therefore
difficult to evaluate by the same criteria applied to economic migrants
from countries that have not experienced similar paroxysms of state- and
insurgent-sponsored violence, devastation, and dislocation.

Fourth, the largest number of Guatemalan immigrants arrived in the United States after the 1980s; prior to that decade, Guatemalans who emigrated to the United States were mostly mestizo (ladino), urban, and from the middle and professional classes. In the last two decades of the twentieth century and onto the twenty-first, the demographic profiles of Guatemalans emigrating to the United States changed. Increasingly, they were Maya fleeing the counterinsurgency campaigns waged by the government mostly in rural, Mayan communities of indigenous campesinos.[11]

The conditions that create the push factors for the out-migration of Guatemalans from their country are not wholly specific to Guatemala. The other two countries of the Northern Triangle (El Salvador and Honduras) have also undergone severe national traumas in recent decades. Chapter 2, which focuses on the broader pattern of immigration from South and Central America, poignantly describes the "dirty war" the government of El Salvador prosecuted against domestic insurgents that resulted in approximately seventy-five thousand deaths. As in Guatemala's civil war, the U.S. government received sustained disapprobation for its complicity in enabling the Salvadoran military and security forces to commit atrocities against its civilian population, particularly Salvadorans who were not insurgents. In both civil wars, the United States provided hundreds of millions of dollars in direct and indirect support to the governments of Guatemala and El Salvador in the form of military equipment, intelligence gathering, logistical support, and counterinsurgency training.

Political instability and the disruption of civil society were also compounded by the U.S.-sponsored Contra War against the Sandinista government of Nicaragua. The U.S.-backed contras launched paramilitary attacks inside Nicaragua from Honduras. The Contra War exacerbated an already weakened economy—a legacy of the Nicaraguan civil war of 1979. Additionally, direct political pressure from the United States and covert CIA operations like the mining of a Nicaraguan harbor contributed to the electoral defeat of the Sandinista government in 1990. Although the U.S. Congress prohibited direct funding of the contras (the Boland I and Boland II Amendments),[12] efforts by the Reagan administration to circumvent the statutory ban precipitated the Iran-Contra Affair and congressional hearings.

The eventual demobilization of rebel forces in Guatemala, El Salvador, and Honduras (the contras) did not completely dismantle the infrastructure of weaponry transportation, logistics, and communication that rebel forces in all three Northern Triangle countries utilized. Elements of that infrastructure have been diverted to the illicit trade in drugs, human trafficking, and organized criminal activity in the three Northern Triangle countries, thereby precipitating ongoing waves of out-migration from Guatemala, El Salvador, and Honduras.[13]

Obstacles to securing stable social and living conditions in these countries have been virtually insurmountable. For example, homicide rates in the Northern Triangle countries are among the highest for countries not at war. Small businesses, public transportation services, and poor neighborhoods are particularly vulnerable to extortion in the Northern Triangle countries, where the equivalent of an estimated $650 million is paid annually in "war taxes"[14] to organized gangs like MS-13 and 18th Street to avoid harassment, violence, and even death. The research and advocacy organization WOLA (Washington Office on Latin America) provides substantial evidence to document these claims.[15] Moreover, the countries of the Northern Triangle have become vital points of transit for the illegal drug trade that flows from the Andean region of South America (particularly Colombia and Peru). The conditions are further compounded by cross-national infiltration and territorial control of transportation networks (Mexico and Guatemala) for drug and human trafficking. Finally, the demobilization of post-conflict combatants (El Salvador and Guatemala) enabled elements of Cold War logistical infrastructures for the movement of weapons and personnel to be redeployed to criminal entities.[16] In Honduras, in particular, a culture of corruption has been institutionalized from the highest levels of government to local public schools, where "ghost" teachers draw government salaries and actual teachers often abandon their students to classrooms without an instructor.[17]

The Proximity of Guatemala to the United States: A History of Interference

Mexico and the United States share a 2,000-mile border from Brownsville, Texas, to San Diego, California. Approximately half of the national territory of Mexico and its nationals living therein were incorporated into the United States through the annexation of Texas (1845) and military conquest (the U.S.-Mexico War of 1848). Puerto Rico was ceded to the United States after the Treaty of Paris (1898) officially ended the Spanish-American War. Puerto Ricans became United States citizens in 1917 through the Jones Act, and the island nation assumed commonwealth status in 1948. Cuba also has close geographic proximity to the United States; it is a mere ninety miles from the southern tip of Florida. Cuba's independence was secured as a provision of the Treaty of Paris, and decades later the country became ground zero for a potentially apocalyptic nuclear confrontation between the United States and the Soviet Union—a confrontation that was barely averted. As noted in chapters 2 and 6, another (Spanish-speaking) Latin American country, the Dominican Republic, also has close (maritime) geographic proximity to a U.S. territory (Puerto Rico) and has a very proximate relationship to the assertion of U.S. power and hegemony in Mexico, Central America, South America, and the Caribbean. As noted in previous chapters, the United States repeatedly intervened politically and militarily in the internal affairs of the Dominican Republic; its military occupation of the country lasted eight years (1916–1924).[18]

The ideological rationale for enforcing an American sphere of influence in the Western Hemisphere was the Monroe Doctrine (1823) and the so-called (Richard) Olney Corollary and the (Theodore) Roosevelt Corollary of 1904.[19] The doctrine and its corollaries were ostensibly advanced as geopolitical strategies to fend off European incursions into the Western Hemisphere to establish, or reestablish, colonial possessions or settle creditor-debtor disputes. Long before these foreign policy principles were articulated, the United States already had engaged in extraterritorial military conflicts in the Western Hemisphere. However, at the turn of the twentieth century, the Roosevelt Corollary became the rationale for asserting the U.S. prerogative to unilaterally "exercise international police power"[20] in Latin American and Caribbean nations to protect American national and commercial interests. The Olney Corollary presaged the Spanish-American War, and the Roosevelt Corollary was pronounced in the immediate aftermath of U.S. support of Panama's independence from Colombia and as the United States forged ahead with construction of the Panama Canal, establishing virtual sovereignty over the Panama Canal Zone. A succession of political and military interventions in Central and South America, including occupations, immediately ensued and persisted throughout the twentieth century.

As early as 1798 and throughout the nineteenth century, the United States repeatedly engaged in unilateralist and expansionist interventions (including filibuster expeditions) against the territorial interests of European powers in the Americas—initially against France's and England's (including Canada in the War of 1812) and then increasingly against Spain's colonies and former colonies, most prominently against Mexico (1846–1848). The United States also prosecuted decades-long wars of attrition and even extermination against Indian nations throughout the nineteenth century, including Indian nations with whom the United States had treaty obligations. Even before the United States became a global power after the Spanish-American War, the country unilaterally prosecuted various small- and large-scale military interventions in Latin America, including in Argentina, Peru, Mexico, Nicaragua, Uruguay, Colombia, and Paraguay.[21]

Guatemala does not have geographic proximity to the United States; the entire length of Mexico separates it from the United States. However, Guatemala has a complex historical proximity to the nation-building process of the United States, particularly during the post–World War II period of U.S. dominance in global politics. The country is a point of origin or transit for the immigrant caravans that have captured national and international attention, as well as for legal and political challenges within the United States and internationally. The Guatemala-Mexico border became the flash point for bilateral negotiations tensions between the United States and Mexico, during both the Obama and Trump administrations, over the detention, processing, and deportation of Central American immigrants and asylum seekers. Both administrations pressured and partially funded the Mexican government to interdict, detain, or deport Central American immigrants and refugees to preempt their arrival at the U.S. border. The Trump administration initially failed but subsequently succeeded in signing a so-called Safe Third Country Agreement with Guatemala.[22] The agreement requires migrants—especially Central American migrants from El Salvador and Honduras—who transit through Guatemala on their way to the United States to have their asylum claims processed in Guatemala, not at U.S. ports of entry. The agreement faces serious challenges, including a ruling from Guatemala's Constitutional Court that Guatemala's president could not negotiate such an agreement without authorization from its Congress. Additionally, human rights and immigration lawyers and members of the U.S. Congress have serious concerns that Guatemala and Mexico can guarantee the rights and safety of migrants. Another serious challenge to the agreement is its potential over-inclusiveness, meaning it could result in the diversion of asylum seekers who had not transited through Guatemala on their way to the United States.[23] A spokesperson for the United Nations High Commissioner for Human Rights asserted that the practice of separating children from their parents is an "arbitrary and unlawful interference in family life, and is a serious violation of the rights of the child."[24]

Race and the Familiar Other

Guatemala has its own intimate familiarity with the structure of race discourse and race relations in the United States in two important respects. First, the tendency in American race discourse to subsume various Hispanic American groups into a monolithic, ethno-racial minority group obscures the complexity within, and the diversity across, these groups; the same is true for differences among their nations of origin. Guatemala is culturally and linguistically quite distinct from the other two countries of the Northern Triangle (El Salvador and Honduras), as well as its northern neighbor, Mexico. The failure to recognize how these differences inform the national identity of these countries parallels the failure to recognize that the primary referent for Hispanic identity in the United States is not a pan-ethnic consciousness, but rather the specific nationalities of (Spanish-speaking) Latin America. Second, Guatemala has a close, historical proximity to the racial regime of Jim Crow in the United States, through the migration of thousands of African Americans from the United States to Guatemala in the final decades of the nineteenth century and the turn of the twentieth century.

As noted in chapter 2, Hispanic Americans do not easily fit the conventional model of assimilation that has historically framed the integration of immigrant groups into the American mainstream. Hispanic Americans do not generally accept the conventional wisdom that Americanization requires monoculturalism, monolingualism, and an exclusively U.S.-centric sense of national identity or affinity. Another problematic feature of race discourse in the United States is the characterization of Hispanic Americans as an immigrant people, which is not literally accurate, since the vast majority of Hispanic Americans are U.S.-born. Even placing Hispanics within the traditional binary (black/white) framework of race discourse in the United States is inconsistent with official government policy that designates Hispanics as an ethnic, not a racial, group. Moreover, the term *Hispanic* does not refer to a single ethnicity but is more appropriately a pan-ethnic category. The primary referent Hispanic Americans typically invoke in describing their Hispanic identity is a specific nationality (e.g., Mexican, Cuban, Dominican, Colombian), not a pan-ethnic sense of affinity or solidarity with Hispanic American groups in general. Most Hispanics do not believe the term *Hispanic* refers to a specific ethnicity. Nor do they self-define according to a single racial category; indeed, Hispanics in the United States and throughout (Spanish-speaking) Latin American are acutely aware (perhaps even hyperaware) of the multiracialism throughout Mexico, Central and South America, and the Caribbean.

The prevailing, though certainly not universal, understanding of race as a socially constructed category also means that race and processes of racialization have been broadened to encompass more than simply phenotype, bloodline, or an immutable racial essence. In previous chapters in the book, we define *racialization* as the process of other-defining groups as a threat (the Racial Other) to the interests of the ethno-racial majority or as exemplary minorities that emulate the majority (the Exceptional Other). This chapter suggests another form of racialization or othering that is a function of the asymmetric power between a regional hegemon, like the United States, and countries that are subjected to political or military interventions. The scope, frequency, and legacy of such interventions shape the self- and other-defining identity formation of both countries, hence the notion of the *Familiar Other.*

An aspect of that (international) familiarity is that a parallel emerges between how a hegemonic power other-defines a nation within its sphere of influence and the members of that nationality within its own borders. If Hispanic American groups in the United States are other-defined by generalizations that obscure important distinctions and differences among them, a similar dynamic will conceal the complexities within and among (Spanish-speaking) countries of Latin America. Guatemala is an important case in point. The vitriol and hyper-partisanship that engulfed immigration politics during the Obama and Trump presidencies effectively foreclosed a nuanced and more informed national conversation about the appropriate political and legal responses to the immigration crisis at the U.S.-Mexico border. Instead, important distinctions between legal immigrants, unauthorized immigrants, refugees, and asylum seekers were collapsed. A similar conflation occurred with important cultural and historical differences between Guatemalans and other Central American immigrants, as well as between Central Americans and Mexicans more generally.

However, Guatemala has a more culturally and linguistically diverse profile than the other two countries of the Northern Triangle (El Salvador and Honduras); the same is true in relation to Mexico. Indeed, in some respects it is even difficult to characterize Guatemala simply as a (Spanish-speaking) Latin American country. The CIA's *World Factbook* estimates that 60.1 percent of the nation is either mestizo (ladino) or European and 40 percent is Mayan.[25] That profile diverges quite markedly from the other two countries of the Northern Triangle. The CIA estimates that Honduras's population is 91 percent mestizo and European, while Amerindians and blacks represent the remaining 9 percent of the country.[26] Even Mexico's substantial indigenous population is not proportionately comparable to the share of Guatemala's population that is indigenous. Approximately 28 percent of Mexico's population is Amerindian; 72 percent are mestizo and European.[27] The same database estimates that 99 percent of El Salvador's population is either mestizo or white; Amerindians, blacks, and "other" make up the remaining 1 percent.[28]

Guatemala is also linguistically distinct from these countries. Although more than two-thirds of Guatemalans speak Spanish, almost one-third (31 percent) of the population speaks one of the twenty-one Mayan languages (K'iche', Q'eqchi', Mam, Kaqchikel, etc.); the country officially recognizes twenty-three national languages that are indigenous.[29] In contrast, the CIA database merely indicates that some Amerindian dialects are spoken in El Salvador and Honduras. In Mexico, only 6.5 percent of the population speaks a non-Spanish Amerindian dialect.[30] Although Guatemala's official language is Spanish, in effect, the country is a multilingual, multiracial, and multicultural nation. Guatemala is, as Octavio Paz said of the United States, a Republic of the Future.

African Americans as the *Familiar Other* in Guatemala

The underlying assumption in the earlier discussion about foreign entanglements between a hegemonic power and the nation it targets for intervention is that the mere act of encounter inextricably links the identity formation processes of both nations. However, some encounters can also occur beyond the realm of geopolitics and realpolitik and reinforce the historical and metaphorical proximity of two countries to each other. An instance of such an encounter is the experience of African Americans who migrated to Guatemala in the latter part of the nineteenth century to seek economic opportunity and escape the racial regime of Jim Crow in the American South. The presence of Afro-descendants in Guatemala, as in other Central American counties, is not entirely a story of the forced importation of Africans during the Atlantic slave trade. Thousands of Caribbean blacks migrated to Guatemala to work in the emerging railroad and plantation systems. African Americans from the U.S. South joined this network of intra-hemispheric migration in the latter decades of the nineteenth century.

Guatemala gained independence from Spain in 1821 and abolished slavery in 1825. Several decades later, businessmen had difficulty compelling indigenous, mestizo, and Garifuna Guatemalans to perform arduous physical labor in areas where the likelihood of being infected by malaria was high.[31] Business interests tied to the burgeoning railroad industry and banana plantations recruited and imported African American (and poor white) workers, as well as blacks from Jamaica and other Caribbean nations. Thousands of African Americans, faced with the ever-present threat of racial violence, political disenfranchisement, post–Reconstruction era racial codes, and severe economic marginalization, responded to these solicitations and became part of the flow of migrant labor into Guatemala. The migration was facilitated by employment recruiters who lured African Americans with offers of better wages, economic opportunities, and homestead guarantees,[32] benefits which seemed to represent better economic and social prospects than what African Americans could expect in the Jim Crow South.

The experience of African Americans in Guatemala was not unilinear. The country had a history of denigrating its small Afro-descendant population, including its Garifuna population of African and Caribbean blacks. Like other Central and South American countries during this period, Guatemala favored white immigration over immigrants of color and routinely privileged white over nonwhite foreigners with higher-paying jobs.[33] Guatemala adopted the social norm that blacks (citizen and foreigner) in the country were presumptively unworthy of the same respect and treatment accorded to white citizens and immigrants, just as the United States had. Repressive work conditions, harassment and discrimination by employers, and employers' failure to pay wages were all reminiscent of the conditions that initially motivated African Americans to emigrate from the United States.

However, Guatemala also enabled African American migrants to improve their socioeconomic status in ways that were more difficult in the United States. Despite obstacles and discrimination, many African American migrants in Guatemala became property and business owners, married interracially, and engaged in social and political activism (e.g., initiating work stoppages against the United Fruit Company and participating in Guatemalan chapters of Marcus Garvey's Universal Negro Improvement Association).[34] The U.S. government, through the Department of State, even intervened to protect African Americans in Guatemala against harassment and discrimination—an intervention by the federal government that would have been unfathomable in the United States at the time. However, such interventions were motivated by concerns among U.S. government officials in Guatemala that unless African Americans were accorded some protections, white U.S. nationals could also be rendered vulnerable to abuses and discrimination.[35] Despite broader latitude for social and economic mobility than in the United States, African Americans in Guatemala encountered a familiar system of racial privilege and advantage for white U.S. nationals and racial harassment and discrimination for people of color like themselves. However, the racialization of social relations that circumscribed the lives of African Americans in Guatemala was primarily de facto, whereas in the United States, the racial regime of Jim Crow was both de facto and de jure. The story of African American emigrants to Guatemala is not unfamiliar to African

Americans. Decades after black Americans abandoned the United States to seek better fortunes in Guatemala, hundreds of African Americans emigrated to the Soviet Union in response to solicitations for labor, but they were also lured by the prospect of living in a more racially accommodating society.[36]

This section began by distinguishing two types of entanglements, or encounters, between nations. The term *foreign entanglements* typically conjures up images of a hegemonic power flexing its power through military or covert interventions into (typically) weaker nation-states. These encounters, or proximities, however violent and disruptive to the targeted nation, nonetheless develop a deep, mutual (metaphorical) familiarity with the national character of each nation, namely their respective identity formation processes. An aspect of this mutual familiarity is the experience of race in both the United States and Guatemala. African American emigrants acceded to the push factor of a repressive racial regime in the Jim Crow South of the United States. Guatemala facilitated this outmigration but subsequently revealed its own, less repressive system of racial privilege and disadvantage. The era of African American migration to Guatemala engendered a historical and metaphorical proximity to each nation's national character in relation to race. That mutual familiarity is not a mere historical footnote; indeed, it resurfaced when predominantly indigenous (Mayan) Guatemalans sought asylum in the United States. The Guatemalan government had, in effect, racialized the country's Mayan population as the *Subversive Other* and prosecuted a brutal and bloody war of extermination. That experience has its own historical and metaphorical proximity to campaigns of extermination against indigenous nations in the United States. Thus, when predominantly indigenous immigrants from Guatemala presented themselves at the U.S.-Mexico border at the height of the Guatemalan civil war, their presence at the border was imbued with a familiarity that is resonant with the American experience.

Conclusion: The Guatemalan American

A decade after graduating from Princeton University, the author returned to his alma mater to assume an administrative role and live in the borough of Princeton, New Jersey. The most indelible impression from the initial period of relocation was discovering that this town, which had helped birth the nation, was home to an emerging Latino community that included Mexicans and Central Americans, many of whom were from Guatemala. In the intervening decade of the author's departure and return to Princeton, a nationwide mobilization had developed throughout many college campuses and cities to protest U.S. covert intervention in Central American civil wars, primarily in El Salvador but also in Guatemala. The Committee in Solidarity with the People of El Salvador (CISPES) was at the forefront of this movement that politicized college campuses in ways unseen since the anti-Vietnam protests of the 1960s. The 1980s also coincided with a shift in the demographic profile of Guatemalans who immigrated to the United States. The Guatemalan government launched a brutal counterinsurgency campaign that concentrated its lethality in primarily Mayan communities of Guatemala. The (racialized) wholesale destruction of many Mayan communities and the death and disappearance of tens of thousands of indigenous Guatemalans created a massive wave of internal and external displacement. Guatemalans in the latter category migrated to southern Mexico, the United States, and Canada. Guatemalan immigrants (authorized and unauthorized) settled in small and large towns and cities throughout the United States, including Princeton, New Jersey. Despite persistent patterns of wage, housing, and social discrimination, the Mexican and Guatemalan community that predominates in the Witherspoon-Jackson neighborhood of Princeton is firmly interwoven into the life of the Princeton community. The municipality supported the "sanctuary city" movement, which the Center for Immigration Studies (an immigration restrictionist advocacy and research organization) estimated encompassed approximately three hundred jurisdictions. Princeton refused to deputize its police force to enforce federal immigration laws.[37]

The political precursor to sanctuary cities was the sanctuary movement of the 1980s in which Christian religious organizations provided safe havens against arrest and deportation to unauthorized immigrants from Guatemala and El Salvador, often in places of worship. The movement began when two houses of worship in Tucson, Arizona, served as safe havens for Guatemalan and Salvadoran refugees. The Reagan administration's rejection of most asylum petitions from Central Americans sparked a national mobilization of religious organizations to defy immigration policies by overtly providing "sanctuary" to Central American migrants. At the height of the movement, 150 religious congregations defied the Reagan administration through overt sponsorship and support of Central American refugee families, and approximately one thousand organizations supported the "concept and practice" of the sanctuary movement.[38] Efforts by the Department of Justice to criminally prosecute individuals associated with the movement led to a class action suit that ultimately resulted in a settlement decree allowing rejected asylum applications from Central American migrants to be reconsidered.[39]

The Guatemalan civil war that killed, disappeared, and displaced hundreds of thousands of Guatemalans, a vast majority of whom were indigenous and Mayan, could not have been prosecuted without the millions of dollars the United States expended to provide the Guatemalan government with military equipment, logistical support, and training and to aid them with intelligence gathering. The CIA also maintained close ties with the Guatemalan army and paramilitary units, even as they perpetuated massacres and egregious human rights violations against Mayan communities suspected of supporting the Marxist insurgents. As noted earlier, the CIA was also intimately involved in the 1954 overthrow of the democratically elected Arbenz government; indeed, it could not have been accomplished without the direct support, or, more accurately stated, sponsorship of the CIA. The overthrow ended a brief period of political and social democracy in Guatemala that had started with the election of Arbenz's predecessor, Juan Joe Arevalo, whose policies favored organized labor, a social security system, and economic development.[40] Upon his election as president, Jacobo Arbenz Guzman instituted a program of progressive land reform and directly challenged the prerogatives of power the United Fruit Company had enjoyed for decades.[41] The intervention of the United States in Guatemala ended a period of democratization that would not be revived until the 1996 peace accords.

A certain historical irony frames the integration of Guatemalan immigrants in Princeton, New Jersey, which is also the home of Princeton University. The university itself has a close, historical proximity to the CIA; the university had a long-standing relationship with the intelligence agency for purposes of recruiting analysts and operatives. Three CIA directors were Princeton graduates, and members of the university faculty participated in research collaborations with the intelligence community. The circuitous route from Princeton University to the CIA, to Guatemala, and now back to Princeton Borough in the form of a vibrant, Guatemalan community represents but one of the varied dimensions of the historical and metaphorical proximity that is shared by the United States and Guatemala. The entanglements between Guatemala and the United States are also a bit more prosaic but are nevertheless vital to both countries.

Thousands of Guatemalans toil daily in all manner of work many Americans would prefer to eschew. The services they provide are also cheaper for American consumers because of the low wages they receive and the absence of many employer-based benefits like health insurance. They are intimately familiar with the American minority and racial experience. The Guatemalan economy benefits enormously from the billions of dollars that flow from Guatemalan Americans in the form of remittances. Guatemala ranks sixth globally in the dollar value of remittances from the United States; the Pew Research Center estimates that in 2017, approximately $7.7 billion was sent from the United States to Guatemala. The two other countries of the Northern Triangle, El Salvador and Honduras, ranked eighth and tenth, respectively.[42]

What does it mean to migrate to a country that has been deeply complicit in upending your own community? The question is not altogether dissimilar to asking what it means for migrants to emigrate from independent, post-colonial nations to their former colonial powers, as is true for millions of migrants who adopt their former colonial overseer as their new home, be it England, France, Portugal, or Spain. On the one hand, the enmity that is woven into the asymmetry of power between the colonizer and the colonized should make emigration back to the colonial power an anathema to one's sense of national pride and identity. On the other, the emigrant is not a stranger in a strange land; indeed, he or she has returned to a nation with which a deep familiarity is quite developed. However, the asymmetry of power between the two nations is not as it was under colonial rule. The emigrant returns with the agency to participate in the reshaping of the self- and other-defining processes for the respective nations as well as for herself or himself.

Notes

1. *Wikipedia,* "Guatemalan Americans."
2. Hong, "Guatemalan Americans."
3. Flores, 2017.
4. Ibid.
5. Ibid.
6. Ibid.
7. Jonas, 2013.
8. Ibid.
9. Gzesh, 2006.
10. Ibid.
11. Hong, "Guatemalan Americans."
12. Brown University.
13. Labrador and Renwick, 2018.
14. Nazario, 2019.
15. Beltrán, 2017.
16. Arnson and Olson, 2011.
17. Ibid.
18. TeleSUR, 2016.
19. U.S. Department of State, "Biographies."

20. U.S. Department of State, "Roosevelt Corollary."
21. Loveman, 2016.
22. Miller and Long, 2019.
23. Blitzer, 2019.
24. Cummings-Bruce, 2018.
25. Central Intelligence Agency, 2019b.
26. Central Intelligence Agency, 2019c.
27. Central Intelligence Agency, 2019d.
28. Central Intelligence Agency, 2019a.
29. Central Intelligence Agency, 2019b.
30. Central Intelligence Agency, 2019d.
31. Garifuna were runaway slaves who settled in communities in Belize, Honduras, and Guatemala.
32. Opie, 2008, p. 587.
33. Ibid., p. 606.
34. Ibid., p. 594.
35. Ibid., p. 601.
36. Simmons, 2014.
37. Norgaard, 2017.
38. Gzesh, 2006.
39. Ibid.
40. Hong, "Guatemalan Americans."
41. Ibid.
42. Pew Research Center, 2019.

References

Arnson, Cynthia, and Eric L. Olson, eds. (2011). "Organized Crime in Central America: The Northern Triangle," *Woodrow Wilson Center Reports on the Americas*, no. 29, September, Woodrow Wilson Center for Scholars, Latin American Program, https://www.wilsoncenter.org/sites/default/files /LAP_single_page.pdf.

Beltrán, Adriana (2017). "Children and Families Fleeing Violence in Central America," WOLA: Advocacy for Human Rights in the Americas, https:// www.wola.org/analysis/people-leaving-central-americas-northern -triangle/.

Blitzer, Jonathan (2019). "How Trump's Safe-Third-Country Agreement with Guatemala Fell Apart," *New Yorker*, https://www.newyorker.com/news /news-desk/how-trumps-safe-third-country-agreement-with-guatemala -fell-apart.

Brown University. "The Counterrevolutionaries (the Contras)," *Understanding the Iran Contra Affairs*, https://www.brown.edu/Research/Understanding _the_Iran_Contra_Affair/n-contrasus.php.

Central Intelligence Agency (2019a). "El Salvador," *The World Factbook*, https://
    www.cia.gov/library/publications/the-world-factbook/geos/es.html.
Central Intelligence Agency (2019b). "Guatemala," *The World Factbook*, https://
    www.cia.gov/library/publications/the-world-factbook/geos/gt.html.
Central Intelligence Agency (2019c). "Honduras," *The World Factbook*, https://
    www.cia.gov/library/publications/the-world-factbook/geos/ho.html.
Central Intelligence Agency (2019d). "Mexico," *The World Factbook*, https://www
    .cia.gov/library/publications/the-world-factbook/geos/mx.html.
Cummings-Bruce, Nick (2018). "Taking Migrant Children from Parents Is Illegal, U.N. Tells U.S.," *New York Times*, https://www.nytimes.com/2018/06
    /05/world/americas/us-un-migrant-children-families.html?smid=nytcore
    -ios-share.
Flores, Antonio (2017). "How the U.S. Hispanic Population Is Changing," Pew
    Research Center, https://www.pewresearch.org/fact-tank/2017/09/18/how
    -the-u-s-hispanic-population-is-changing/.
Gzesh, Susa (2006). "Central Americans and Asylum Policy in the Reagan Era,"
    Migration Policy Institute, https://www.migrationpolicy.org/article/central
    -americans-and-asylum-policy-reagan-era/.
Hong, Maria. "Guatemalan Americans," Countries and their Cultures, accessed
    July 27, 2019, https://www.everyculture.com/multi/Du-Ha/Guatemalan
    -Americans.html.
Jonas, Susanne (2013). "Guatemalan Migration in Times of Civil War and Post-War Challenges," Migration Policy Institute, https://www.migrationpolicy
    .org/article/guatemalan-migration-times-civil-war-and-post-war-challenges.
Labrador, Rocio Cara, and Danielle Renwick (2018). "Central America's Violent
    Northern Triangle," Council on Foreign Relations, https://www.cfr.org
    /backgrounder/central-americas-violent-northern-triangle.
Loveman, Brian (2016). "U.S. Foreign Policy toward Latin America in the 19th
    Century," *Oxford Research Encyclopedias*, https://oxfordre.com/latinamerican
    history/view/10.1093/acrefore/9780199366439.001.0001/acrefore
    -9780199366439-e-41.
Miller, Zeke, and Colleen Long (2019). "U.S., Guatemala Sign Agreement to
    Restrict Asylum Cases," *AP News*, https://news.yahoo.com/trump-says
    -guatemala-signing-deal-201217093.html.
Nazario, Sonia (2019). "Pay or Die," *New York Times*, https://www.nytimes.com
    /interactive/2019/07/25/opinion/honduras-corruption-ms-13.html?smid
    =nytcore-ios-share.
Norgaard, Lara (2017). "Living in the Shadows: The Life of Undocumented
    Immigrants in Princeton," *Community News*, March 31, accessed July 27,
    2019, https://communitynews.org/2017/03/31/living-in-the-shadows-the
    -life-of-undocumented-immigrants-in-princeton/.
Opie, Frederick Douglas (2008). "Black Americans and the State in Turn-of-the-Century Guatemala," *The Americas* 64, no. 4: 583–609.

Pew Research Center (2019). "Remittance Flows Worldwide in 2017," https://www.pewresearch.org/global/interactives/remittance-flows-by-country/.

Simmons, Ann (2014). "Great Read: In Russia, Early African American Migrants Found the Good Life," *Los Angeles Times*, https://www.latimes.com/world/la-fg-c1-black-russian-americans-20141119-story.html.

TeleSUR (2016). "A Century of U.S. Intervention in the Dominican Republic," https://www.telesurenglish.net/analysis/A-Century-of-U.S.-Intervention-in-the-Dominican-Republic-20160921-0034.html.

U.S. Department of State. "Biographies of the Secretaries of State: Richard Olney (1835–1917)," Office of the Historian, https://history.state.gov/departmenthistory/people/olney-richard.

U.S. Department of State. "Roosevelt Corollary to the Monroe Doctrine, 1904," Office of the Historian, https://history.state.gov/milestones/1899-1913/roosevelt-and-monroe-doctrine.

Wikipedia. "Guatemalan Americans," https://en.wikipedia.org/wiki/Guatemalan_Americans#Cities_with_largest_Guatemalan_population.

CHAPTER TEN

Race, Ethnicity, and the Future of Hispanic Identity

I'm Latina but I'm not colored. My family is from Venezuela. We are not colored people. We're white people.

—Alejandra, age 21

Introduction

Race is the pseudoscientific concept that has shaped all human interaction in the history of the United States of America.[1] What began as contact between foreign cultures eventually mushroomed into a global system of human interaction based on a belief in white superiority. It was the European explorers, or those we identify as members of the Caucasian race, who helped spread the notion of white supremacy throughout the developing New World. Historically, there are numerous examples of how European imperialism, coupled with the ideology of racial supremacy, exploited human societies on every continent and destroyed cultures and social systems for economic and political gain.[2] However, our focus has been on issues surrounding race and identity for members of the Hispanic/Latino community in the United States of America.

Race and Identity

As demonstrated throughout these readings, the Hispanic community has rapidly expanded over the past fifty years. Estimated at a national population of more than fifty-seven million, or 17.8 percent of the nation's total, Hispanic Americans are frequently described by government officials as the nation's largest ethnic or racial minority.[3] However, they are far from being monolithic, and to describe them as a singular ethnic or racial group is a complete misnomer. The Hispanic community is comprised of many ethnic and racial groups originating from countries south of the border.[4] By far, the overwhelming majority of Hispanic Americans are of Mexican heritage—an estimated two-thirds of the Hispanic population.[5] However, this ever-growing ethno-racial population includes individuals whose ethnic heritage is rooted in countries like Cuba, Costa Rica, the Dominican Republic, Guatemala, Honduras, Nicaragua, Panama, El Salvador, Bolivia, Chile, Colombia, Ecuador, Paraguay, Peru, Venezuela, and Puerto Rico, a commonwealth of the United States. What all of these nations shared in common is a history of domination and control by the once powerful Spanish Empire; thus, for individuals whose primary heritage is tied to these countries, their first language is Spanish. In addition to a shared language and certain cultural characteristics, a history of racial domination, racial prejudice, and racial privilege is embedded in their national heritage, where membership in a socially designated racial category predetermined social standing, social opportunities, and the quality of life. It is an undeniable fact that the racial and social stratification that existed in these countries placed members of the white community at the top of the social hierarchy. To be a member of the Amerindian, African, mixed-race, or other communities carried social consequences and obstacles that were, at times, difficult to overcome. Immigration patterns (coupled with the historic annexation of Mexican territories by the United States) resulted in the relocation of millions of Spanish-speaking individuals. Now, as citizens of the United States, generations of Hispanics have become familiar with our own unique form of American race and American racism.

Understanding the social significance of race, color, and ethnic identification and their relationship to class and social mobility is part of the epic memory of the Hispanic American community. While some members may identify themselves as descendants of the indigenous people, enslaved Africans, or mixed-race populations of their native lands, others prefer to identify with the European colonizers who seized the land and all of its resources, developing the Spanish culture in the New World. In a variety of different ways, members of the community seek to embrace a self-defined social identity that reflects a sense of pride and acceptance of their racial and ethnic background. However, placing oneself in a racial group reflective of social perceptions or social reality has proven to be a confusing and challenging task for many Hispanic Americans. For others, racial and ethnic identities overlap. While ethnicity is understood to refer to the original place of origin, race may subsequently be described under the generic group terminology as *Hispanic* or *Latino*.

The Hispanic community has many social descriptors and ascribed social labels, such as *Spanish-speaking, Latino, Latinx, immigrant, brown people, people of color, minority*, and *miscegan*. It remains up to the individual to determine if the racial category they belong to is white, black, brown, or other. As we reviewed the unique social and historical characteristics of many of these communities, we have noted the inconsistencies between how members of the community self-identify and the numerous categorical labels they are assigned by scholars, government officials, and even the general public.

There is no universal agreement on how best to describe the nation's "largest ethno-racial minority group." It was during the early 1970s when the U.S. government first used the term *Hispanic* to describe a person's region of origin. According to the early government definition, Hispanics were individuals coming from Mexico and South or Central America. (Several decades later, with a quick stroke of the pen and changes in the language on census forms, the government designated the entire group coming from the southern region of the Western Hemisphere as Latinos!) As previously emphasized, Hispanics are not a singular ethnic group; their heritage is representative of the multiple nations listed above, as well as of an American-born population whose parents or grandparents were born in foreign nations.

Nor are Hispanic Americans a singular racial group; members proudly identify themselves as white, black, brown, and other. There is no agreement on the use of the terms *Hispanic, Latino, Latinx*, or *Spanish-speaking*, the nomenclature used to describe membership in the group. While most indicate and acknowledge their Spanish heritage, not all members identify Spanish as their first language; this is especially true for first- and second-generation Hispanics born in the United States. According to the 2017 Pew Research Center study, only 70 percent of those identifying themselves as Latino speak Spanish in their homes and consider Spanish to be their first language.[6] When given a choice, most prefer to identify themselves based on the place of their national origin or of that of a previous generation (i.e., I am Mexican, Cuban, Costa Rican, Dominican, Columbian, Honduran, and/or Puerto Rican). However, one's embrace of ethnic heritage decreases over time. Second- and third-generation members of the community may prefer to use more general terms: I am Latino, Latinx, white American, black American, or

American. For example, Mexicans in the United States decreasingly describe themselves as Mexican or Hispanic/Latino while increasingly considering themselves as American generally and as "typical" Americans more specifically. Slightly more than half of Mexican Americans indicate they are "white" in the census race question. This response is most likely reflective of the community's lived experience; part acculturation and part assimilation, to be "American" is to embrace the Anglo lifestyle and identity of the majority.

Furthermore, extensive ethnic and racial mixing has also resulted in the decision by many members of the Hispanic community to acknowledge or simply prefer one part of their heritage over the other. As described in a previous chapter on the Dominican American experience, extensive intermarriage of Dominicans with partners of other ethnicities sometimes creates circumstances that, depending on the dominant ethnic presence in the environment surrounding the family, may lead the children to identify with the ancestry of one of their parents rather than the other. Intermarriage with members of non-Hispanic and other racial groups also presents its own challenges. For example, as shared by eighteen-year-old Alex, "My mother is Cuban. She married my father, a white American. My brothers and I know a few words, but we do not speak Spanish. When anyone asked, we always referred to ourselves as Americans, white Americans, and no, we are not members of a minority group."

As revealed in previous chapters, the Hispanic/Latino community has undergone a process of racialization. Racialization is defined here as the sociopolitical phenomenon that perceives and treats a class of persons according to readily identifiable markers of identity, such as phenotype, culture, or national origin. Thus, a group can be racialized even though it may not constitute a "race" in the traditional understanding of the term. Race is socially constructed; historically, members of the majority group have been free to determine which characteristics constitute a racial grouping. The observable, genetically transferred physical characteristics that initially formed the basis of a racial grouping have been extended to include culture, language, religion, and even place of origin. For example, social discourse around race has resulted in the false notion that Spanish-speaking people are a race, Jewish people are a race, Muslims are a race, and Middle Easterners are a race. Positive or negative characteristics are assigned to each group, resulting in the perception that membership in one group is preferred or superior to others. In America, race is also viewed through the prism of assimilability, i.e., which groups are best suited for adaptability to the American way of life?

Culture and Identity

Culture is defined as a way of life.[7] It is the way we live—our values, beliefs, social customs, and practices. Culture is also commonly understood to include language, food, music, art, religion, and family traditions. What is the common or shared culture in the Hispanic American community?

Spanish as the first language, spoken in the home, in primary, intimate settings, and at Hispanic community functions, is the most commonly shared cultural characteristic. As a group, Hispanic Americans maintain close relationships with religious organizations and are overwhelmingly Catholic (although the same could be said for Irish and Italian Americans). Salsa and merengue are embraced as traditional forms of music and dance, and strong family ties (*familismo*) bind the nuclear and extended family units. The stereotypical meal of beans, rice, and plantains coupled with chicken and pork is considered a staple in the home, and holidays (Christmas, Holy Week, and birthdays, especially quinceañeras) are observed with traditional Spanish customs. Cinco de Mayo, a celebration of Mexican independence, is also a cause for celebration in the Latino community, and Hispanic Heritage Month, which started as a weeklong celebration in 1968, was expanded to a monthlong celebration in 1988. While there are optimistic views toward the development of a Hispanic/Latino transnational identity, it appears that specific ethnic identifications, or a form of ethnic multiculturalism, supersede the desire to be identified generically as Hispanic. Many racial groups (Asian, Indian, and African) have attempted pan-ethnic unity, some more successfully than others.[8] The level of cohesiveness among the varying subgroups is much dependent upon their understanding and willingness to embrace a common goal or agenda, more specifically: Why are we all in this thing together?

Common Causes

According to a 2017 Pew Research Center study, more than two-thirds of Latinos see Hispanic as a pan-ethnic category while less than one-third see being Latino as a common culture.[9] These findings are consistent with self-identity reports from other sources; if given the choice, the majority prefers to describe themselves based on ethnic identity. However, most acknowledge that they are members of a community that is uniquely different from the American majority. But are the differences and/or similarities enough to unite the community into a powerful social or cultural force that is a representative voice of Hispanic Americans?

There are many issues of social concern to Hispanic Americans, but to assume that the majority of the Hispanic community is uniformly in agreement on pressing issues of the day would be erroneous. From an aspirational point of view, the many sub-ethnic groups in the Hispanic community should unite to help strengthen their ability to fight for a common cause. However, any form of coalition or alliance among groups with varying interests and agendas invariably faces internal conflict.[10] The same is true for Hispanic Americans. Moreover, some ethnic groups within the Hispanic community may be more, or less, revered than others. Consider the sign posted, in English, in a major shopping mart by a local vendor and purveyor of specialty food products: "WE ARE NOT MEXICANS! WE ARE PROUD AMERICAN PUERTO RICANS!" What are some of the issues and concerns that would serve to help galvanize the Hispanic American community?

Bilingual Education Movement

As the number of immigrant and Spanish-speaking children increased in the nation's public schools, due in part to the lifting of immigration restrictions against non-English-speaking countries, there was a growing cry for the implementation of bilingual education programs. Theoretically, bilingual education would involve the establishment of a curriculum whereby the academic content was taught in two languages; in the United States, the main focus was on Spanish and English. The basic premise of the movement was to acknowledge the learning obstacles that children who were not fully fluent in English faced. According to its many proponents, a bilingual education program fosters an environment in which non-English-speaking students can develop efficiency in the English language while retaining the ability to speak and learn in their native tongue.[11] Arguments about the need to preserve the "cultural heritage" of minority children, as well as the need to provide high-quality education, were also put forth. To many, it was a sound educational approach to the ever-growing challenge of educating foreign language students.

The 1968 Bilingual Act, an extension of Title VII of the Elementary and Secondary Education Act of 1965, was the federal legislation that provided funding to school districts to develop bilingual education programs. The legislation recognized the special needs of students with limited English-speaking ability and created guidelines to fund bilingual programs. The program was a federal subsidy to assist with the development and implementation of bilingual programs; local school districts and state governments were required to obtain the additional funding needed for full implementation. The Act has undergone numerous revisions in the more than fifty years since its passing. However, the primary focus continues to be the ability to address non-English-speaking students' needs.[12]

The movement for bilingual education has been embroiled in controversy from the very beginning. What specific target group was to be the focus of the bilingual programs? Spanish-speaking populations were the largest number of non-English-speaking children entering the public school systems, but what about other non-English-speaking populations? Were there enough qualified educators to teach in bilingual programs? How could we best determine the effectiveness of bilingual education, and, most importantly, were taxpayers expected to bear the cost of bilingual education?

While supporters of the bilingual education movements extolled the many positive effects of bilingual programs, opponents questioned if an English-only language of instruction should be required for all public schools. They cited examples of the millions of immigrants who arrived at the turn of the twentieth century, all of whom were absorbed in the public school system with English-only instruction. Some would argue that gaining fluency in the English language facilitated the process of assimilation to the American way of life. External forces (the English-only movement) also gained momentum as states began passing laws making English the official language.[13] These efforts were not limited to attacks on bilingual education, but also included initiatives to require English-only in the transaction of government, business, and private affairs and included prominent conservative voices from the Hispanic community.[14]

In addition to the overall concerns about the need for bilingual education, there have also been disagreements around which programs and approaches are most effective in serving student needs. For example, in June 2019, the Trenton, New Jersey, Board of Education (black, brown, and white members) put forth a proposal to create a separate high school for bilingual students. The Trenton Global Academy would serve four hundred of the city's English-language-learning students. According to the board, the district's "current bilingual program has 'significant gaps,' and the creation of a school entirely for recently immigrated, new to the American school system, will better serve the English Language Learning, or ELL, students."[15] The board-approved proposal was based on the changing demographics of the City of Trenton, which historically has had a sizable Spanish-speaking population, but one that was continuing to witness a rapid growth.[16] An estimated one-third of the city self-identified as Hispanic/Latino. Regarding student enrollment, for the school year 2018–2019, 19.3 percent of the student population were enrolled in the

ELL curriculum. The board argued that the "district had to think differently about how to meet the needs of a population of students who are unable to access the traditional educational system due to language barriers."[17] However, members of the Teachers Education Association and the community pushed back. Of primary concern were questions about segregation: A high school, which specialized in ELL instruction, segregates the mostly Hispanic students from the mainstream population. This is inherently wrong . . . or is it?

Immigration

Bilingual education may or may not be a rallying point for members of the Hispanic community, but what about the questions surrounding immigration and immigration reform? Illegal and legal immigration and immigration reform have become hot-button issues in American public discourse. Two opposing forces shape the public view: one decries America's broken immigration system, which leads to millions of legal and illegal immigrants coming into the United States, and the other uplifts our heritage as a country of immigrants and decries the current restrictive approaches taken toward the populations from south of the border.[18] Issues surrounding immigration have proven to be divisive for the American people. While one can easily recognize the explosive nature of the contemporary debate, American immigration policy has a controversial past, one with obvious racial overtones. It is true that America is a nation of immigrants. Columbus's moment of "discovery" was the beginning of a worldwide immigration pattern that resulted in millions of foreigners relocating to U.S. shores.[19] The most desired have always been those from European (white) nations whose immigrant populations overflowed into the Western Hemisphere from the sixteenth through the early twentieth centuries. The early open-door policy was welcoming to most, but there were some contentious moments, with nativists arguing about which populations were more desirable than others. The Irish, for example, were long considered to be one of America's most suffering immigrant groups.[20] Arriving in extremely large numbers during the middle of the nineteenth century, they were considered to be poor, diseased, and ignorant, a population unlikely to be fully integrated into the American mainstream. Their racial purity was also questioned, with opponents arguing that they were not part of the great white Anglo-Saxon race. Similar arguments occurred at the end of the century, as large numbers of Greeks and Italians poured into the country.[21] Northern Europeans and those from the Mediterranean were deemed biologically and morally inferior. And in 1916,

American Madison Grant published *The Passing of the Great Race: Or, The Racial Basis of European History*.[22] A devout believer in eugenics, Grant was a leader in promoting a theory of Nordic superiority, laying the foundation for the scientific racism that emerged in the twentieth century.[23] This was a period in which ignorance, deceit, falsehoods, and notions of white supremacy reigned supreme. As recently cited by conservative columnist George Will "If you think we have reached peak stupidity—that America's per-capita quantity has never been higher—there is solace, of sorts, in Daniel Okrent's guided tour through the immigration debate that was heading toward a nasty legislative conclusion a century ago. *The Guarded Gate: Bigotry, Eugenics, and the Law That Kept Two Generations of Jews, Italians, and Other European Immigrants Out of America* provides evidence that today's public arguments are comparatively enlightened."[24] Okrent's book provides an in-depth analysis of the mood of the country (particularly of leading politicians and the intellectual elite) when the U.S. government developed restrictive immigration policies based on race.[25] It was not the first time the federal legislation targeted a particular racial group. The 1882 Chinese Exclusion Act was the first federal law to restrict immigration based on race and ethnicity. "Cheap" Chinese labor was viewed as a threat to the white American workforce.[26] The Immigration Act of 1924, or Johnson-Reed Act, placed restrictions on non-European immigrants with the use of a quota system. Severe limitations were also placed on those seeking entry to the United States from Africa, Asia, and South America.[27] Following the Immigration Reform Act of 1965, the pattern of immigration shifted from the European countries to nations populated by people of color. And as noted previously, the nation's largest wave of immigration occurred during the latter part of the twentieth century and into the twenty-first, whereby the majority of this new immigration population was coming from south of the border.[28]

Are immigration issues a priority concern for most Hispanic Americans? The answer to that question is dependent upon specific issues and specific populations. Mexican Americans may be more heavily impacted by restrictive immigration policies affecting family and extended family members. Members of the Mexican American community are estimated to have an "illegal" alien population of 20 percent. Issues surrounding "The Dreamers" and DACA (Deferred Action for Childhood Arrivals) have a profound impact on this community as well, given that the overwhelming majority of Dreamers and DACA seekers are from Mexico.[29] Immigrant families from Guatemala, Honduras, and El Salvador may also rank immigration reform as their number one priority issue. Could this become the rallying point for Hispanic America? While there are likely to be positive sentiments about the struggles the Mexican, Honduran, Guatemalan, and Salvador American communities face around immigration status, DACA, Dreamers, and deportation issues, these issues are not prioritized in other Spanish-speaking communities. For example, for Puerto Ricans, issues of statehood or independence, along with the recovery of the island from Hurricane Maria, are dominant concerns.[30] Cuban Americans remain focused on restrictive U.S. economic policy toward the nation;[31] Venezuelan Americans feel powerless to effect change in their homeland, which threatens the mere survival of millions of people;[32] and Dominican and Costa Rican immigrants, who faced less restrictive obstacles as they made their way into the United States, express concern over economic and financial stability.[33] Furthermore, there is disagreement within the Mexican American/Latino community about U.S. immigration policy. As Donald Trump described Mexicans seeking access to the United States as "drug dealers, criminals, and rapists" and threatened to shut down the border to prohibit the entry of immigrants seeking legal status, many were surprised to see that a significant number of his supporters were from the Mexican American community.[34] And various polls conducted during the 2016 presidential race placed Hispanic support for Trump anywhere between 18 percent and 32 percent.[35]

The humanitarian crisis at the border, where children and families are trapped in America's broken immigration system, has touched the American people.[36] How we respond differs, based not so much on race and ethnicity, but on a clear demarcation along political lines. The Democratic leadership offers one form of interpretation or strategy, the Republicans another.

Political Empowerment

Political empowerment is an agreed-upon goal for many "minority" communities. We need racial, ethnic, gender, age, class, and religious diversity represented in political office. How is that best achieved among the Hispanic community? In regard to participation in the political process, how can we organize and develop a bloc of Hispanic Americans voters who would have a measurable impact on the political process? The predictability of the bloc vote of special interest groups is part of the American political process. For example, polling data suggests that Southern whites are more likely to vote Republican and Southern blacks, Democrat. Northern white liberals are more likely Democrats. The high school educated, white working class are more likely Republicans. Elite, college-educated whites are more likely Independents. "Minority" groups, in general, lean toward affiliation with the Democratic Party, and blacks remain overwhelmingly Democratic, regardless of regional location, etc. These are the popular trends among likely voters. What level of uniformity or predictability can one offer about the increasingly expanding Latino vote?

Hispanic voters are more likely to affiliate with the Democratic Party, which is viewed as socially progressive and more sensitive to minority issues. This pattern of support is fairly consistent in the Hispanic community. A 2018 Pew Research Center report reveals that "by more than two-to-one (63% to 28%), Hispanic voters are more likely to affiliate with or lean toward the Democratic Party than the GOP. The overall balance of partisan orientation among Hispanics is little changed over the last decade."[37] The growth in the number of Hispanics eligible to vote caught the attention of both major political parties. As Jens Manuel Krogstad noted in 2016, prior to the presidential election, "Significant growth in the number of Latino eligible voters has helped make the U.S. electorate more racially and ethnically diverse than ever . . . a record 27.3 million Latinos are eligible to cast ballots, representing 12% of all eligible voters."[38] The Hispanic vote was the fastest-growing demographic for all eligible voters, fueled in part by the large number of U.S.-born millennials who were eligible as first-time voters. Would their participation in the 2016 or future elections have a significant impact on the outcome? While the majority of Hispanic voters has leaned toward the Democratic Party, Krogstad also noted that their electoral impact has long been limited by low voter turnout and a population concentrated in non-battleground states. More specifically, recent polling and demographic data (2016) suggests that the ten largest states with Latino voters are, predictably, red or blue. From the state with the great percentage to the smallest, we note the following: New Mexico (red), Texas (red), California (blue), Arizona (red), Nevada (blue), Florida (red), Colorado (blue), New Jersey (blue), New York (blue), and Illinois (blue).[39] A seismic shift in Hispanic voting patterns, or a unified Hispanic vote, could impact the outcome of local, state, and national elections.

Prioritizing Key Issues

While immigration, immigration reform, voter participation, and rising political clout continue to dominate the news, they are not the most important issues of concern for Hispanic Americans. A 2014 Pew Research Center study found that, when surveyed, the Hispanic community consistently ranks several issues higher than that of immigration. "In 2013, some 57% of Hispanic registered voters called education an 'extremely important' issue facing the nation today. That's compared with jobs and the economy (52%) and health care (43%). Just 32% said immigration." Moreover, and not surprisingly, those who indicated that immigration or immigration reform was their number one priority (80 percent) were overwhelmingly recent immigrants rather than the American-born Hispanic population (57 percent).[40]

There are numerous organizations, both political and nonpolitical, working toward prioritizing what they believe to be issues of concern to the Latino community. UnidosUS, formerly known as the National Council of La Raza (NCLR), was founded in 1968 as a nonpartisan voice for Latinos. According to their website, "We serve the Hispanic community through our research, policy analysis, and state and national advocacy efforts, as well as in our program work in communities nationwide. And we partner with a national network of nearly 300 Affiliates across the country to serve millions of Latinos in the areas of civic engagement, civil rights and immigration, education, workforce and the economy, health, and housing." They further indicate that their goal is to "build a stronger America by creating opportunities for Latinos. We envision an America where economic, political, and social advancement is a reality for all Latinos, where all Hispanics thrive, and where our community's contributions are recognized."[41]

In their 2019 publication, "Stronger Communities, Stronger America: A Latino Policy Agenda for the 116th Congress," UnidosUS identifies key issues of concern to the Latino community, including civil rights and criminal justice, economic security, education, health and well-being, and immigration. The policy document offers specific recommendations regarding what actions would address these issues. For example, Congress should address voter suppression, racial profiling, and mass incarceration, all of which disproportionately impact the Latino community. Efforts should be made to increase employment opportunities for quality jobs, income, wage equity, and wealth building. Additional investments are needed in pre-K, early childhood, K–12, and higher education. Increased access to health care is needed, particularly in light of recent statistics that suggest the significantly smaller number of Hispanic families who have health-care insurance are vulnerable to preventable diseases, as is greater access to healthy, affordable food. Finally, immigration remains a high priority. UnidosUS calls for the modernization of the immigration system and protection of family unity by focusing on and achieving permanent protections for longtime residents.[42]

The Congressional Hispanic Caucus (CHC) is a congressional member organization of the U.S. House of Representatives. It was founded in 1976 by five Hispanic congressmen: Herman Badillo, Baltasar Corrada del Rio, Kika de la Garza, Henry Gonzalez, and Edward Roybal. What initially started as a bipartisan group evolved into a Democrat-only organization when Republican congressmen left the group in the late 1990s due to policy differences.[43] In 2003, the Congressional Hispanic Conference (CHC), which also uses the same initials as the Congressional Hispanic Caucus, was formed by Florida Congressman Mario Diaz-Balart. Three of his Republican colleagues joined him.[44] Both organizations are composed of members of Hispanic/Latino or Portuguese descent and portend to support legislative initiatives of concern to the Hispanic community.

According to their website, the Congressional Hispanic Caucus "aims to address national and international issues and the impact these policies have on the Hispanic community. The function of the Caucus is to serve as a forum for the Hispanic Members of Congress to coalesce around a collective legislative agenda. The Caucus is dedicated to voicing and advancing, through the legislative process, issues affecting Hispanics in the United States, Puerto Rico and the Commonwealth of the Northern Mariana Islands." The Congressional Hispanic Conference "seeks to emphasize both national and international issues that have a significant impact on the Hispanic community in the United States. The members believe that Hispanics play a vital role in our democracy and must be actively engaged in all the issues facing our nation." Reflecting on their historic disagreements with an overwhelmingly Democratic body, the Congressional Hispanic Conference further emphasize that "for too long, Hispanics have been framed as a single-issue community. The Congressional Hispanic Conference creates a forum for Members of Congress to collaborate in the creation of a cohesive legislative agenda, and is dedicated to promoting the interests of all Hispanics."[45]

In 2019, the 116th Congress had thirty-eight members in the Congressional Hispanic Caucus; it had six in the Congressional Hispanic Conference. While both organizations work toward further empowerment of the Hispanic community, their philosophical, ideological, and political differences keep them apart.

Why Race Still Matters

Membership in America's Hispanic community means embracing some aspect of one's ethnic heritage and linking it to the larger ethno-racial group. The diversity that exists in today's Latino community is reflective of more than four hundred years of history, one in which those of

Mexican heritage became the disproportionately largest Spanish-speaking group in America. In twenty-first-century America, the nation's largest minority includes multiple generations of American-born Hispanics as well as the hundreds of thousands who continue to arrive in the country as new immigrants. And one can attribute the boom in the Hispanic population and the interest in the various cultures to the explosive increase in the immigration patterns in the past fifty years. It is the ongoing addition of new immigrants, as well as the constant exchange between American-born Hispanics and the people and culture of their places of origin, that help to maintain a growing and vibrant Hispanic culture.

For Hispanic America, questions surrounding race and identity remain fluid. While there is much validity to the argument that the entire Latino community has been racialized, what remains are distinct racial identities among many Hispanic Americans. Why do questions about race still matter?

Scholar, public intellectual, and social activist Cornel West raised that specific question in his 1993 publication of *Race Matters*.[46] While focusing on a range of issues that impacted the black community, West reminded America that we could not escape the history of race and racism and its impact on contemporary American life. In the United States of America, everyone is viewed through the prism of race. Race is a social construct, fully developed and forcibly imposed on the American people for more than four hundred years. The ramifications of racially imposed social stratification can be seen everywhere. As a socially constructed concept, race has created a system of social injustice, unfairly distributing the nation's valuable social resources to the white majority and interfering with the ability of others to develop their fullest human potential. Patterns of racial discrimination are ubiquitous. America's communities are racially segregated, with whites continuing to benefit from these historical patterns of segregation. The nation's ghettoes, barrios, slums, and reservations, where substandard housing, poor schooling, and limited employment are the norm, are filled with people of color. In the majority of these communities, residents are forced to deal with higher crime rates, drug trafficking, police brutality, alcoholism, and substance abuse. There is an undeniable link between race, poverty, and class. The persistence of racial disparities in educational achievement, as provided by the nation's public schools, further demonstrates the advantages to being born white rather than a person of color in America. The seats of power are dominated and controlled by the white majority, who give little credence to the substantial impact that race, racism, and racial discrimination have wrought on the American people.[47] Hispanic America has been victimized by American racism.

The ongoing battle against racism and colorism is one of the many challenges facing the Hispanic community. For too many, whiteness is seen as the most desired and privileged status. The Afro-Latino, miscegan (brown), and self-identified "others" are more fully cognizant of the impact of race and color discrimination. Overcoming the social inequities resulting from racial bias must also be a priority for the Hispanic community. Those who cling to whiteness must confront issues surrounding white privilege in the Latino community.

Ed Morales's cautionary warning to Hispanic America is worth repeating. Striving for whiteness through marriage or by rejecting the multiracial backgrounds of the Latino community will not serve to unify the people.[48] Beliefs in white superiority must be rejected. The ability to embrace ourselves and be comfortable in our own skin is key to strengthening our identity as Hispanic Americans. He further notes:

> Whether we choose to identify ourselves as Hispanic, Latino, or the increasingly popular Latinx, these labels help us find our place in American society and culture. While there will always be Hispanics who no longer need or want to identify, the forces in society that create "included" and "excluded" groups on the basis of what one's race or ethnicity *appears* to be are not going away. From the early 20th-century activism of W.E.B. Dubois and Marcus Garvey through the civil rights movement, African-Americans have consolidated a powerful notion of identity based on racial solidarity. This approach pushed back against anti-black racism and yielded tangible political results, as well as power and influence in American society. Such leverage will remain elusive to Hispanics if we move away from acknowledging and embracing our "difference."[49]

Hispanic America must demonstrate a willingness to fully interrogate the race (and color) question and develop a greater understanding of the far-reaching implication of race and American racism on the multiracial and multiethnic members of the community.

Notes

1. Reid-Merritt, 2017.
2. Rodney, 2011.
3. U.S. Census Bureau, 2017.
4. Arreola, 2004.
5. U.S. Census Bureau, 2017.
6. Flores, 2017.

7. Ferris and Stein, 2016.

8. Schaefer, 2018.

9. Flores, 2017.

10. Karenga, 2010.

11. Krashen, 1999.

12. Orr, 2019.

13. Crawford, 2000.

14. Chávez, 1995.

15. Rizzo, 2019.

16. Suburban Stats.

17. Rizzo, 2019.

18. Clark-Ibanez and Swan, 2019; ProCon.org, 2019.

19. Wright, 2008; Schaefer, 2018.

20. Daniels, 2002; Rose, 2014.

21. Moskos, 1989; Ciongoli and Parini, 2002.

22. Grant, 2017.

23. McDaniel, 1997.

24. Wills, 2019.

25. Okrent, 2019.

26. Schaefer, 2018.

27. Workmen's Circle, 2019.

28. Schaefer, 2018.

29. Krogstad, 2014.

30. Diaz, 2019; Camarda and Gonzalez, 2018.

31. Piccone, 2018.

32. Maupin, 2016.

33. Torres-Saillant, 2012; Hernández and Rivera-Batiz, 2003.

34. BBC News, 2016; Capatides, 2016.

35. Shepard, 2016.

36. AFT, 2019; Isacson, Beltrán, and Meyer, 2019.

37. Pew Research Center, 2018.

38. Krogstad, 2016.

39. Gass, 2016.

40. Krogstad, 2014.

41. UnidosUS, 2019a, 2019b.

42. Ibid.

43. Ballotpedia, 2019a.

44. Ballotpedia 2019b.

45. Congressional Hispanic Caucus, 2019.

46. West, 1993.

47. Reid-Merritt, 2017.

48. Morales, 2018.

49. Ibid.

References

American Federation of Teachers (AFT) (2019). "Humanitarian Crisis at the U.S. Border," https://www.aft.org/our-community/immigration/humanitarian -crisis-us-border.

Arreola, Daniel (2004). *Hispanic Spaces, Latino Places: Community and Cultural Diversity in Contemporary America*, Houston: University of Texas Press.

Ballotpedia (2019a). "Congressional Hispanic Caucus," https://ballotpedia.org /Congressional_Hispanic_Caucus.

Ballotpedia (2019b). "Congressional Hispanic Conference," https://ballotpedia.org /Congressional_Hispanic_Conference.

BBC News (2016). "'Drug Dealers, Criminals, Rapists': What Trump Thinks of Mexicans," August 31, https://www.bbc.com/news/av/world-us-canada-37 230916/drug-dealers-criminals-rapists-what-trump-thinks-of-mexicans.

Camarda, Bonnie, and Will Gonzalez (2018). "'We Remain Frustrated by the President's Response.' What's Next for Puerto Rican Evacuees in Phila- delphia," *Philadelphia Inquirer*, May 3, https://www.inquirer.com/philly /opinion/commentary/unidos-pa-pr-hurricane-maria-philadelphia-evacuees -20180503.html.

Capatides, Christina (2016). "Meet the Mexican Americans Who Agree with Donald Trump on Immigration," *CBS News*, June 1, https://www.cbsnews .com/news/meet-the-mexican-americans-who-agree-with-donald -trump-on-immigration/.

Chávez, Linda (1995). "One Nation, One Common Language," *Reader's Digest* (August): 87–91.

Ciongoli, A. Kenneth, and Jay Parini (2002). *Passage to Liberty: The Story of Italian Immigration and the Rebirth of America*, New York: Regan Books.

Clark-Ibanez, Marisol, and Richelle S. Swan (2019). *Unauthorized Portraits of Latino Immigrants*, Lanham: Rowman & Littlefield Publishers.

Congressional Hispanic Caucus (2019). "About Us," https://congressional hispaniccaucus-castro.house.gov/about.

Crawford, James (2000). "Anatomy of the English-Only Movement," https:// benjamins.com/catalog/impact.2.09cra.

Daniels, Roger (2002). *Coming to America: The History of Immigration and Ethnicity in American Life*, New York: Perennial Publishing.

Diaz, Rubén, Sr. (2019). "Statehood for Puerto Rico," *The Bronx Times*, May 23, https://bronx.com/statehood-for-puerto-rico/.

Ferris, Kerry, and Jill Stein (2016). *The Real World: An Introduction to Sociology*, 5th ed., New York: W. W. Norton & Company.

Flores, Antonio (2017). "2015, Hispanic Population in the United States Statistical Portrait: Statistical Portrait of Hispanics in the United States," Pew Research Center, https://www.pewresearch.org/hispanic/2017/09/18/2015 -statistical-information-on-hispanics-in-united-states/.

Gass, Nick (2016). "Gallup: Red States Now Outnumber Blue States," *Politico*, February 3, https://www.politico.com/story/2016/02/how-many-red-states -blue-states-are-there-218672.

Grant, Madison (2017). *The Passing of a Great Race*, Eastford: Martino Fine Books.

Hernández, Ramona, and Francisco Rivera-Batiz (2003). *Dominicans in the United States: A Socioeconomic Profile 2000*, New York: CUNY Academic Works.

Isacson, Adam, Adriana Beltrán, and Maureen Meyer (2019). "There Is a Crisis at the U.S.-Mexican Border: But It's Manageable," WOLA, https://www.wola .org/analysis/fix-us-mexico-border-humanitarian-crisis/.

Karenga, Maulana (2010). *Introduction to Black Studies*, 4th ed., Los Angeles: San-kore Press.

Krashen, S.D. (1999). "Bilingual Education: Arguments for and (Bogus) Argument Against," in *Language in Our Time: Bilingual Education and Official English, Ebonics and Standard English, Immigration and the Unz Initiative*, James E. Alatis and Ai-Hui Tan, eds., https://repository.library.georgetown .edu/handle/10822/551456.

Krogstad, Jens Manuel (2014). "Top Issue for Hispanics? Hint: It's Not Immigra-tion," Pew Research Center, https://www.pewresearch.org/fact-tank/2014 /06/02/top-issue-for-hispanics-hint-its-not-immigration/.

Krogstad, Jens Manuel (2016). "Key Facts about the Latino Vote in 2016," Pew Research Center, https://www.pewresearch.org/fact-tank/2016/10/14 /key-facts-about-the-latino-vote-in-2016/.

Maupin, Caleb T. (2016). "U.S.-Led Economic War, Not Socialism, Is Tearing Venezuela Apart," *Mint Press*, July 12, https://www.mintpressnews.com /us-led-economic-war-not-socialism-tearing-venezuela-apart/218335/.

McDaniel, George (1997). "Madison Grant and the Racialist Movement," *American Renaissance*, December, https://www.amren.com/news/2010/07/madison _grant_a/.

Morales, Ed (2018). "A New Report Says Hispanic Identity Is Fading. Is That Really Good for America?" *The Washington Post*, https://edmorales .net/2018/07/01/a-new-report-says-hispanic-identity-is-fading-is -that-really-good-for-america/.

Moskos, Charles (1989). *Greek Americans: Struggle and Success*, 2nd ed., New Brunswick: Transaction Publishers.

Okrent, David (2019). *The Guarded Gate: Bigotry, Eugenics and the Law That Kept Two Generations of Jews, Italians, and Other European Immigrants Out of America*, New York: Scribner.

Orr, Amy (2019). "The Bilingual Act of 1968," Immigration to the United States, http://www.immigrationtounitedstates.org/379-bilingual-education -act-of-1968.html.

Pew Research Center (2018). "Trends in Party Affiliation among Demographic Groups," https://www.people-press.org/2018/03/20/1-trends-in-party-affil iation-among-demographic-groups/.

Piccone, Ted (2018). "From Order to Chaos: U.S. Cuban Relations Are about to Get Worse," Brookings Institute, April 16, https://www.brookings.edu

/blog/order-from-chaos/2018/04/16/u-s-cuban-relations-are-about-to -get-worse/.

ProCon.org (2019). "Should the Government Allow Immigrants Who Are Here Illegally to Become U.S. Citizens?" https://immigration.procon.org/.

Reid-Merritt, Patricia, ed. (2017). *Race in America: How a Pseudoscientific Concept Shaped Human Interaction*, Santa Barbara: Praeger.

Rizzo, Olivia (2019). "School Plan Segregates Kids, Foes Say." *Times of Trenton*, June 23, 1.

Rodney, Walter (2011). *How Europe Underdeveloped Africa*, Baltimore: Black Classic Press.

Rose, Peter (2014). *They and We: Racial and Ethnic relations in the United States and Beyond*, 7th ed., New York: Routledge.

Schaefer, Richard T. (2018). *Racial and Ethnic Groups*, 15th ed., Boston: Pearson-Prentice Hall.

Shepard, Steven (2016). "How Popular Is Trump with Hispanic Voters?" *Politico*, June 3, https://www.politico.com/story/2016/06/donald-trump-hispanic -voters-223845.

Suburban Stats. "Population Demographics for Trenton, New Jersey in 2019, 2018," https://suburbanstats.org/population/new-jersey/how-many-people-live -in-trenton.

Torres-Saillant, Silvio (2012). *Introduction to Dominican Blackness*, New York: CUNY Academic Works.

UnidosUS (2019a). "WE ARE UNIDOS US," https://www.unidosus.org/about-us/.

UnidosUS (2019b). "Stronger Communities, Stronger America: A Latino Policy Agenda for the 116th Congress," http://publications.unidosus.org/handle /123456789/1935.

U.S. Census Bureau (2017). "Facts for Features: Hispanic Heritage Month 2017," https://www.census.gov/newsroom/facts-for-features/2017/hispanic -heritage.html.

West, Cornel (1993). *Race Matters*, New York: Vintage Press.

Wills, George (2019). "George Will column: Last Century's Immigration Debate Makes Today's Seem Enlightened," *Richmond Times-Dispatch*, June 29, https://www.richmond.com/opinion/their-opinion/george-will-column -last-century-s-immigration-debate-makes-today/article_d8a7a648 -8367-5496-9831-14e98175bc80.html.

Workmen's Circle (2019). "The Immigration Act of 1924 (The Johnson-Reed Act)," http://circle.org/jsource/the-immigration-act-of-1924-the-johnson -reed-act/.

Wright, Russell O. (2008). *Chronology of Immigration in the United States*, Jefferson: McFarland & Company.

Bibliography

Acosta, Teresa Palomo. "In Re Ricardo Rodriguez," *Handbook of Texas Online*, http://www.tshaonline.org/handbook/online/articles/pqitw.

Acuna, Rodolfo F. (2014). *Occupied America: A History of Chicanos*, 8th ed., New York: Pearson.

Aguero, Felipe (2016). "How More Accurate Census Data Can Shape Social Justice in Colombia and Peru," The Ford Foundation, https://www.fordfoundation.org/ideas/equals-change-blog/posts/how-more-accurate-census-data-can-shape-social-justice-in-colombia-and-peru/.

Alsema, Adriaan (2018). "Portrait of Colombia's Only Black President Returns to Presidential Gallery," *Colombia Reports*, August 2, https://colombiareports.com/portrait-of-colombias-only-black-president-returns-to-presidential-gallery/.

Alvarez, Roberto (1986). "The Lemon Grove Incident," *The Journal of San Diego History* 32, no. 2, https://sandiegohistory.org/journal/1986/april/lemongrove/.

American Federation of Teachers (2019). "Humanitarian Crisis at the U.S. Border," https://www.aft.org/our-community/immigration/humanitarian-crisis-us-border.

Anderson, Theodore (1971). "Bilingual Education: The American Experience," *The Modern Language Journal* 55, no. 7: 427–440.

Aponte, Sarah (1999). *Dominican Migrations to the United States: 1970–1997*, New York: CUNY Academic Works.

Arnson, Cynthia, and Eric L. Olson, eds. (2011). "Organized Crime in Central America: The Northern Triangle," *Woodrow Wilson Center Reports on the Americas*, no. 29, September, Woodrow Wilson Center for Scholars, Latin American Program.

Arocha, Jaime (1998). "Inclusion of Afro-Colombians: Unreachable National Goal?" *Latin American Perspective* 25, no. 3: 70–89.

Arreola, Daniel (2004). *Hispanic Spaces, Latino Places: Community and Cultural Diversity in Contemporary America*, Houston: University of Texas Press.

Auber, Tamar (2018). "CNN Commentator Swipes at Toobin: Puerto Rico Is Not Case of Trump 'Ignoring People of Color,'" https://www.mediaite.com/tv /cnn-commentator-swipes-at-toobin-puerto-rico-is-not-case-of-trump -ignoring-people-of-color.

Ballotpedia (2019). "Congressional Hispanic Caucus," https://ballotpedia.org /Congressional_Hispanic_Caucus.

Ballotpedia (2019). "Congressional Hispanic Conference," https://ballotpedia.org /Congressional_Hispanic_Conference.

Baralt, Guillermo A. (2014). *Slave Revolts in Puerto Rico: Conspiracies and Uprisings, 1795–1873*, Princeton: Markus Wiener Publishers.

Batalova, Jeanne, and Alicia Lee (2012). "Frequently Requested Statistics on Immigrants and Immigration in the United States," Migration Policy Institute, https://www.migrationpolicy.org/article/frequently-requested -statistics-immigrants-and-immigration-united-states-2#1b.

Batalova, Jeanne, and Alicia Lee (2012). "Frequently Requested Statistics on Immigrants and Immigration in the United States," Migration Policy Institute, https://www.migrationpolicy.org/article/frequently-requested -statistics-immigrants-and-immigration-united-states-2#6.

BBC News (2016). "'Drug Dealers, Criminals, Rapists': What Trump Thinks of Mexicans," August 31, https://www.bbc.com/news/av/world-us-canada -37230916/drug-dealers-criminals-rapists-what-trump-thinks-of -mexicans.

Bhopal, Raj (2007). "The Beautiful Skull and Blumenbach's Errors: The Birth of the Scientific Concept of Race," *British Medical Journal* 335: 1308.

Bonilla-Silva, Eduardo (2001). *White Supremacy and Racism in the Post-Civil Rights Era*, Boulder: Lynne Rienner Publishers.

Brown, James, and Bruce Tucker (1986). *James Brown: The Godfather of Soul*, New York: Thunder's Mouth Press.

Buffington, Sean (2019). "Dominican Americans," Countries and Their Culture, https://www.everyculture.com/multi/Bu-Dr/Dominican-Americans.html #ixzz5nubZufEU.

Calleros, Charles (2012). *Readings in Persuasion:* Briefs That Changed the World (Part Two), https://arizona-asu-primo.hosted.exlibrisgroup.com/primo -explore/fulldisplay?docid=01ASU_ALMA21909171470003841 &context=L&vid=01ASU&lang=en_US&search_scope=Everything &adaptor=Local%20Search%20Engine&tab=default_tab&query= any,contains,Calleros,%20Charles.&o.

Camarda, Bonnie, and Will Gonzalez (2018). "'We Remain Frustrated by the President's Response.' What's Next for Puerto Rican Evacuees in Philadelphia," *Philadelphia Inquirer* (May 3), https://www.inquirer.com/philly /opinion/commentary/unidos-pa-pr-hurricane-maria-philadelphia -evacuees-20180503.html.

Capatides, Christina (2016). "Meet the Mexican Americans Who Agree with Donald Trump on Immigration," *CBS News,* June 1, https://www.cbsnews

.com/news/meet-the-mexican-americans-who-agree-with-donald-trump
-on-immigration/.

Carter, Nimbi, and Pearl Ford Dowe (2015). "The Racial Exceptionalism of Barak Obama," *Journal of African American Studies* 19, no. 2: 105–119.

Castro, Fatimah Williams (2013). "Afro-Colombians and the Cosmopolitan City: New Negotiations of Race and Space in Bogotá, Colombia," *Latin American Perspectives* 40, no. 2: 105–117.

Censo (2011). "X National Population Census and VI Housing Census, Costa Rica" (English version), https://unstats.un.org/unsd/demographic/sources /census/quest/CRI2011en.pdf.

Central Intelligence Agency (2019). "Central America: Costa Rica," *The World Factbook*, https://www.cia.gov/-library/publications/the-world-factbook /geos/cs.html.

Central Intelligence Agency (2019). "Country Comparison: Distribution of Family Income—Gini Index," *The World Factbook*, https://www.cia.gov/library /publications/the-world-factbook/rankorder/2172rank.html.

Central Intelligence Agency (2019). "Country Comparison: Health Expenditures," *The World Factbook*, https://www.cia.gov/-library/publications/the -world-factbook/fields/358rank.html#CS.

Chase, Cida S. "Costa Rican Americans," https://www.everyculture.com/multi /Bu-Dr/Costa-Rican-Americans.html.

Chaves, Margarita, and Marta Zambrano (2006). "From Blanqueamiento to Reindigenización: Paradoxes of Mestizaje and Multiculturalism in Contemporary Colombia," *European Review of Latin American and Caribbean Studies /Revista Europea de Estudies Latinoamericanos y del Caribe*, no. 80: 5–23.

Chávez, Linda (1995). "One Nation, One Common Language," *Reader's Digest* (August): 87–91.

Childs, Matt D. (1970). *The 1812 Aponte Rebellion in Cuba and the Struggle against Atlantic Slavery*, Chapel Hill: The University of North Carolina Press.

Chomsky, Aviva, Barry Carr, and Pamela Maria Smorkaloff, eds. (2004). *The Cuba Reader: History, Culture, Politics*, Durham: Duke University Press.

Ciongoli, A. Kenneth, and Jay Parini (2002). *Passage to Liberty: The Story of Italian Immigration and the Rebirth of America*, New York: Regan Books.

The City College of New York (2019). "CUNY Dominican Studies Institute," https://www.ccny.cuny.edu/dsi/.

Clark-Ibanez, Marisol, and Richelle S. Swan (2019). *Unauthorized Portraits of Latino Immigrants*, Lanham: Rowman & Littlefield Publishers.

Clary, Mike (1997). "Black, Cuban Racial Chasm Splits Miami," *The Los Angeles Times*, https://www.latimes.com/archives/la-xpm-1997-03-23-mn-41392 -story.html.

Cline, Sarah (2000). "Native Peoples of Colonial Central Mexico," in *The Cambridge History of the Native Peoples of the Americas*, Bruce G. Trigger and Wilcomb E. Washburn, eds., Cambridge: Cambridge University Press, 2: 187–222.

Cocco De Filippis, Daisy (2000). *Documents of Dissidence: Selected Writings by Dominican Women,* New York: CUNY Academic Works.

Cohen, Richard (2008). "Meet 'Juan Crow,'" Southern Poverty Law Center, https://www.splcenter.org/news/2008/06/16/meet-juan-crow.

Comas, Juan (1971). "Historical Reality and the Detractors of Father Las Casas," in *Bartolomé de las Casas in History: Toward an Understanding of the Man and His Work* (Collection Spéciale: CER), Juan Friede and Benjamin Keen, eds., DeKalb: Northern Illinois University Press, 487–539.

Congressional Hispanic Caucus (2019). "About Us," https://congressionalhispaniccaucus-castro.house.gov/about.

Congressional Hispanic Conference (2019). "About Us," https://hispanicconference-mariodiazbalart.house.gov/about-us.

Cooke, Julia (2015). "Among Sweeping Changes in U.S. Relations: Cuba's Race Problem Persists," http://america.aljazeera.com/articles/2015/8/13/amid-sweeping-changes-in-us-relations-cubas-race-problem-persists.html.

Corzo, Gabino La Rosa (2003). *Runaway Slave Settlements in Cuba: Resistance and Repression,* Chapel Hill: The University of North Carolina Press.

Crawford, James (1992). *Hold Your Tongue: Bilingualism and the Politics of "English Only,"* Reading: Addison-Wesley.

Crawford, James, ed. (1992). *Language Loyalties: A Source Book on the Official English Controversy,* Chicago: University of Chicago Press.

Crawford, James (1995). *Bilingual Education: History, Politics, Theory, and Practice,* 3rd ed., Los Angeles: Bilingual Educational Services.

Crawford, James (2000). "Anatomy of the English-Only Movement," https://benjamins.com/catalog/impact.2.09cra.

CTL News (2014). "Hispanics More Likely to Choose 'Other Race' in U.S. Census—Prefer to Be Identified by Country of Origin," https://ctlatinonews.com/hispanics-more-likely-to-choose-other-race-in-u-s-census-prefer-to-be-identified-by-country-of-origin/.

Cubanos por el Mundo (2010). "U.S. Census Report: Facts about Cuban Americans," https://cubanosporelmundo.com/2013/01/14/u-s-census-bureau-2010-facts-about-cuban-americans/.

Daniel, G. Reginald (2002). *More Than Black? Multiracial Identity and the New Racial Order,* Philadelphia: Temple University Press.

Daniels, Roger (2002). *Coming to America: A History of Immigration and Ethnicity in American Life,* New York: Perennial Publishing.

Daniels, Roger (2011). *Coming to America: A History of Immigration and Ethnicity in American Life,* 2nd ed., New York: Harper Perennial.

Daniels, Roger, and Harry H. L. Kitano (1970). *American Racism: Exploration of the Nature of Prejudice,* New York: Prentice Hall.

Davis, Julie Hirschfeld (2019). "After Trump Accuses Four Democratic Congresswomen of Hating U.S., They Fire Back," *New York Times,* https://www.nytimes.com/2019/07/15/us/politics/trump-go-back-tweet-racism.html.

Denis, Nelson A. (2016). *War against All Puerto Ricans: Revolution and Terror in America's Colony*, New York: Nation Books.

Department of Homeland Security (2017). "Persons Naturalized by Region and Country of Birth: Fiscal Years 2015–2017," https://www.dhs.gov/immi gration-statistics/yearbook/2017/table21.

Desilver, Drew (2013). "How Mexicans in the United States See Their Identity," Pew Research Center, http://www.pewresearch.org/fact-tank/2013/05/03 /how-mexicans-in-the-united-states-see-their-identity/.

Diaz, Rubén, Sr. (2019). "Statehood for Puerto Rico," *The Bronx Times*, May 23, https://bronx.com/statehood-for-puerto-rico/.

Diouf, Sylviane A. (2016). *Slavery's Exiles: The Story of the American Maroons*, New York: NYU Press.

Dobratz, Betty A., and Stephanie Shanks-Meile (2000). *White Power, White Pride!: The White Separatist Movement in the United States*, Baltimore: Johns Hopkins University Press.

DominicanRepublic.com (2019). "Demographics," https://www.dominicanrepub lic.com/demographics/.

DPLA (2019). "Puerto Rican Migration to the U.S.," https://dp.la/primary-source -sets/puerto-rican-migration-to-the-us.

Duany, Jorge (2000). "Neither White nor Black: The Politics of Race and Ethnicity among Puerto Ricans on the Island and in the U.S. Mainland," presented at The Meaning of Race and Blackness in the Americas: Contemporary Perspectives, Brown University, Providence, Rhode Island.

Duany, Jorge (2002). *The Puerto Rican Nation on the Move: Identities on the Island and in the United States*, Chapel Hill and London: University of North Carolina Press.

Encyclopaedia Britannica. "Belize," https://www.britannica.com/place/Belize /Languages.

Encyclopaedia Britannica. "Rodrigo Carazo Odio, President of Costa Rica," https:// www.britannica.com/biography/Rodrigo-Carazo-Odio.

Ennis, Sharon R., Merarys Ríos-Vargas, and Nora G. Albert (2011). "The Hispanic Population: 2010," U.S. Census Bureau, https://www.census.gov /prod/cen2010/briefs/c2010br-04.pdf.

Falcon, Angelo (2018). "Latinos and the 'Of Color' Problem," *Al Día*, April 3, https://aldianews.com/articles/opinion/latinos-and-color-problem /52221.

Fernández-Armesto, Felipe (2014). *Our America: A Hispanic History of the United States*, New York: W. W. Norton and Company.

Fernandez De Castro, Rafa (2015). "Mexico 'Discovers' 1.4 Million Black Mexicans—They Just Had to Ask," *FUSION*, accessed June 2, 2019, https:// fusion.tv/story/245192/mexico-discovers-1-4-million-black-mexicans -they-just-had-to-ask/.

Ferrer, Ada (2014). *Freedom's Mirror: Cuba and Haiti in the Age of Revolution*, New York: Cambridge University Press.

Ferris, Kerry, and Jill Stein (2016). *The Real World: An Introduction to Sociology*, 5th ed., New York: W. W. Norton and Company.

Figueroa, Luis A. (2005). *Sugar, Slavery and Freedom in Nineteenth-Century Puerto Rico*, Chapel Hill: University of North Carolina Press.

Findlay, Eileen J. Suárez (1999). *Imposing Decency: The Politics of Sexuality and Race in Puerto Rico, 1870–1920*, Durham and London: Duke University Press.

Flores, Antonio (2015). "Facts on U.S. Latinos, 2015: Statistical Portrait of Hispanics in the U.S.," Pew Research Center, https://www.pewresearch.org/hispanic/2017/09/18/2015-statistical-information-on-hispanics-in-united-states-trend-data/.

Flores, Antonio (2017). "How the U.S. Hispanic Population Is Changing," Pew Research Center, https://www.pewresearch.org/fact-tank/2017/09/18/how-the-u-s-hispanic-population-is-changing/.

Flores, Antonio (2017). "2015, Hispanic Population in the United States Statistical Portrait: Statistical Portrait of Hispanics in the United States," Pew Research Center," https://www.pewresearch.org/hispanic/2017/09/18/2015-statistical-information-on-hispanics-in-united-states/.

Flores, Antonio, Gustavo López, and Jynnah Radford (2017). "2015, Hispanic Population in the United States Statistical Portrait: Statistical Portrait of Hispanics in the United States," Pew Research Center, https://www.pewresearch.org/hispanic/2017/09/18/2015-statistical-information-on-hispanics-in-united-states-current-data/.

Florido, Adrian (2016). "An Emerging Entry in America's Multiracial Vocabulary: 'Blaxican,'" *NPR*, https://www.npr.org/sections/codeswitch/2016/03/08/467358961/an-emerging-entry-in-americas-multiracial-vocabulary-blaxican.

Fox, Cybelle, and Thomas Guglielmo (2012). "Defining America's Racial Boundaries: Blacks, Mexicans, and European Immigrants, 1890–1945," *American Journal of Sociology* 118: 327–379.

Franklin, John Hope, and Alfred Moss (2000). *From Slavery to Freedom*, New York: McGraw Hill.

Gale Encyclopedia of Multicultural America (2019). "Colombian Americans," https://search.credoreference.com/content/entry/galegale/colombian_americans/0.

Galeano, Eduardo (1997). *Open Veins of Latin America: Five Centuries of the Pillage of a Continent*, New York: Monthly Review Press.

Gándara, Patricia, and Frances Contreras (2010). *The Latino Education Crisis: The Consequences of Failed Social Policies*, Cambridge: Harvard University Press.

Garcia, Justin, D. (2017). "Hispanic/Latino Identity as Racial Misnomer," in *Race in America: How a Pseudoscientific Concept Shaped Human Interaction*, Patricia Reid-Merritt, ed., Santa Barbara: Praeger, 155–180.

Gass, Nick (2016). "Gallup: Red States Now Outnumber Blue States," *Politico*, February 3, https://www.politico.com/story/2016/02/how-many-red-states-blue-states-are-there-218672.

Gates, Henry Louis (2011). "Black in Latin America" (episode 1), PBS, https://www.pbs.org/video/black-in-latin-america-black-in-latin-americas-henry-louis-gates/.

Gibson, Carrie (2017). "How Colonialism and Racism Explain the Inept U.S. Response to Hurricane Maria," *Vox*, https://www.vox.com/the-big-idea/2017/10/5/16426082/colonialism-racism-american-response-puerto-rico-maria.

Girard, Phillippe R. (2010). *Haiti: The Tumultuous History—From Pearl of the Caribbean to Broken Nation*, New York: St. Martin's Griffin.

Girard, Phillippe R. (2011). *The Slaves Who Defeated Napoleon: Toussaint Louverture and the Haitian War of Independence, 1801–1804*, Tuscaloosa: University of Alabama Press.

Gomez, Alan (2017). "Obama Ends 'Wet Foot, Dry Foot' Policy for Cubans," *USA TODAY*, January 12, https://www.usatoday.com/story/news/world/2017/01/12/obama-ends-wet-foot-dry-foot-policy-cubans/96505172/.

Gonzalez, Juan (2011). *Harvest of Empire: A History of Latinos in America*, New York: Penguin Books.

González-Wippler, Migene (2017). *Santeria: African Magic in Latin America*, 2nd rev. ed., New York: Original Publication.

Gordon-Reed, Annette (2017). "America's Original Sin: Slavery and the Legacy of White Supremacy," *Foreign Affairs*, https://www.foreignaffairs.com/articles/united-states/2017-12-12/americas-original-sin.

Gott, Richard (2005). *Cuba: A New History*, New Haven: Yale University Press.

Gradin, Carlos (2013). "Race, Ethnicity and Living Conditions in Costa Rica," paper presented for the IARW-IBGE Conference on Income, Wealth, and Well-Being in Latin America, Rio de Janeiro, Brazil, September 11–14: 1–27.

Graham, Richard, ed. (1990). *The Idea of Race in Latin America, 1870–1940*, Austin: University of Texas Press.

Granberry, Julian, and Gary Vescelius (1992). *Languages of the Pre-Columbian Antilles*, Tuscaloosa: University of Alabama Press.

Grant, Madison (1970). *Passing of the Great Race, Or, the Racial Basis of European History* (American Immigration Collection, Series 2), Buffalo: Ayer Co Publishers.

Grillo, Evelio (2000). *Black Cuban, Black American: A Memoir*, Houston: Arte Público Press.

Helg, Aline (1967). *Our Rightful Share: The Afro-Cuban Struggle for Equality, 1886–1912*, Chapel Hill: University of North Carolina Press, 28.

Helliwell, John, Richard Layard, and Jeffrey Sachs (2018). *World Happiness Report 2018*, accessed May 3, 2019, https://s3.amazonaws.com/happiness-report/2018/WHR_web.pdf.

Hernández, Ramona, and Francisco Rivera-Batiz (2003). *Dominicans in the United States: A Socioeconomic Profile 2000*, New York: CUNY Academic Works.

Higginbotham, A. L. (1978). *In the Matter of Color: Race, and the American Legal Process*, New York: Oxford University Press.

History.com. "Rafael Trujillo," https://www.history.com/topics/1960s/rafael-trujillo.

History.com. "U.S. Troops Land in Dominican Republic," https://www.history
.com/this-day-in-history/u-s-troops-land-in-the-dominican-republic.

HistoryofCuba.com. "End of Slavery in Cuba," http://www.historyofcuba.com
/history/race/EndSlave.htm.

Hong, Maria. "Guatemalan Americans," Countries and their Cultures, accessed
July 27, 2019, https://www.everyculture.com/multi/Du-Ha/Guatemalan
-Americans.html.

H. Res. 194 (110th), (2008). "Apologizing for the Enslavement and Racial Segregation of African-Americans," GovTrack.us, https://www.govtrack.us
/congress/bills/110/hres194.

Hudson, Rex (2010). "Colombia: A Country Study," Federal Research Division,
Library of Congress., U.S. Government Printing Office, 1–364.

Ignatiev, Noel (2008). *How the Irish Became White* (Routledge Classics, vol. 137),
1st ed., Oxford: Routledge.

Immigration to the United States. "Immigration and Naturalization Act of 1965,"
http://immigrationtounitedstates.org/594-immigration-and-nationality
-act-of-1965.html.

Isacson, Adam, Adriana Beltrán, and Maureen Meyer (2019). "There Is a Crisis at
the U.S.-Mexican Border: But It's Manageable," WOLA, https://www.wola
.org/analysis/fix-us-mexico-border-humanitarian-crisis/.

Jessop, Alicia (2013). "The Secrets behind the Dominican Republic's Success in
the World Baseball Classic and MLB," *Forbes*, March 19, https://www
.forbes.com/sites/aliciajessop/2013/03/19/the-secrets-behind-the-dominican
-republics-success-in-the-world-baseball-classic-and-mlb/#58f25716285f.

Jones, Grant D. (2000). "The Lowland Maya from the Conquest to the Present,"
in *The Cambridge History of the Native Peoples of the Americas*, Bruce G.
Trigger and Wilcomb E. Washburn, eds., Cambridge: Cambridge University Press, 2: 346–391.

Joyner, James (2007). "Biden: Obama Clean, Articulate, Bright African American,"
Outside the Beltway, https://www.outsidethebeltway.com/biden_obama_
clean_articulate_bright_african-american/.

Kamen, Henry (2004). *Empire: How Spain Became a World Power, 1492–1763*, New
York: HarperCollins.

Karenga, Maulana (2010). *Introduction to Black Studies*, 4th ed., Los Angeles: San-
kore Press.

Kendi, Ibram X. (2016). *Stamped from the Beginning: The Definitive History of Racist
Ideas in America,* New York: Nations Books.

Kinsbruner, Jay (1996). *Not of Pure Blood: The Free People of Color and Racial
Prejudice in Nineteenth-Century Puerto Rico*, Durham: Duke University
Press.

Klein, Herbert S. (1967). *Slavery in the Americas: A Comparative Study of Virginia
and Cuba*, Chicago: University of Chicago Press.

Kornbluh, Peter (1998). *Bay of Pigs Declassified: The Secret CIA Report on the Invasion of Cuba* (National Security Archive Documents), New York: W.W Norton & Company.

Korrol, Virginia Sánchez, and Pedro Juan Hernández (2010). *Pioneros II: Puerto Ricans in New York City 1948–1998* (Images of America) (English, Spanish and English Edition), Charleston: Arcadia Publishing.

Krashen, S. D. (1999). "Bilingual Education: Arguments for and (Bogus) Argument against," https://repository.library.georgetown.edu/handle/10822/551456.

Krogstad, Jens Manuel (2014). "Top Issue for Hispanics? Hint: It's Not Immigration," Pew Research Center, https://www.pewresearch.org/fact-tank/2014/06/02/top-issue-for-hispanics-hint-its-not-immigration/.

Krogstad, Jens Manuel (2016). "Key Facts about the Latino Vote in 2016," Pew Research Center, https://www.pewresearch.org/fact-tank/2016/10/14/key-facts-about-the-latino-vote-in-2016/.

Lee, Michelle Ye Hee (2015). "Donald Trump's False Comments Connecting Mexican Immigrants and Crime," *The Washington Post*, https://www.washingtonpost.com/news/fact-checker/wp/2015/07/08/donald-trumps-false-comments-connecting-mexican-immigrants-and-crime/.

Levinson, Sarah H., and Franklin W. Knight (2018). "Cuba," https://www.britannica.com/place/Cuba.

Linnaeus, Carolus (1758). *Systema naturae per regna tria naturae: secundum classes, ordines, genera, species, cum characteribus, differentiis, synonymis, locis* (in Latin), 10th ed., Stockholm: Laurentius Salvius.

Little, Becky (2018). "Why Mexican Americans Say 'The Border Crossed Us': How White Settlers Edged Out Mexicans in Their Own Backyard," https://www.history.com/news/texas-mexico-border-history-laws.

Longley, Kyle (1993). "Peaceful Costa Rica, the First Battleground: The United States and the Costa Rican Revolution of 1948," *The Americas* 50, no. 2: 149–175.

Lopez, Gustavo (2015). "Hispanics of Colombian Origin in the United States, 2013: Statistical Profile," Pew Research Center, https://www.pewhispanic.org/2015/09/15/hispanics-of-colombian-origin-in-the-united-states-2013/.

López, Gustavo (2015). "Hispanics of Dominican Origin in the United States, 2013, Statistical Profile," Pew Research Center, https://www.pewhispanic.org/2015/09/15/hispanics-of-dominican-origin-in-the-united-states-2013/.

Lopez, Gustavo, and Eileen Patten (2015). "The Impact of Slowing Immigration: Foreign-Born Share Falls among 14 Largest U.S. Hispanic Origin Groups, Appendix: Additional Tables and Charts," Pew Research Center, https://www.pewhispanic.org/2015/09/15/appendix-additional-tables-and-charts/.

Lopez, Mark Hugo, Ana Gonzalez-Barrera, and Gustavo Lopez (2017). "Hispanic Identity Fades Across Generations as Immigrant Connections Fall Away," Pew Research Center, https://www.pewresearch.org/hispanic/2017/12/20 /hispanic-identity-fades-across-generations-as-immigrant-connections-fall -away/.

Loshe, Russell (2013). "'La Negrita' Queen of the Ticos: The Black Roots of Costa Rica's Patron Saint," *The Americas* 69, no. 3: 323–355.

Loveman, Mara, and Jeronimo O. Muñiz (2007). "How Puerto Rico Became White: Boundary Dynamics and Intercensus Racial Reclassification," *American Sociological Review* 72: 915–939, https://doi.org/10.1177 /000312240707200604.

Loving v. Virginia, 388 U.S. 1 (1967), JUSTIA U.S. Supreme Court, accessed May 23, 2019, https://supreme.justia.com/cases/federal/us/388/1/.

Luxner, Larry (2015). "Welcome to Bound Brook, New Jersey, Ground Zero of Costa Rican Migration to the U.S.," *The Tico Times Costa Rica*, December 22, https://ticotimes.net/2015/12/22/welcome-to-bound-brook-new-jersey -ground-zero-of-costa-rican-migration-to-the-us.

Lyons, James J. (1990). "The Past and Future Directions of Federal Bilingual-Education Policy," *Annals of the American Academy of Political and Social Science* 508: 66–80.

Madrigal, Cándida (2013). "Colombians in the United States: A Study of Their Well-Being," *Advances in Social Work* 14, no. 1: 26–48.

Manrique, Linnete (2016). "Dreaming of a Cosmic Race: José Vasconcelos and the Politics of Race in Mexico, 1920s–1930s," *Cogent Arts & Humanities*, https://www.tandfonline.com/doi/pdf/10.1080/23311983.2016.1218316.

Marrow, Helen (2005). "Colombian Americans," in the *Encyclopedia Latina: History, Culture, Society*, Ilan Stavans, ed., New York: Grolier. http://helenm arrow.com/wp-content/uploads/2011/10/Marrow_2005_EL_Colombi anAmers.pdf.

Martinez, Robert A. (2013). "African Aspects of the Puerto Rican Personality," accessed October 31, 2018, https://urayoan-comentarios.blogspot.com /2013/12/african-aspects-of-puerto-rican.html.

Maupin, Caleb T. (2016). "U.S.-Led Economic War, Not Socialism, Is Tearing Venezuela Apart," *Mint Press*, July 12, https://www.mintpressnews.com /us-led-economic-war-not-socialism-tearing-venezuela-apart/218335/.

McDaniel, George (1997). "Madison Grant and the Racialist Movement," *American Renaissance*, December, https://www.amren.com/news/2010/07/madison _grant_a/.

Middeldyk, R. A. Van (2016). *The History of Puerto Rico: From the Spanish Discovery to the American Occupation*, North Charleston: CreateSpace Independent Publishing Platform.

Minster, Christopher (2019). "The U.S. Occupation of the Dominican Republic," ThoughtCo, https://www.thoughtco.com/us-occupation-of-the-dominican -republic-2136380.

Mintz, Steven. "Historical Context: Facts about the Slave Trade & Slavery," *History Now*, https://www.gilderlehrman.org/content/historical-context-facts-about-slave-trade-and-slavery.

Molina, Natalia (2010). "'In a Race All Their Own': The Quest to Make Mexicans Ineligible for U.S. Citizenship," *Pacific Historical Review* 79, no. 2: 167–201.

Morales, Ed (2018). "A New Report Says Hispanic Identity Is Fading. Is That Really Good for America?" *The Washington Post*, https://www.washingtonpost.com/news/post-nation/wp/2018/02/02/a-new-report-says-more-hispanic-identity-is-fading-is-that-really-good-for-america/.

Moreno, Christina (2015). "9 Outrageous Things Donald Trump Has Said about Latinos," *The Huffington Post*, https://www.huffingtonpost.com/entry/9-outrageous-things-donald-trump-has-said-about-latinos_us_55e483a1e4b0c818f618904b.

Moskos, Charles (1989). *Greek Americans: Struggle and Success*, 2nd ed., New Brunswick: Transaction Publishers.

Moya Pon, Frank (2010). *The Dominican Republic: A National History*, 3rd ed., Princeton: Markus Wiener Publishing Inc.

Murillo, Enrique, Jr. (2019). *Critical Readings on Latinos and Education*, New York: Routledge Press.

National Office of Statistics of Cuba. "Censos en Cuba" (Spanish version), http://www.one.cu/loscensos.htm.

NationMaster (2019). "Colombia Geography Stats," https://www.nationmaster.com/country-info/profiles/Colombia/Geography.

Nations Online Project. "History of Cuba," https://www.nationsonline.org/oneworld/History/Cuba-history.htm.

Norgaard, Lara (2017). "Living in the Shadows: The Life of Undocumented Immigrants in Princeton," *Community News*, March 31, accessed July 27, 2019, https://communitynews.org/2017/03/31/living-in-the-shadows-the-life-of-undocumented-immigrants-in-princeton/.

Okrent, David (2019). *The Guarded Gate: Bigotry, Eugenics and the Law That Kept Two Generations of Jews, Italians, and Other European Immigrants Out of America*, New York: Scribner.

Opie, Frederick Douglas (2008). "Black Americans and the State in Turn-of-the-Century Guatemala," *The Americas* 64, no. 4: 583–609.

Orr, Amy (2019). "The Bilingual Act of 1968," Immigration to the United States, http://www.immigrationtounitedstates.org/379-bilingual-education-act-of-1968.html.

Ortiz, Paul (2018). *An African American and Latinx History of the United States* (ReVisioning American History Book 4), Boston: Beacon Press.

O'Toole, G. (1986). *The Spanish War: An American Epic 1898*, New York: W. W. Norton and Company.

Pace v. Alabama, 106 U.S. 583 (1883), JUSTIA U.S. Supreme Court, accessed May 23, 2019, https://supreme.justia.com/cases/federal/us/106/583/.

Parker, Kim, Juliana Menasce Horowitz, Rich Morin, and Mark Hugo Lopez (2015). "Multiracial in America: Proud, Diverse, and Growing in Numbers," Pew Research Center, https://www.pewsocialtrends.org/2015/06/11/multiracial-in-america/.

Partlow, Joshua (2019). "'My Whole Town Practically Lived There': From Costa Rica to New Jersey, a Pipeline of Illegal Workers for Trump Goes Back Years," *The Washington Post*, February 8, https://www.washingtonpost.com/politics/my-whole-town-practically-lived-there-from-costa-rica-to-new-jersey-a-pipeline-of-illegal-workers-for-trump-goes-back-years/2019/02/08/8cdbc1dc-2971-11e9-97b3-ae59fbae7960_story.html.

Pew Research Center (2017). "Hispanic America Studies," https://www.pewresearch.org/fact-tank/2019/09/16/key-facts-about-u-s-hispanics/.

Pew Research Center (2018). "Trends in Party Affiliation among Demographic Groups," https://www.people-press.org/2018/03/20/1-trends-in-party-affiliation-among-demographic-groups/.

Piccone, Ted (2018). "From Order to Chaos: U.S. Cuban Relations Are About to Get Worse," Brookings Institute, April 16, https://www.brookings.edu/blog/order-from-chaos/2018/04/16/u-s-cuban-relations-are-about-to-get-worse/.

ProCon.org (2019). "Should the Government Allow Immigrants Who Are Here Illegally to Become U.S. Citizens?" https://immigration.procon.org/.

Radford, Jynnah, and Luis Noe-Bustamente (2019). "Facts on U.S. Immigrants, 2017: Statistical Portrait of the Foreign-Born Population in the United States," Pew Research Center, https://www.pewresearch.org/hispanic/2019/06/03/facts-on-u-s-immigrants/.

Reid-Merritt, Patricia, ed. (2017). *Race in America: How a Pseudoscientific Concept Shaped Human Interaction*, Santa Barbara: Praeger.

Reid-Merritt, Patricia, ed. (2018). *A State-by-State History of Race and Racism in the United States*, Santa Barbara, CA: Greenwood Press.

"Resultados Preliminares: Censo Nacional de Población y Vivienda 2018," http://geoapps.esri.co/censo2018/index.html.

Reyner, Solange (2017). "Rice: America Born with a Birth Defect, 'Slavery,'" *Newsmax*, https://www.newsmax.com/US/condoleezza-rice-slavery-america-cbs/2017/05/07/id/788639/.

Rich, Sarah, and Salah Troudi (2006). "Hard Times: Arab TESOL Students' Experiences of Racialization and Othering in the United Kingdom," *TESOL Quarterly* 40, no. 3: 615–627.

Ríos, Merarys, Fabián Romero, and Roberto Ramirez (2014). "Race Reporting among Hispanics: 2010," Population Division, U.S. Census Bureau, Working Paper, no. 102: 1–20.

Rizzo, Olivia (2019). "School Plan Segregates Kids, Foes Say," *Times of Trenton*, June 23, 1.

Rodney, Walter (2011). *How Europe Underdeveloped Africa*, Baltimore: Black Classic Press.

Rogler, Charles C. (1972 [1946]). "The Morality of Race Mixing in Puerto Rico," in *Portrait of a Society: Readings on Puerto Rican Sociology*, Eugenio Fernández Méndez, ed., Rio Piedras: University of Puerto Rico Press, 57–64.

Romer, Astrid Hernández (2005). "La Visibilización Estadística de los Grupos Étnicos Colombianos," *DANE*, https://www.dane.gov.co/files/censo2005 /etnia/sys/visibilidad_estadistica_etnicos.pdf.

Rosales, F. Arturo, and Francisco A. Rosales (1997). *Chicano! The History of the Mexican American Civil Rights Movement (Hispanic Civil Rights)*, 2nd rev. ed., Houston: Arte Publico Press.

Rose, Peter (2014). *They and We: Racial and Ethnic Relations in the United States and Beyond*, 7th ed., New York: Routledge.

Rosentiel, Tom (2012). "Latino? Hispanic Neither? A Conversation on Identity," Pew Research Center, https://www.pewresearch.org/2012/05/30/latino -hispanic-neither-a-conversation-on-identity/.

Roth, Wendy (2012). *Race Migrations: Latinos and the Cultural Transformation of Race*, Stanford: Stanford University Press.

Rouse, Irving (1992). *The Tainos: Rise and Decline of the People Who Greeted Columbus*, New Haven: Yale University Press.

Rumbaut, Ruben G. (1992). "The Americans: Latin American and Caribbean Peoples in the United States," in *Americas: New Interpretive Essays*, Alfred Stepan, ed., Oxford: Oxford University Press, 275–307.

Sánchez, Juan O. (2016). *The Ku Klux Klan's Campaign against Hispanics, 1921– 1925: Rhetoric, Violence and Response in the American Southwest*, Jefferson: McFarland & Company.

Saneaux, Sully, and Ramona Hernández (2013). *La República Dominicana y la prensa extranjera: Mayo 1961–Septiembre 1963* (Desde la desaparición de Trujillo hasta Juan Bosch), New York: CUNY Academic Works.

Saunders, Nicholas J. (2005). *The Peoples of the Caribbean: An Encyclopedia of Archeology and Traditional Culture*, Santa Barbara: ABC-CLIO.

Schaefer, Richard T. (2011). *Racial and Ethnic Groups*, 12th ed., Boston: Pearson-Prentice Hall.

Schaefer, Richard T. (2018). *Racial and Ethnic Groups*, 15th ed., Boston: Pearson-Prentice Hall.

Scheina, Robert L. (2003). *Latin America's Wars, Volume I: The Age of the Caudillo, 1791–1899*, Dulles: Brassey's.

S. Con. Res. 26 (111th), (2009). "A Concurrent Resolution Apologizing for the Enslavement and Racial Segregation of African Americans," GovTrack.us, accessed May 11, 2019, https://www.govtrack.us/congress/bills/111 /sconres26.

Seelye, Catherine (1998). "Clinton Comment on Slavery Draws a Republican's Ire," *New York Times*, March 28, https://www.nytimes.com/1998/03/28 /us/clinton-comment-on-slavery-draws-a-republican-s-ire.html.

Sharman, Russell Leigh (2001). "The Caribbean Carretera: Race, Space and Social Liminality in Costa Rica," *Bulletin of Latin American Research* 20, no. 1: 46–62.

Shepard, Steven (2016). "How Popular Is Trump with Hispanic Voters?" *Politico*, June 3, https://www.politico.com/story/2016/06/donald-trump-hispanic-voters-223845.

Staten, Clifford L. (2005). *The History of Cuba* (Palgrave Essential Histories Series), New York: St. Martin's Press.

Steiner, Stan (1974). *The Islands: The Worlds of the Puerto Ricans*, New York: Harper & Row.

Stocking, George W. (1968). *Race, Culture and Evolution: Essays in the History of Anthropology*, New York: Free Press.

Suburban Stats. "Population Demographics for Trenton, New Jersey in 2019, 2018," https://suburbanstats.org/population/new-jersey/how-many-people-live-in-trenton.

Taylor, Paul, Mark Hugo Lopez, Jessica Martínez, and Gabriel Velasco (2012). "When Labels Don't Fit: Hispanics and Their Views of Identity," Pew Research Center, http://www.pewhispanic.org/2012/04/04/when-labels-dont-fit-hispanics-and-their-views-of-identity/.

TCRN Staff (2018). "Costa Rica Celebrates Black and Afro-Costa Rican Culture Day on August 31st," *The Costa Rica News*, August 31, accessed May 12, 2019, https://thecostaricanews.com/costa-rica-celebrates-black-and-afro-costa-rican-culture-day-on-august-31st/.

Thomas, Hugh (2010). *Cuba: A History*, New York: Penguin Books.

Torres-Saillant, Silvio (2012). *Introduction to Dominican Blackness*, New York: CUNY Academic Works.

Torres-Saillant, Silvio (2015). "Dominican-American Literature," in *The Routledge Companion to Latino/a Literature*, Suzanne Bost and Frances R. Aparicio, eds., London: Routledge, Taylor & Francis Group, 41–53.

Torroni, Antonio, Michael D. Brown, Marie T. Lott, Nancy J. Newman, and Douglas C. Wallace (1995). "African, Native American, and European Mitochondrial DNAs in Cubans from Pinar del Rio Province and Implications for the Recent Epidemic Neuropathy in Cuba," *Human Mutation* 5, no. 4: 310–307. https://doi.org/10.1002/humu.1380050407.

Trasancos, Stacy A. (2016). *Particles of Faith: A Catholic Guide to Navigating Science*, Notre Dame: Ave Maria Press.

UnderstandingRace.Org (2009). "The Story of Race: A History," https://youtu.be/No5ai6LZLFg.

UnidosUS (2019). "WE ARE UNIDOS US," https://www.unidosus.org/about-us/.

UnidosUS (2019). "Stronger Communities, Stronger America: A Latino Policy Agenda for the 116th Congress," http://publications.unidosus.org/handle/123456789/1935.

United Nations (2019). "Costa Rica Commits to Fully Decarbonize by 2050," https://unfccc.int/news/costa-rica-commits-to-fully-decarbonize-by-2050.

U.S. Census Bureau (2010). "United States Census Questionnaire 2010," https://www.census.gov/2010census/pdf/2010_Questionnaire_Info.pdf.

U.S. Census Bureau (2017). "Facts for Features: Hispanic Heritage Month 2017," https://www.census.gov/newsroom/facts-for-features/2017/hispanic-heritage.html.

U.S. Department of Commerce, Bureau of the Census (1913). "Thirteenth Census of the United States Taken in the Year 1910: Statistics for Porto Rico," Washington, D.C.: Government Printing Office.

U.S. Department of State (2019). "US Relations with Costa Rica, fact sheet," *Bureau of Western Hemisphere Affairs*, https://www.state.gov/r/pa/ei/bgn/2019.htm.

Veltman, Calvin (1988). *The Future of the Spanish Language in the United States*, Washington, D.C.: Hispanic Policy Development Project.

Verin-Shapiro, Penny (2000). "Why 'Nuyoricans' Are Given the Cold-Shoulder by Other Puerto Ricans," https://eric.ed.gov/?id=ED456178.

Waibel, Leo (1939). "White Settlement in Costa Rica," *The Geographical Review* 29, no. 4: 529–560.

West, Cornel (1993). *Race Matters*, New York: Vintage Press.

West, Cornel (2017). "Cornel West to Activists, Immigrants: Let's Dump the Democratic Party," https://www.colorlines.com/articles/cornel-west-activists-immigrants-lets-dump-democratic-party.

Wiese, Ann-Marie, and Eugene E. Garcia (2001). "The Bilingual Education Act: Language Minority Students and U.S. Federal Educational Policy," *International Journal of Bilingual Education and Bilingualism* 4, no. 4: 29–48.

Wikipedia. "Costa Rican Americans," https://en.wikipedia.org/wiki/Costa_Rican_Americans.

Williams, Janice (2017). "From Black to White: Why Sammy Sosa and Others Are Bleaching Their Skin," *Newsweek*, https://www.newsweek.com/sammy-sosa-skin-bleaching-lightening-636516.

Wills, George (2019). "Last Century's Immigration Debate Makes Today's Seem Enlightened," *Richmond Times-Dispatch*, June 29, https://www.richmond.com/opinion/their-opinion/george-will-column-last-century-s-immigration-debate-makes-today/article_d8a7a648-8367-5496-9831-14e98175bc80.html.

Workmen's Circle (2019). "The Immigration Act of 1924 (The Johnson-Reed Act)," http://circle.org/jsource/the-immigration-act-of-1924-the-johnson-reed-act/.

World History Project. "United States Occupation of the Dominican Republic 1916," https://worldhistoryproject.org/1916/1916-united-states-occupation-of-the-dominican-republic.

World Population Review (2019). "Colombia Population 2019," http://worldpopulationreview.com/countries/colombia-population/.

Wright, Russell O. (2008). *Chronology of Immigration in the United States*, Jefferson: McFarland & Company.

Yeager, Timothy (1995). "Encomienda or Slavery? The Spanish Crown's Choice of Labor Organization in Sixteenth-Century Spanish America," *The Journal of Economic History* 55: 842–859, accessed July 19, 2013, http://www.latinamericanstudies.org/colonial/encomienda-slavery.pdf.

Zong, Jie, and Jeanne Batalova (2018). "South American Immigrants in the United States," Migration Policy Institute, https://www.migrationpolicy.org/article/south-american-immigrants-united-states#EnglishProficiency.

Index

About the Authors

Patricia Reid-Merritt, DSW, is Distinguished Professor of Africana Studies and Social Work and at Stockton University. She is the author of *Sister Power: How Phenomenal Black Women Are Rising to the Top*, *Righteous Self-Determination: The Black Social Work Movement in America*, and *Tarnished Legacy: A Reluctant Memoir*. She is the editor of *Race in America: How a Pseudoscientific Concept Shaped Human Interaction* and *A State-by-State History of Race and Racism in the United States*.

Michael S. Rodriguez, PhD, is Associate Professor of Political Science and the campus liaison for the Washington internship program at Stockton University. He is author of "Race and the Quest for U.S. Citizenship: Birthright Restrictionism and American Constitutionalism" in *Race in America: How a Pseudoscientific Concept Shaped Human Interaction*.